PAINT IT BLACK

Paint It Black

The Murder of Brian Jones

Geoffrey Giuliano

To Vrinda for the faith, Virgin for the chance and Brian for the story. Let's hope this helps finally to set the record straight.

First published in Great Britain in 1994 by
Virgin Books
an imprint of Virgin Publishing Ltd
332 Ladbroke Grove
London W10 5AH

Copyright © Indigo Editions 1994

The right of Geoffrey Giuliano to be identified as the author of this work has been asserted by him in accordance with the Copyright Designs and Patents Act 1988

A catalogue record for this book is available from the British Library

ISBN 1 85227 424 7

Typeset by Phoenix Photosetting, Chatham, Kent
Printed and bound in Great Britain by
Mackays of Chatham PLC, Chatham, Kent

'There were plenty of people who wanted him dead and for very good reasons. Some day the truth will come out.'

Keith Richards, 1989

Contents

Illustrations

Acknowledgements

Senior Editor: Mal Peachey
Executive Researchers: Brenda Giuliano and Sesa Nichole Giuliano
Intern: Devin Giuliano

The author would like to thank the following people for their kindness and selfless hard work in helping to realise this book: Sriman Jagannatha Dasa Adikari; Charles Artley; Sylvia Baily; Robin Bayer; Dr Mirza Beg; Deborah Lynn Black; Srimati Vrinda Rani Devi Dasi; Enzo of Valentino's; Jim Fitzgerald; Paul Forty; Robin Scot Giuliano; Avalon and India Giuliano; ISKCON; Dr Michael Klapper; Allan Lang; Timothy Leary; Leaf Leavesley; Marcus Lecky; Donald Lehr; Andrew Lownie; His Divine Grace B. H. Mangalniloy Goswami Maharaja; Mark Studios, Clarence, New York; David Lloyd McIntyre; Tony Mullikan; Michelle Ogden; Phyllis Phipps; His Divine Grave A. C. Bhakitivedanta Swami Prabhupada; Rob Shreeve; Self Realization Institute of America (SRI); Steven Rosen; Jo Smart; Sean Smith; Wendell and Joan Smith; Paul Slovak; Something Fishy Productions Ltd; Dave Thompson; Touch Productions; Edward Veltman; Robert Wallace; Gill Woolcott; Dr Ronald Zucker.

*The main timeframe of this story runs from November 1966
to mid July 1969*

Introduction

BRIAN WASN'T EASY. If there was one theme that ran through my three-years-plus research on the man it was that he was generally very hard work. But I understand that. As a matter of fact, people often say the same about me. I'm sure it has something to do with the innate urgency of wanting to leave some kind of a mark, but maybe more with the red-hot passion of *having* to create. And Brian Jones was a very creative bloke.

With almost a single, masterful stroke he created The Rolling Stones, which, they will tell you, are the greatest rock 'n' roll band in the world. Like Athena, Greek goddess of wisdom, who sprang fully grown out of her father Zeus's brow, so too The Stones were very much Brian's baby. In bearing The Stones of course, Mr Shampoo (as manager Andrew Loog Oldham sometimes called him) also helped to engender much that the eternal swinging sixties were and are. Still, Brian's most important creation, the one he laboured longest on, must always be himself.

A bright kid from middle-class pretensions he was reared to become a dentist but ended up a naughty bluesman who kissed the girls and made them cry. Mum and dad were mortified. Brian split to Sweden. While there he fell desperately in love with the smoky image of the tawny-blond he saw in every mirror. A significant key to Brian, a man who, his girlfriend Suki Potier once charged, had really only ever made love to himself.

On a day-to-day basis Jones was at varying times petulant, bossy, divisive, dishonest, lazy, violent, incompetent and just plain mean. Conversely, he was just as apt to be intensely charming and, by the way, hysterically funny and upbeat. You never knew which way the wind would blow. As Keith Richards once said of his late colleague, 'Brian was a nice bunch of guys.' As far as I'm concerned, the indelible hallmark of a true artist.

Introduction

When he finally ground himself down to the point that a coup was staged and he was ousted from The Stones, Brian had nowhere to go but up. Unfortunately he never did. And that is what this book is about: the crime of murder. In this case the unlawful taking of a young, especially promising life.

Like I said, Brian was definitely a pain in the ass – but there's no way he deserved to be held under the water by some moron until the life spun out of him. In fact, there was nothing wrong with Brian Jones that a good few months at the Betty Ford Clinic and a timely measure of genuine affection couldn't have put right. Unfortunately, that didn't happen and Brian Jones soared into rock history as the fucked-up kid who got too loaded on drugs and fell asleep in his backyard pool. In that sense perhaps Brian was murdered twice.

As for those responsible for Brian's early end, be warned: if I can help to nail you I will. It isn't often an author gets the chance to try and right a wrong as big as this one. Or at least shed some light on it.

For years, rumours have circulated that The Stones or their management had something to hide about Brian's death. For all the attendant nastiness that went on regarding Brian's final exit, there is no question that any of The Rolling Stones were in any way implicated in his tragic and unjustified death. The same goes for the organisation that surrounded them. When Brian died, it was a terrible tragedy for everyone connected to The Stones, and a great loss to the world.

'Skyfield'
6 April 1994

1 BAD MOON RISING
Rejected Youth

THE ANONYMOUS EPITAPH chiselled on his headstone in Cheltenham's St Mary's churchyard says it all, 'In Affectionate Remembrance of Brian Jones.' A testament bereft of emotion and conspicuous in its indifference, more suited to a fond acquaintance or loyal pet than a loving son.

Even beyond the grave, the estrangement endured by Jones was to be perpetuated by a family either unable, or unwilling, to claim their lost boy. The calculated alienation that had shaped the life of this young man on a slow tumble towards his tragic destiny was now forever etched in dusty marble.

Lewis Brian Hopkin-Jones, born 28 February 1942, the eldest child of Welsh aeronautical engineer, Lewis, and his wife, Louisa, was bright, inquisitive, animated but overtly sensitive and somewhat withdrawn. Neighbours remember him contentedly roaming the pavements with his pet goat, and his inseparable feline companion, Rollader. Things, however, weren't quite as wonderful at home.

At barely four years of age tragedy invaded the household when Jones lost his baby sister, Pauline, to leukaemia. Lewis and Louisa, locked in their own private pain, didn't invite Brian into their grief. Lost and alone, the little boy wandered around the hushed, strained house in terrified confusion, fearing his beloved sister had been given away and that he too might share the same fate.

'I remember this awful feeling of doom and gloom,' recalled Jones near the end of his life. 'My poor sister. I had no idea what had happened to her. I was terribly afraid. Instead of drawing me closer my parents seemed to push me away. But why? What had I done to anyone? It still hurts terribly to this day.'

His isolation was compounded when Jones suffered a severe bout of croup, giving way to a lifelong battle with chronic bronchitis and asthma. Thereafter Brian was condemned to not only emotional, but physical quarantine, looking on from afar while other children played happily.

Then suddenly young Jones was no longer alone. He found in music his one true companion. His parents were initially delighted when it became apparent that Brian inherited their own keen musical ear; with Louisa a piano teacher and Lewis organist and choir director for St Mary's. Six-year-old Brian took to his lessons with immediate flair and enthusiasm, displaying an amazing natural aptitude, quickly absorbing complicated theory and even sight-reading. Revelling in his parents' all too occasional display of approval he excelled at a rate which astonished his teachers. Before long, he picked up the recorder and clarinet with equal ease. Lewis began to envision a career for his son as a classical musician. Perhaps as first chair in a prestigious symphony or even an accomplished soloist. Not quite the sober dental career he had carved out for his son initially, but still a noble profession to suit the family's upwardly mobile ambitions.

Jones's early school days were eased along with the help of his near genius IQ of 135. Easily mastering all the required academic disciplines, it was the arts where he really excelled, providing an outlet for his burgeoning creativity. In his favourite subject, English, Brian would pen imaginative science fiction tales, deeply impressing his masters at Dean Close Junior Public, but not particularly his parents. In art class he transformed his love of trains into spectacular locomotive designs of minute detail and accuracy. Not surprisingly, he also played clarinet in the school orchestra.

Inevitably, the inquisitive mind and hyperactive temperament common in gifted children launched the emergence of a rebellious streak in Brian. Regular incidents included dyeing the family pets with a brilliant host of vivid food colourings, hiding his dreaded school uniform and eyeglasses, and melting down his regiment of tin soldiers into a puddle of hot lead.

Phil Kent, one of Brian's early playmates recalls in Laura Jackson's *Golden Stone* how young Jones took macabre delight in pushing the limits of childhood play: 'Risking his dad catching him, Brian would take a baking tray, heap on what ever came to hand – usually Airfix models – and create a crash. Then, with some pinched matches he'd set it alight. For just those few illicit seconds, as the flames blazed, there was this little drama going on before our eyes.'

In 1953 Jones's antics took a more serious turn as he entered Cheltenham's distinguished Pates Grammar School in the town's exclusive Promenade district. Still a brilliant student who could pass a test with only a last minute perusal of his notes, Jones recognised the need for a real challenge. Stimulation that began with the harmless use of his mortarboard as a boomerang and tramping about the halls in football boots soon escalated into enticing his classmates to forsake their usual milk-break for the more hearty, and illicit, ale. Eventually, Brian was suspended for instigating a small riot against the school's holier-than-thou prefects.

Not only did these escapades garner the attention he was so desperately seeking at home, but pitted school authorities against his father who later confessed, 'He exasperated me beyond measure in his younger days.'

According to *Golden Stone*, headmaster Dr Bell said, 'Brian's father was forever turning up in my study, totally unannounced, with complaints. He was on Brian's back all the time. Brian was a clever boy, an intelligent rebel, introverted, withdrawn, but he wasn't a bad lad.'

Like most adolescents, Jones was encouraged to run off his excess energy in sports. Defying his somewhat tenuous constitution, Brian excelled in a wide range of physical disciplines, from soccer to judo, and proved himself a swimmer and diver of outstanding stamina. Despite his aptitude, Jones deemed these activities a waste of time. 'I just couldn't take to games,' he said. 'I skived whenever possible and my regrets were that I simply had to turn up and play on some occasions. But the funny thing was, that almost despite my attitude I wasn't bad at badminton. At least there was a bit of action in that sport. Mostly though, it was just that I couldn't stand being bored.'

As Jones moved into his teens he became acutely aware of the confines of conservative Cheltenham. One hundred miles west of London and centuries removed, Cheltenham, untouched by two world wars, was perched contentedly on the lush, bucolic Cotswolds.

Keith Richards had this to say about his future colleague's oh-so-provincial home town: 'It's a very genteel city of old ladies where it used to be fashionable to take baths once a year at Cheltenham Spa. Now it's a seedy sort of place full of aspirations to be an aristocratic town. Pretty in its own way, but Dullsville. It rubs off on anyone who comes from there.'

It was a place too, where old world values had been ingrained within the brick and mortar of the well preserved Regency houses that lined the streets. Psychotherapist and author Mandy Aftel observes, 'Cheltenhamians do not confine their concern for appearance to the town's landscape. They are extremely self-conscious and strive to do the 'proper thing'. They occupy themselves with propriety to the point of lifting their little finger when they drink tea, a mannerism Brian Jones assumed when the spirit moved him. Much of Brian's personality was formed in Cheltenham and although he often loathed those parts of himself he could never divorce himself from them.'

Meanwhile, in the whitewashed, semi-detached home at 35 Hatherly Road with its single bay window and sunrise gate identical to every other, Brian discovered jazz at the tender age of thirteen. Abruptly abandoning the piano, to the particular horror of his mother, he sold his clarinet and purchased a second-hand alto saxophone. Within a few hours the first tentative notes came chortling from his room, wafting melodically through the neighbourhood. Not long afterwards, Jones formed his first band, a local skiffle outfit where he played, among other instruments, a washboard.

'My music was always for *me*,' said Brian candidly. 'I needed something and that was it. In the beginning I thought maybe my parents would be proud of me, but they never were. Just the opposite really. At that point I thought, "Okay, fuck you then. I'll make it without you." And I did. Sometimes though I do look back and think that something really important was lost. What was it? Don't ask me, man.'

A thoroughly disenchanted Lewis stated, 'He was obsessed with music. He used to play modern jazz morning, noon and night. I saw it as a positive evil in his life.'

Dick Hattrell, an accomplished bassist and early cohort of Jones revealed in A. E. Hotchner's book, *Blown Away*, 'He was having the same kind of trouble at home as I had. His father was as strait-laced as mine. As long as Brian was playing classical music on the piano and clarinet he had no problems. But his father loathed the sound of jazz and by the time Brian was thirteen he had renounced classical music to the consternation of his father, who told Brian he didn't want "that music" in the house, as it gave him a migraine.'

Thus, for the Jones family music became a pivotal point of controversy, a killing ground which not only pitted Brian against his parents, but polarised relations with his sister, Barbara. The further Brian bucked the borders of conventionality, the more Louisa overtly favoured her daughter. She was after all, the model child, sober, religious, with aspirations towards teaching, whose dutiful obedience was already turning her into a skilled pianist and violinist. Brian conversely, was depicted as a blight on the family name and thus, like a contagion, had to be isolated from his sister, lest she succumb to his disreputable influence. The result was a devastating estrangement that could never quite be bridged. It was the kind of insidious emotional abuse that slowly and surely began to erode Jones's fragile, porcelain psyche.

Yet part of Brian wanted desperately to conform, setting up an internal tug-of-war he would wage all of his life. Jones would spend hours reading the Bible, maintaining his exemplary school grades, and honed a personal manner that could be at once genteel, polite and gracious.

Being shunned left Brian suffering from such low self-esteem he pursued a quick fix that lay just next door to Pates Grammar, in the equally posh Girls' Grammar School. Jones, now well beyond gawky adolescence, was a handsome, though diminutive rogue whose irresistible Cheshire-cat grin and tart wit was dangerously attractive to the neighbouring ingénues. While his school peers could only fantasise their carnal conquests, Brian was actually living them, plunging heedlessly into a sequence of illicit trysts and leaving his stunned mates in gaping envy.

At home he was a condemned failure; at school, however, he was idolised as a legend. Said Brian later, 'I found myself accepted by the older boys and I was in.'

Suddenly, it all backfired one dark day in 1958, when his brazen sexcapades landed a fourteen-year-old girl, named Valerie, pregnant. To Jones, the sum of his previous recklessness couldn't begin to match this unthinkable, unforgivable scandal. Lewis and Louisa quickly spirited him away for two weeks in Germany in the hopes of hushing up the unsavoury and humiliating situation. An abortion was discussed and favoured by Brian, but in the end Valerie went through with the birth and put the child, a boy, up for adoption.

Meanwhile, returning home, the after shocks of the scandal rocked the entire community and even made the local papers. At school Brian was no longer the fashionable James Dean rebel, but an ostracised pariah banished in disgrace. So Brian drew inward, locking himself away in his room dreaming about one day becoming a musician, and playing with the cherished wooden bus with flashing lights his father had made for him a lifetime ago.

For Lewis Jones it became frustratingly clear he could not stamp out his son's life like one of his aeroplane designs. 'I had high hopes that he would go to Cambridge or Oxford,' he confessed, 'but it was not to be. I think the mild rebellion he displayed was due to the fact that at school they wanted to make him a scientist of some kind, when essentially he was more inclined towards the arts. Had he devoted as much time to his studies as he did to music I think he would have been a brilliant scholar. Our clash was not so much one of personality as of ambition.'

Speaking of that turbulent time Brian has said, 'When I left school I felt completely at sea. Everyone regarded me as a lazy, good-for-nothing layabout, including my parents, and I suppose I was in a way.'

At seventeen he packed his clothes, slung his £3 Spanish guitar over his shoulder and boldly hitchhiked his way through Scandinavia over the summer of 1959. Jones later referred to the period as, 'The most free and happy time of my life.' Busking for his keep Brian revelled in his new found liberation, mingling with bistro musicians and free-thinking Bohemians as well as loving and leaving the willowy, willing Swedish women.

Finally out of money and on the brink of starvation, Jones had no option but to struggle home in November. To his surprise some significant changes had taken place in his absence. By 1960 the coffee bar craze that swept across the rest of the civilised world had at long last managed to infiltrate Cheltenham. Not only was Brian able to fine tune his musical skills by sitting in with a host of jazz combos, here too was the ideal outlet to avoid the increasingly intolerable situation at home.

These often seedy hang-outs with names like the Patio, Aztec and El Flamenco, attracted a wide spectrum of avant-garde artists, musicians and social outcasts providing just the stimulation Jones's eager, restless mind craved. A favourite haunt was the Barbeque Waikiki of which school chum, Pete Boswell observed to author Jackson, 'Here Brian would hang out with his crowd, scoffing burgers and Cokes and generally killing time by talking music and surveying the skirts.'

His voracious sexual appetite soon landed a 23-year-old married Guildford woman 'in the club' as a result of a one-night stand in celebration of Jones's eighteenth birthday. On 4 August she delivered Brian's second illegitimate child, a girl, of whose existence Jones was never informed. In 1986 Stones' bassist Bill Wyman met up with the young woman and made a curious discovery. She'd uncovered her famous father's identity at age fifteen and upon investigation found in him similar behaviour patterns attributed to her bouts with epilepsy.

'I learned that sometimes he didn't know whether he was here, there or anywhere. That tallied exactly with one of the epileptic symptoms I suffer from. I have since discovered there were so many times when

Brian went ill. It's possible the epileptic symptoms I have are inherited from him.'

Wyman, intrigued over the theory offered, 'What she said seems to me to throw a revealing light on his demeanour and antics inside The Stones, behaviour which puzzled us for so many years: His tantrums, illnesses and absences, and general contrariness. Her theories about the father she never met also have an important bearing on the still mysterious circumstances surrounding his death in the swimming pool. This makes me wonder, did Brian have a debility that affected his life, The Stones' career and even his death?'

Among the most zealous patrons of the coffee house circuit were Cheltenham's boistrous teen population. The talented but aloof musician, however, always carefully kept his distance providing an intriguing enigma. What they couldn't guess was that Jones's history of parental dominance and peer alienation, coupled with his superior intellect and innate shyness, crippled his ability to interact with his own age group. The musicians in the trad bands were a generation removed and he therefore felt comfortable in their company, rarely mixing with the younger regulars.

At the Aztec, Jones met and became involved with fifteen-year-old Patricia Andrews who worked at Boots. 'People described him as a bit of a loner, an oddball with a shady reputation,' Pat says in *Golden Stone*. 'When I got my first glimpse of him I thought, no way! God, he was wearing a Harris tweed suit like my dad looking dead out of place in the coffee bar. I felt sorry for him because he seemed so lonely and I was curious to find out why people wouldn't talk to him.'

Although Andrews admitted a healthy appreciation of his Welsh good looks and easy charm, it was his keen mind that captured her attention. 'He was intelligent,' she said, 'really clever. He also listened. That was the beauty about Brian. He wouldn't just spout off. He wanted feedback, to listen to people.'

Hailing from a staunchly working-class background Pat wanted desperately to better herself. Brian, obviously well-read on a variety of subjects and graced with an eloquent, cultured voice was the perfect conduit.

In Pat, conversely, Brian found not just another coquette ready to swoon at one glance of his magnetic blue eyes, but a steady young woman of strength and outspoken sincerity that peered beyond the tiring and vacuous veneer of appearances.

The hub that turned their relationship was a mutual interest in music which they would discuss for hours on end. 'Brian without music would be like a man without arms,' revealed Pat to Laura Jackson. 'He had an incredible feel for music and an even more incredible burning desire to play it. Everything else was very much a poor second.

'Seventy-five per cent of the time Brian was miserable because he was so thwarted musically at home. He loved his parents a great deal, but he was very sad and hurt that they couldn't accept his lifestyle and didn't conform to the person they wanted him to be.'

Later on that year Jones also struck up a friendship with John Appleby at the popular El Flamenco club. Ten years older, with a kindly, unflappable manner, Appleby proved a steadying influence on the often confused, insecure musician. In their relationship Jones found the warm, nurturing father/son camaraderie he had always craved.

Brian and John shared a zealous fascination with British trams, John being a member of the Tramway Museum Society. As the pair spent long hours restoring vintage trams, they developed a friendship that lasted well into The Stones.

Years later they stepped inside a pub together and were promptly swamped with fans. One approached John and asked, 'What's it like to be a rock star's father?' As Appleby groped to explain he wasn't Brian's dad, Jones proudly bellowed out, 'John's my second father!' Even Lewis Jones was to acknowledge on several occasions, 'John knew Brian better than I did.'

Yet even this budding friendship was rudely invaded by the Jones's behind-the-scenes power plays. Louisa, quietly steaming over her son's club-hopping and eccentric musical hobby in lieu of a steady job, had her own agenda. One night she commandeered Appleby in the living room. 'I must have a word with you about Brian,' she said, tight-lipped. 'He's in and out of the Waikiki and all the rest and goes to parties every night. He doesn't seem the least inclined to do any work. Please see what you can do about it.'

Appleby duly arranged a position for Brian as a conductor on the double-decker buses. As it turned out, young Jones embraced the opportunity as a chance to live out his childhood obsession with buses. The reality of the early morning hours, however, coupled with a passing fancy that quickly grew old, Brian lasted all of three weeks.

Finding the pressures at home unbearable Jones boarded with Pat's sister and her husband Bernie Taylor. He followed his first job with a series of short-lived, futile tenures as a sales assistant, coal man (he lasted only three days) and factory worker. Still trying to please his parents he took a post as junior assistant with the architects' department of the Gloucestershire County Council. Jones was showing real promise until he charmed a colleague into footing the bill for a £30 overcoat, never repaying the debt. A trait that, not coincidentally, spilled over to several missed payments on his rent.

The council position was going so well that Jones took it one step further by applying to the Cheltenham School of Architecture. His academic record of nine GCE O levels and Advanced level passes in chemistry and physics made for impressive qualifications. Following his initial acceptance, however, just two days later his application was abruptly withdrawn. Bernie Taylor, incensed over Jones's outstanding debt, reportedly informed the school's principal that their newly admitted candidate was, in fact, 'An irresponsible drifter and potentially poor student.'

Furthermore, according to friends, Brian was banned from the school because of his unrestricted womanising. Even on his own substantial merits it seemed, Jones could not get a break.

Back home once again Brian was so ashamed of the stifling, judgemental atmosphere, he never brought friends around to Hatherly Road. Instead, he spent a lot of time at the warm, close-knit family home of Dick Hattrell. 'Brian got on extremely well with my father,' confirmed Dick. 'He was very well educated and they would talk about Shakespeare, Dickens, cricket, all sorts of things which, quite honestly, were a bit over my head. My father became very fond of Brian and often invited us to Sunday lunch.'

Such was not the case, however, at the sober and repressed Jones household. In fact if not for a job-related car accident Jones had over the frigid winter of 1960 (in which he lost a tooth and injured a leg) Pat might never have got a look at the Jones family.

She recalls being led through a spotless and sterile house where a formidable atmosphere crackled tensely beneath the polite veneer of its occupants. 'I was reminded of a Victorian household, with its very sombre, very serious, foreboding atmosphere,' describes Andrews. 'There was no joy, no laughter, no happiness, nothing I knew at my home.'

Pat remembers being taken to a back room at the house where a centre table was covered in starched white linen. 'When Mrs Jones lifted up the cloth I was shocked. It was the middle of winter and she had done cucumber sandwiches and cake. Here Brian had just lost his tooth and had it screwed back in and she was doing up a tea as if nothing had happened. All I could think of was Brian feeling like death with his aching, bloody mouth.

'Mrs Jones asked, "What do you do, dear?"

' "I work at Boots." Even as I said it I felt a deep chill. That was it. She immediately looked down her nose at me as if to say, "Oh my God, our son is going out with a shop girl!" When she found out my father worked at Dowty Rotel, the same company as Brian's father, but on the shop floor, that really did me in. It became clear as she went on about his previous girlfriend that I wasn't what she considered a good match for her son.'

Following this strained moment the family retired to the lounge where Pat got her first and only glimpse of fifteen-year-old Barbara Jones. Andrews remembers that Mrs Jones sat on one of the room's two couches, her arms protectively about her daughter while Brian remained on the opposite side. 'He subsequently told me that his mother ordered him to stay away from Barbara and that she was to stay away from him,' reveals Pat. 'He would sit in one room, they would be in another.'

Barely a month later, Andrews's sixteenth birthday in December marked a critical turning-point in Brian's deteriorating family situation. In preparation for a special celebration Jones decided to stop-off at home for a change of clothes, only to find the house closed up and locked. To his amazement Brian found stashed in the bushes a suitcase with his belongings bearing a note that his parents had gone on holiday. The message was devastatingly clear; Brian was no longer welcome in his own home. To worsen an already catastrophic turn of events Jones, forced to break-in through a French window to collect the rest of his things, was accosted by police who had been called by neighbours. Thereafter he turned his back forever on Hatherly Road, leaving home for good.

Lewis Jones would later say in defence of that difficult period, 'Brian became involved in Cheltenham in a sphere that was quite foreign to my understanding. At the time, the idea that he could achieve success in the music world looked ridiculous to me. A complete barrier built up between us.'

By 1961, Jones moved with his reliable, trusted mate, Dick Hattrell, into a tiny flat at 73 Prestbury Road in Cheltenham's art college district. Here Brian immersed himself totally in his music, playing in a pair of trad bands and forming a successful rock'n'roll instrumental combo called The Ramrods.

Explained Dick: 'His father never tried to understand what Brian wanted, which was why Brian tried to make a success of what began as an interest, developed into an obsession and finally, became a career.'

Jones, however, encountered a severe stumbling block with Pat's announcement just a few months later that she was expecting Brian's child, his third, in late autumn. His reaction was predictably conflicting. On one hand he was caught up in the momentary illusion of home and family, repeatedly referring to Pat as his fiancée. Yet reality, as always, pulled him towards his one true North: Music.

Jones clearly had a one-track mind. He and Dick had gone up to London's trendy Marquee Club to witness the legendary blues master, Muddy Waters, in his first performance on electric guitar. Dick remembers: 'After that night it was as if Brian had found his mission in life. He got himself electrified and never stopped practising for hours at a stretch.'

In Jackson's book, Andrews recalls his impassioned determination to acquire the rare and difficult art of the slide guitar. Brian hauled her on a frenzied midnight search for a homemade slide-bar that took the pair to a plumber's yard. 'We looked and looked through this filthy scrapheap for this bloody bit of piping, just something he could cut to size. Finally, in a garage tip we found it, about two-inches long and it fitted Brian's finger perfectly. He was happy.'

By mid-1961, Pat moved into the flat with Dick and Brian, filled with a sixteen-year-old's romantic notions of an idyllic love-nest. But her romantic notions quickly dissolved into bitter reality. Every payday Jones would wait for her outside Boots to snatch her wages for the purchase of new guitar strings and records.

Jones also proved himself a philanderer, something Pat tried to brush off as Brian's insecure need to 'prove his male instincts'. A jealous argument erupted leaving Pat with a blackened eye, exposing the deep-seated anger and pain normally cloaked under Brian's cultured guise. Although she clung desperately to the hope that once the baby arrived Brian would settle down and they would be a real family, Pat could not avoid the truth.

'It wasn't so much losing him physically,' she remembered in *Golden Stone*, 'it was that I could feel I was losing him emotionally. He was slipping away from me, to his music. He was so carried away with the guitar, his fingers bled and he never even noticed.'

The baby was finally born on 23 October 1961, a six-pound boy, the startling image of his father. An excited Brian named him Julian Mark, in honour of his jazz sax idol, Julian 'Cannonball' Adderley. In a touching display, Brian burst into the Victoria Nursing Home bearing an enormous bouquet of red roses he had purchased with the sale of his treasured record collection. 'The sacrifice was enormous for Brian,' Pat recalled to Laura Jackson. 'You had to really know him to appreciate that. But he really did have a kind nature and it showed when he'd go and do things like that.'

The gift, however, along with some baby clothes was the last she would ever receive. As Brian moved on to yet another flat, Pat took the baby home to her parents.

Brian initially embraced Mark with all the gusto of a child who'd got a brand new toy for Christmas. 'For the first few months he was quite proud of Mark,' admits Pat. 'He would carry him about, take him everywhere. He was really interested and absorbed. Then his manager said, that due to the publicity he shouldn't go around with Mark, he mustn't associate with me and Mark. That got me mad and I told Brian so. "It's just one of those things you'll have to put up with for a few months," Brian said to me. "As soon as we've made it we won't worry about that kind of thing." When he made a record and became pretty well known he began to drift away.'

There were increasingly frequent trips to London, specifically to the Ealing Jazz Club to hear Alexis Korner and his revolutionary rhythm and blues ensemble, Blues Incorporated. This was the music that stirred Brian's soul as no other; *the blues*, raw and primitive, like coal mined from deep within the earth. Korner recalls being dramatically accosted off stage by a very enthusiastic fan: 'It was Brian, of course, accompanied by a mate of his who said nothing. Not that anyone else could, because Brian was this pent-up ball of obsessive energy, talking away ten-to-the-dozen in an incredibly intense manner.'

Driven by an overwhelming need to play this brave new sound he was allowed to sit in with the band, showing a prowess and innate feel on slide guitar that won immediate adulation from the packed house. Not surprisingly he grew ever more aware of his charismatic appeal with each subsequent performance. Notably impressed was Korner himself. 'He learned how to bait an audience long before anything like that occurred to Mick. You should have seen those kids' reactions when Brian picked up a tambourine and gave it one tiny little shake in their faces.'

Korner, a generous man, fourteen years Jones's senior, took the budding star under his wing, representing another surrogate father, and one of the few genuinely concerned about Brian's welfare throughout his short life. 'He had a way of talking that was all his own,' grinned Korner. 'It was a beautiful mixture of good manners and rudeness. No one really knew very much about Brian's home life because he was very careful not to involve his escape route – music – with the middle-class past he was escaping.'

Encouraged by his success, Brian and Dick decided to make the permanent break to London. Pat, suddenly seeing it all slipping away, made one last desperate attempt to salvage the relationship. She packed up Mark, took a bus to London and showed up on Brian's Notting Hill doorstep at 3 a.m.

The move was to prove disastrous. Jones was now circling in another orbit, enmeshed in what his father termed 'his absolute religion to music'. Mingling with the likes of blues heavyweights Muddy Waters, Bo Diddley and Chuck Berry while Pat sat all but ignored in a corner. When Brian did pay her attention he often erupted in jealous tantrums forcing her to quit a number of jobs over some imagined infidelity.

As Hattrell put it, 'Brian didn't really want to be with her. He wanted the bright lights and beautiful girls who made eyes at him while he was performing. Pat was a very ordinary, frumpy girl, not at all artistic. She was convenient, someone to clean the flat, cook his food and provide a sexual outlet.'

Beyond the obvious, Andrews was seeing something happening to Brian. It wasn't just the endless string of disposable dollybirds tucked under his arm, like the fourteen-year-old schoolgirl he openly paraded about town; nor the snazzy Italian box-jacket and winklepicker shoes he had purchased from her wages while she'd gone hungry. This was rather a new confidence, cocky, steely, manifesting itself on several fronts. He dropped his name, now calling himself Elmo Jones after his latest blues idol, Elmore James. Thrown off too were the last vestiges of parental dominance by abandoning his brief studies at the prestigious London College of Optics, Mr Jones's last-gasp attempt to rope Brian into professional respectability.

Even beyond such superficial alterations, however, Pat noticed changes even more disturbing. Gone was the early playful Brian she'd fallen in love with, who for all his faults and hang-ups had initially displayed a certain degree of innocence, even sweetness. Now in its place emerged a callous toughness increasingly devoid of genuine warmth, 'A little Welsh bull,' as Keith Richards would dub him.

As his popularity continued to grow Andrews witnessed an ever-burgeoning display of ego. Inevitably his fellow musicians gathered around inviting him to join their groups, 'I don't join other people's bands,' he haughtily announced, 'people join mine.'

Eventually Pat came to the inevitable realisation that she didn't know him anymore, and in September she and Mark left London and Brian for good. 'It was the only thing to do. I didn't tell Brian. I bottled out and left a note.'

Pat, however, had one final trip to make to Hatherly Road. As she explained, 'My father felt that people at work were talking about him because of Mark being born. He felt Mr Jones was behind this, that maybe they wanted to ease him out.

'I rushed over like a hurricane to their doorstep, Mr Jones hurriedly closed the door behind him so Brian's mother wouldn't see.

' "Listen, I'm very upset about the way my father's being treated at work," I told him. "I've seen how you've treated Brian and you're certainly not going to treat Mark like that. If you've got any ideas of seeing your grandson while you're behaving in this manner, you can forget it." '

Seeing Lewis Jones's look of haughty disdain she finally recognised what she was just beginning to see in Brian. The sins of the father visited upon the son. Brian, like so many victims, would go on to victimise not only himself, but others around him.

Years later, while Jones was earning £1,000 a week as a Rolling Stone and not contributing a penny to his son, Andrews had this to say: 'The one thing I feel badly about is when I'm walking down the road and Mark sees some toy and I can't afford to get it for him. I say to myself, Brian's got enough money, why can't he buy him something? But I never hear from him. I feel quite sorry for him in a way, the kind of person he is Brian can never be happy, can never have true friends. The only friends he has probably like him because of who he is. If he was turned out on to the streets no one would want to know Brian. He's not the kind of person you take to. He's cynical, he's got no feelings for anybody. He uses people for his own good and throws them aside.'

'You're signing a part of you away when you get married,' Brian once said in reference to his many fallen relationships. 'I think you sign your whole life away. Perhaps if I could, I'd get married for a year, just sign a year's contract.'

Even though Jones finally managed to sever the physical ties to Cheltenham, it remained a place filled with emotional scars that would haunt him forever after. At the height of his popularity and fame as a Rolling Stone, he and chauffeur Brian Palastanga stopped for a rare visit home. Palastanga remembers a warm summer evening on the front lawn, talking with Lewis Jones when he happened to look up and see Brian standing at his bedroom window peering out wistfully, a veritable little boy lost.

'Why were you looking like that?' the chauffeur asked when he came down.

'I wish I could be back here,' he mused quietly.

But it was just one more illusion. For Brian, home had never been a refuge, no more than the childhood fantasy he would try to recreate years later at Cotchford Farm. Although he would spend his life searching for his lost innocence, a blissful haven of love and security, in the end, there was no safe place for Brian Jones.

2 GILDED CAGE
Fame, Money and Madness

As TIME PASSED, being perceived a leader was more important to Brian Jones than even his music. The need to dominate and control, as he was once dominated and controlled, became an all-consuming ambition Jones was determined to achieve. It was an ironic twist that that which all of Cheltenham had disdained – Brian's profound lack of discipline, his thoughtless philandering and the endless scandals – were now used to his full advantage.

Or as Ian Stewart, the piano playing 'sixth Stone' put it, 'Brian's highly suspect character paved the way to his international success.'

The first time the would-be rebels, Mick Jagger and Keith Richards, saw him perform during a 7 April appearance at the Ealing Club, they were overawed by his presence on stage: daring, wild and musically far superior. As Richards put it: 'We were dead impressed.'

'They were very much in awe of him,' friend 'Spanish' Tony Sanchez recalled in *Up and Down with the Rolling Stones*: 'It wasn't just that his musical knowledge and ability dwarfed theirs, it was their thinly concealed envy for the fact that he lived dangerously and walked firmly on the wild side of life, while they combined rebellion with a cosy life at home with mum and dad. Keith, particularly, talked about fights he'd been in and things he'd shoplifted, but even he couldn't hide his shock when Brian casually mentioned his worry over his two illegitimate children.'

Anita Pallenberg put it even more succinctly: 'Brian wanted to catch your attention when he was speaking; to captivate you. Then he had the way he moved and his hair, which was captivating, and I'm sure The Stones fell for it. Keith in a cynical way maybe, Mick, he fell for it. Brian was so far ahead of them you wouldn't believe it. Here are Mick and Keith trying to learn how to be sex objects; they were still schoolboys and Brian already had two illegitimate children.'

The early relationship between Jagger and Jones was certainly one of hero worship on the part of the younger, more inexperienced Mick. Jagger idolised Jones for his ability to read music, his accomplished musicianship, and mostly, for those goading, slightly effeminate displays Brian threw off on stage. Jones patiently taught him the fundamentals of blues harmonica despite his blatant disrespect for singers who weren't musicians. They were also similarly drawn together by some early recordings they'd made at IBC Studios in Portland Place.

As Marianne Faithfull observed: 'Although in the end, Mick became intent on replacing Brian, in the beginning Brian was, in effect, his role model.'

The 'little Welsh bull' quickly proved worthy of his nickname; hustling gigs, relentlessly soliciting investors and badgering club owners to give The Stones a chance. He fought to keep the fledgling band going over the brutally cold snowbound winter of 1962/63, London's worst in over a hundred years. Jagger and Jones, together with Dick moved into a two-room bedsit in Edith Grove, Chelsea, a rat-infested dump without working plumbing and only a few naked light bulbs that operated via an electric coin meter.

They just about managed the rent via Jagger's £7 a week London School of Economics grant and Jones's shop assistant job at Whitley's department store, fending off starvation by stealing into neighbours' flats and nicking empty bottles for the deposit. Their daily diet of pork pies and stale bread was supplemented by a rare treat of eggs and potatoes stolen from markets along the Fulham Road.

'We were so good at it,' boasted Brian, 'they never once suspected us.' Jones would regularly exploit any means to accomplish his goals, including regular dips into the cash register at Whitley's. He wasn't even above poaching Keith's last pound out of his pocket while he slept.

Like a childhood bully, Jones preyed mercilessly on those weaker than himself, such as Dick Hattrell, who'd shown up unexpectedly with an £80 stipend from his stint in the Territorial Army. Jones first whipped the sweater off his back and handed it to a shivering Keith while taking Hattrell's coat for himself. He then not only snatched the entire paycheque for food and booze, but bought himself a spanking-new guitar as well.

As he struggled single-mindedly to keep his dream aloft, Jones secretly worried that Jagger was becoming a problem. The resident student was wavering about staying with the band, leaning more towards the sure money of an accountant's career than the itinerant life of an aspiring muso. Jones feared if Jagger decided to quit The Stones, he'd take Richards with him, the one guy he couldn't really afford to lose. After all, Richards and Jagger were boyhood friends from Dartford, part of London's outer-ring suburbs from which all The Stones hailed, with the exception of Brian.

Jones masterfully utilised those long winter days when Jagger was at college to hone both a musical and personal camaraderie with Richards. They had much in common, including the strained relationship with their fathers. Bert Richards, ironically, was an engineer like Lewis Jones. Keith's particular situation was so bad he wouldn't even speak with his dad for some twenty years.

Brian and Keith's shared passion for the blues ultimately produced that rarest of all musical gifts, an identity that defined their emerging sound. 'The whole secret behind The Stones,' explained Richards, 'is the way we work two guitars together. Brian and I worked on guitar together intensely; it was the cheapest way to stay warm.'

According to Ian Stewart, Jones's strategy worked brilliantly. 'During this period Keith and Brian developed a relationship as close as their guitar playing and I sensed that Jagger was beginning to feel left out, jealous and resentful of Brian. I could see him looking at Brian in a way that was quite menacing. I could sense back then the beginning of Mick's desire to distance Keith from Brian. When people live together all the bloody time you're never sure whether they mean what they say or whether they're laughing at you all the time. I used to think they were fucking insane at times.'

In Jones's obsessive drive to achieve, anyone was expendable. Predictably, the first on his list was the ever malleable Dick Hattrell, with his dubious position as band roadie. The bespectacled 5′ 3″, rotund rock wannabe followed Brian around like a lapdog. Jones however, wanting to distance himself from anything remotely close to his provincial roots, always made Hattrell walk a respectful ten yards behind. During rare meals taken at the Wimpy Bar, Jones would demand that Hattrell hand over his money and then make the poor guy wait outside in the cold while he and Keith went inside to eat.

On another of those frigid winter nights Brian sent Hattrell out for cigarettes and then bolted the door behind him. 'Brian had a very cruel streak,' remembers Hattrell. 'I thought he'd keep me out in the cold for only a short while and then relent, but no, I was locked out until morning and I damn near froze to death.'

Finally, when Hattrell could no longer contribute any money, Jones decided one snowy night it was time to cut him loose. 'It ended up with us stripping him off and trying to electrocute him,' says Richards. 'Brian and I came back to the pad and he was in Brian's bed. Brian got very annoyed that he was in his bed asleep. We had all these cables lyin' around and Brian pulled out this wire: "This end is plugged in, baby, and I'm coming after you." Brian ran after him with this long piece of cable attached to an amplifier, electric sparks flying around the room. Dick ran down the stairs, out into the street with nothing on screaming, "Don't go up there, they're trying to electrocute me!"'

'Stay out on the doorstep or else I'll give you 220 volts!' threatened Jones as he slammed the door. Despite his despicable treatment at the hands of Jones, Hattrell remained a loyal friend to Brian right up until the very end.

Brian though, didn't confine his sadistic behaviour to his flatmates. One-time friend, Kathy Etchingham, most noted for her high profile relationship with Jimi Hendrix, was subject to many a twisted prank. 'He did some bloody evil things to me. We went to this party together and he told me that the drinks were in the garage. So I went marching back there. What he didn't tell me was there was a big hole in the floor and I went straight into it. He thought it was very funny. I had no skin on my knees and elbows. He was behind me when I walked in and brought a few friends to watch.' Little wonder that Jones didn't endear himself to many people.

If Jones could dish it out, by contrast, he couldn't really take it. Keith and Mick took some delight in ganging up on their flatmate, mercilessly chiding him for his fetish of washing his hair twice daily; they also performed caustic characterisations of Jones's thick neck and short, stubby legs. The highly sensitive Stone was often, and easily, reduced to tears.

As the band slowly started to marshal a following at the Ealing and Marquee, Brian, still desperate to win approval at home, decided this was the time to break the news to his parents. He gathered up his courage and phoned them one evening telling Lewis and Louisa he had formed a new group and wanted to stop by and discuss it with them.

'To me,' said the elder Jones, 'this was evidence that in spite of our early disagreements he still regarded me as his confidant. He came to Cheltenham to see us and was full of ambition for the future. He appeared to have found what he was looking for; a chance to become a competent jazz musician. From that moment on there was a complete and lasting reconciliation.'

But that's not how Keith Richards saw it. Even after he'd been successful with The Stones, Jones was still searching for parental recognition. 'Brian would sit up for two days and nights writing and rewriting letters to his parents. What he wanted was an admission at last that he'd got his own thing together. He'd come back from visits with his parents and would always say he couldn't communicate with them.'

Jones's girlfriend at the time, model Linda Lawrence, claimed Brian's parents totally ignored him and that it was only after he'd made a successful record they even acknowledged his birthday. 'The contact was because he had made it, money,' affirmed Lawrence, 'but that wasn't the contact he was looking for.' Later incidents would also contest Lewis Jones's declaration of restored father/son harmony.

Meanwhile, thanks to Jones's relentless promotional blitz and the boy's blossoming talent, by the spring of 1963 The Rolling Stones were suddenly the hottest band in London. Giorgio Gomelsky, owner of Richmond's Crawdaddy Club, stated, 'There was no doubt that Brian was the leader of the band, the energy in the band. Brian reigned over every single move that happened to them, he was the organising one.'

Echoed legendary blues man Bo Diddley: 'Brian was a feisty little dude that was trying to pull the group ahead. I saw him as the leader. He didn't take no mess. He was a fantastic cat who handled the group beautifully.'

A long-time friend of Jones, whom we will call Derrick, points out how Brian's background and experience was turned to full advantage: 'At the beginning of the Stones thing Brian was the most worldly – he'd been a bohemian. Mick and Keith had come out of a lower suburban existence and hadn't really been around the scene like Brian had and so they resented it, but he was in fact the initial attitude and drive behind what The Stones were. He was showing them "Look, it can be done," and they slowly caught on to it.'

Eventually, Jones proved himself every bit the electrifying Marquee draw he'd once been with Alexis Korner. Observed Korner: 'He had a very good sense of tactics, he knew how to get an audience. When The Stones came on stage Mick would drop his lip and dribble a little bit, but once they started performing he would just sing. Brian was the aggressive member of The Stones. He'd do that funny tiptoe dance of his, right to the edge of the stage and slap the tambourine in the audience's face as if to say, "Fuck you!" then he'd drop back again, leering at you all the time so as to make you really angry.'

Cream percussionist Ginger Baker, who originally suggested bringing in Charlie Watts as The Stones' drummer, remembers Jones as a
born performer right from the beginning. Recalling one of the band's
first gigs at the Cy Laurie Club on Windmill Street Ginger said, 'I
noticed that Mick just stood at the mike, almost motionless and sang. It
was Brian who was the showman, leaping about, playing on his knees
and running into the crowd with his guitar. When you went to see The
Stones in the early days Brian was the one you wanted to see.'

According to London journalist Judith Simonds, Jones's snarling
stage persona was, at least in part, an outgrowth of his continued
struggle with asthma. The attacks, which he often experienced some
three times a week had over the years built up a pattern of anxiety and
panic. Jones was terrified of having an attack in the middle of a performance. Said Simonds, 'Through his asthma, stage work was agony
for him. Working to counteract his fear of an attack he promoted the
most unsmiling, violent image of the group.'

A crucial turning point in Jones's fortunes occurred on 3 May 1963
when The Stones signed on the management team of young Andrew
Loog Oldham and established show biz agent, Eric Easton. Oldham, a
former publicist for The Beatles, was a nineteen-year-old wonder-boy
determined to carry away a chunk of the big time for himself – whatever it took.

Jones, despite taking an immediate, instinctive dislike to Oldham
sensed the pair was going to take them places. He promptly signed a
management agreement on behalf of all The Stones, with a separate
confidential deal for himself whereby he bagged an extra £5 weekly – a
move which would ever after come back to haunt both Jones and his
unforgiving colleagues in The Stones.

Oldham though, saw some immediate house-clearing to be done.
With his prominent lantern jaw resulting from a childhood calcium
deficiency, Ian Stewart, resembling more a meat packer than a rock
star, was doomed. 'He just doesn't look the part,' reasoned Oldham,
'plus six is too many for fans to remember the faces in the picture.'

As band leader it was Jones's task to deliver the bad news. 'It wasn't
done very nicely,' remembered the burly piano player. 'I just turned up
one day to find the others had stage suits and there was no suit for me.
Brian said "Don't worry about it. You're a part of The Stones, you'll
still get a sixth share, I promise you."'

But like so many of Brian's self-serving promises this one too was not
to be. Even though Stew agreed to stay on as the group's road manager

24

and remained an integral part of the band, according to his wife Cynthia he was devastated by the brutality of his dismissal. 'He did care about being relegated. Andrew loved the pretty, thin, long-haired boys. Stew felt bitter, not because he was not up there on stage, but about the savage way he was kicked to one side.'

Another suggestion for change came from Easton. He wanted to drop Jagger from the band, concluding his voice was too weak and that the vocalist was still only comfortable singing twelve-bar blues. 'I don't think Jagger's any good,' he said to Brian in the office one day.

'Okay, we'll get rid of him then,' Jones coolly replied.

Brian was only too willing to comply. Not only was this his chance to bring in Paul Jones, who'd been singing with Korner and had always been Brian's first choice for lead vocalist, but it meant an opportunity for him to promote the harmonies he'd been working out with new bassist Bill Wyman.

'Brian always fancied himself as a back-up vocalist,' said Richards. 'He was really hot into this thing of harmonies. But Mick and I knew the band wasn't really capable of playing that kind of stuff. Brian's voice wasn't his forte. It was like a rasp.'

Fatefully, Oldham overruled Easton, and Jagger's position within the band was firmly established. With Andrew's strategy to play up the look and persona of the band, allegiances once more shifted, this time briefly tying Brian and Mick together. Jones further refined Jagger's harmonica technique and advised him on his stilted stage movements. Jagger, a quick study, was learning all too well.

Of the constantly shifting triangle Richards has said, 'There was always this incredible conflict between Brian, Mick and myself. It was imbalanced in one way or another. There was something between us that didn't quite make it somewhere. Maybe it's in the stars. He was a Pisces, I'm a Sagittarius and Mick's a Leo. Maybe those three can't ever completely connect all together at the same time for very long.'

By September of 1963, Jones moved in with his girlfriend, Linda Lawrence and her family in Windsor, while Richards and Jagger took a flat with Oldham in north London. The move signalled a slow, steady shift of power with the triumvirate of Keith, Mick and Andrew leaving Brian, once more, on the periphery.

Remarked Alex Lawrence, Linda's father in *Golden Stone*: 'We used to go up to The Stones' office in London and Andrew was there. We never liked him. He was very snotty and was very obviously in cahoots with Mick and Keith against Brian. Mick seemed jealous of Brian.'

Noel Redding, bassist for The Jimi Hendrix Experience, further explained to Jackson: 'Mick tried to take Brian on, right, because Jones frankly was getting more attention than him. It's well known that Mick really resented the attention Brian got. I mean, he really hated it.'

Jagger was fast emerging as the star of the group, aided by his power-position as lead vocalist, leaving Jones in an increasingly hopeless position. 'You don't realise it on stage, but the strength of the spotlight on the singer is much brighter than that on the rest of the musicians,' explains Richards.

Although for a time Jones remained the crowd favourite, Jagger's popularity was beginning to grow even as they embarked on their first tour of Great Britain on 29 September 1963. As writer/photographer Nick Kent noted: 'Brian Jones was the most respectably middle-class and there were like five girls backstage who were totally enchanted, but also very frightened. They all went to Brian, but they were looking at Jagger who was standing next to them with the attitude, "Okay, talk to me. What you talkin' to that cunt for?" '

Jones bitterly watched Jagger prance about the stage having all but stolen his manoeuvres in what could only be termed a blatant act of betrayal. As Philip Norman wrote in his fine biography *The Stones*: 'Brian in particular, loved to see "bother" starting and encouraged it by brief shakes of his hair and tambourine. It was largely from this trick of Brian's that Mick Jagger learned how small, tantalising body movements could tease up conventional screams to a banshee-like howl. He too began to slip off his Cecil Gee Italian jacket and dangle it on his forefinger like a stripper's G-string.'

None of this went unnoticed by Oldham, whose loyalty to front-man Mick, his cash cow, was obvious. As Bill Wyman put it, the cagey manager initiated a 'whispering campaign about Brian'. He chose the tour to drop the bombshell that Jones was receiving £5 a week more than the other members.

'Everybody freaked,' recalls Richards. 'We said, "Fuck you!" It was ridiculous for Brian to tout himself as the leader. The Stones were formed with nothing like that in mind. The extra £5 a week has got to go towards fixing an amplifier!'

If that didn't put a definite chill on The Stones' relationship with their founder, Ian Stewart remembers Jones lost his leadership position for good one night when the band stopped to discuss their lodgings. 'Look, I'm the leader of this band,' boasted Jones, 'so all of you can stay in a twenty-five-bob-a-night hotel while I stay in a thirty-five bob one. I'll see you in the morning.'

'Brian really blew it that night,' confirmed Stew. 'That's when the band made up their minds he was never going to be leader. Brian always fancied himself a leader, but mostly all he did was make a lot of noise about it. He didn't have it in him; after all, leaders are born, not made. Brian got exactly what he was asking for. He'd been such an asshole to everyone.'

Jones's vulnerability to sickness caused him to often miss gigs. He was on constant medication for back problems, ear infections, sore throats and frequently came away from health clinics diagnosed with 'nervous strain'. 'Brian's illnesses became a band joke,' said Wyman. 'Mick and Keith would say sarcastically, "Oh, Brian's ill again, does he have a doctor's certificate?" He seemed a hypochondriac and when you're young you haven't time for other people's illnesses.'

Being stripped of his authority was a blow to Jones that was temporarily waylaid by the skyrocketing stardom The Stones were finally achieving. He relished cruising around town in his flashy Humber sports car, club-hopping at such trendy nightspots as The Establishment, the exclusive Ad Lib and Whipp's. He adored being nominated as *Rave Magazine*'s 'Best Dressed Pop Star of the Week' for his racks of fashionable threads culled from pricey Carnaby Street boutiques. Mostly though, it was the recognition and fame he craved, feeding on the instantaneous, though admittedly shallow, adulation that came with it.

'That was the thing that really fucked Brian up. He was so desperate for attention,' says Jagger. 'He wanted to be admired and loved and all that, which he was by a lot of people, but it was never enough for him.'

Linda Lawrence maintains that Brian's behaviour stemmed from an absolute need to be a celebrity. 'He felt he had to be a star because he wasn't a star in his family; he wanted to be a star in another way. It wasn't his ego. It was something he wanted to fulfil, that he hadn't got from his childhood.'

Lawrence too became victim to Jones's childish, often dangerous pranks: He would take her on boat rides down the river, lurching dangerously to the edge of a waterfall before swerving around the other way; driving her out to a deserted forest at night, he would get out of the car, lock the doors and make menacing gestures. Ultimately, Linda would endure endless rounds of physical abuse, with Jones knocking her around violently. 'I never felt he was cruel,' notes Lawrence curiously, 'but rather releasing something hurtful from his past that made him angry.'

Linda delivered Brian's fourth child in June 1964, a son whom he callously once again named Julian, and summarily discarded from his world. Said Stones' secretary, Shirley Arnold, 'He was so rude about that poor little kid. He used to call it Broad Bean Head.'

Whether out of fear, or simple disinterest, Jones didn't even bother telling his parents of the new arrival. Linda's mother then took it upon herself to inform the Joneses of the existence of their grandson. Lewis Jones coldly wrote back: 'Many aspects of the situation seem very mysterious. You say the baby is nine months old, implying it was born last June. We saw Linda in May and never had the slightest suspicion. I spoke to Linda on 1 June and again at the end of June. Nothing said was remotely suggestive of such an event. Brian and Linda stayed with us in October. Nothing in their conversation or manner aroused any suspicions. So after nine months of most successful secrecy you have now told me and I cannot understand why . . .'

Even as Jones was achieving his dream, he found himself in a dilemma caused by the direction in which Oldham was spinning the band.

To play up the rivalry with the wholesome Beatles, The Stones' manager packaged the band as, 'Threatening, uncouth and animalistic,' a ruffian image dramatically heightened by his catch phrase, 'Would You Like Your Daughter to Marry A Rolling Stone?' His ploys of sending The Stones to London's five-star hotels with photographers to document their getting thrown out, and instructions to act 'disgracefully and be abominably rude' with the press were increasingly disdained by the cultured, ever more refined Jones.

If there's one area in which Brian's superior upbringing and education served him well it was in talking to the media. Brian Jones in another time without the drugs, long hair, crazy clothes and loud music might have been a sophisticated young politician, barrister, or fledgling diplomat. He was that good with the spoken word. Although today there are precious few examples of Brian's repartee, one very rare interview did surface early this decade. It was recorded during The Stones' turbulent, ground breaking 1964 tour of America.

Question: Why do you think The Rolling Stones became such a fantastic success?

Brian: We've just provided the right thing at the right time. We've come along with a very raw sort of music where everything is rather sweet and things were getting sort of sloppy and sentimental. In

England they were anyway. I believe so in America too, you know, with Cliff Richard and that sort of thing. A new tough element seems to be growing up. I don't mean tough kids, but a new vital urge seems to be growing up amongst the young people. And we provide a music with the same sort of vitality. It hasn't happened all that quickly. We've been around in England for about eighteen months now and some groups make big records with their first ones – we haven't. It's like America is taking time to build.

Question: As a matter of fact, there seems to be a great deal of resistance to the group. How would you account for that?

Brian: Well, I suppose there's always resistance to something new, isn't there? Always. To every action there's a reaction, isn't there? It's true with pop music as well.

Question: I've read many magazine articles on The Rolling Stones that were practically libellous. I've never seen any British group described in the way The Rolling Stones have been. You've got very long hair, but you certainly don't look dirty and this is an allegation I have read so many times and I just can't understand it.

Brian: It's very difficult to explain. All I can do really is deny it and say that I am speaking for myself, and I resent it very much. If anyone called me dirty to my face I wouldn't take it lying down. When you read it in magazines there's very little you can do. You're really at the mercy of the magazine writers, what they write, people believe, and they've written so much dirty rubbish about us I do feel very resentful about it. I just hope this time around we can show people we're not dirty, we're not really scruffy and we're not thick.

Still, even as Brian's leadership was being usurped and his opposition to their Neanderthal personae ignored, there was one area where Jones had always remained king, the music. Yet even his vision for the purist blues approach, achieved so well on vinyl on The Stones' first self-titled EP, was slowly starting to crumble in the face of Oldham's bullheaded drive to mass popularity.

Said Brian: 'When we left the club scene we also left the diehard R&B fanatics and we made a compromise to cope with the pop fans we came across in dance halls and on tours.'

Once again, Jones could not wage a lone battle against forces determined to make a faster, more ruthless climb to the top. Already, in mid-1964, the crack in The Stones' unadulterated blues vein came via Jagger and Richards's first feeble attempts at song writing. Included in an otherwise raw and primitive collection of R&B covers culled from the tour circuit for their first LP was the song, 'Tell Me'. A Jagger/Richards composition, it was merely an amateurish imitation of the Merseybeat sound, complete with Mick's 'Whoa yeah' Beatlesque ending.

The tune's mere presence on the album, however, was enough to rattle the unsettled guitarist whose firm grip on both the band and his own emotional well-being had begun to be forcibly prised loose.

Meanwhile, in the footsteps of their 'fab' rivals, The Stones were poised to conquer America over June 1964 and once more, Jones's problems were temporarily pushed aside in anticipation of this new challenge. 'It's the people I want to see, not so much the places,' he was saying. 'I want to meet up with people who have the same musical ideas as we do, Muddy Waters, and Bo Diddley. Obviously we hope for success, but I don't believe in anything good until it happens.'

Jones's comments were prophetic, as The Stones had not yet caught on in the States. Night after night the band would play to as few as 600 fans in a 15,000-capacity venue. Disappointing to the organisation, for Brian, away from the pressures of home, it was like a fresh beginning. Once again the stage was home where he could dance, preen and gaily toss his silky blond locks.

Enthused one fan: 'Brian had so much energy. You could see him really getting high behind the music especially when he played harmonica. It completely turned him on. It was almost like Mick Jagger's spotlight was equally Brian's.'

'America was parties and everything you could possibly dream of,' hailed Jones. 'It was there, laid on us.' But it would be the final time he would hold the stage hostage as his own.

Back home in London that tumultuous autumn of 1964, Jones faced the full force of his long awaited celebrity. Much to Oldham's surprise and delight, The Stones were now viewed as moral outlaws, clashing rebellious teens against their ever-conservative parents. Although Brian loved the mass adulation, for the fragile Stone it soon got out of hand. 'When fans really start raving they seem almost like enemies,' he publicly stated. 'You know in your heart that all they're trying to do is make contact, touch you or talk to you. But what it seems is that thousands of kids are trying to tear you apart, to throw things at you, to knock you over, this drives us into ourselves so that the only people we speak to properly are the other people in the group.'

The mob scenes too seemed to bring out Brian's near paralysing fear:

Jones had a pronounced phobia about anyone touching his hair. He even refused to have a barber cut it, only those he trusted, usually a girlfriend. Fans, of course, were driven wild by his shaggy golden mop and inevitably wanted to reach out and grab it, which drove Brian berserk. During the many uncontrollable riots, Brian was often dragged off stage fending for his life, with his clothes being ripped away.

It left him so terrorised he often called Linda's father following a gig: 'I'm scared to go out because of all the people. Please come and get me.'

On several occasions Mr Lawrence had to drive Jones to the venue and actually carry him in his arms, like a petrified child, backstage to the dressing-room.

In his book *Stone Alone*, Bill Wyman tells how on their way to a gig one night Jones wanted to make a phone call and the band took off in the van leaving him running for his life to escape hordes of fans who managed to tear off his jacket, leave his shirt in shreds and even make off with his shoes. 'We all thought it was hilarious, but Brian didn't see the joke. Brian always felt a little left-out because of his bloody stupidity,' said Stewart. 'He used to do such dumb things, anything to upset people. Then he would get all pathetic and say, "Nobody loves me. Why is everybody against me?"'

Jones's insecurities were growing daily. Brian would ask Linda, 'Do you think Mick is better than me? Do the fans like that type of person better? Who do you think gets the most fan letters?' Linda revealed how it got so bad that Brian would often break down in tears because he felt he was losing control of the band.

'He would question whether the fans came to see The Stones because of Mick, or did they come because of the actual music, which was what I felt Brian was representing.'

Overshadowed and neglected, Brian desperately looked for avenues to garner attention. Gered Mankowitz came on board as photographer for The Stones' second highly successful American tour, which began on 24 October 1964 in New York and ended in Chicago on 15 November. In Hotchner's book *Blown Away*, he recalled: 'Brian was very well-spoken, terribly full of social grace. But there was another side to him, a manipulative side that was very difficult to cope with. He could be very hard, very cruel. He enjoyed laughing at people's mistakes. He would try and screw up pictures just to make my life difficult. He'd play games to be a difficult sort of elf, a little naughty boy. I think he became paranoid about his role in the band because he had initiated it.'

That autumn tour was also noteworthy for two developments. The

first was the birth to Jones's casual girlfriend, Dawn Malloy, of a boy –
Jones's fifth child. Dawn went straight to the band's management and
announced the blessed event, throwing Brian into a tailspin. Andrew
hastily prepared the following document, witnessed by Mick: 'I have
received a cheque for £700 from Andrew Loog Oldham Ltd, paid to me
by the said company on behalf of Brian Jones in full settlement of any
claims arising, damages and inconveniences caused, by me, by the birth
of my son and I understand completely that the matter is now closed
and that I will make no statement about Brian Jones or the child to any
members of the press or public.' Once again, Jones – who had no
knowledge of the document – slithered out of a dicey situation.

It was on this tour too that Jones was introduced to the world of illicit pharmaceuticals. Drug use, combined with his delicate condition
quickly took its toll. Once Jones had to be rushed to a Milwaukee Hospital, the official word had Brian suffering from bronchitis and extreme
exhaustion, but in fact, he was delirious and in such a rundown condition from a steady diet of uppers and cocaine that he had to be fed
intravenously.

As Charlie Watts said: 'I think Brian liked drink and he liked drugs,
but they weren't very good for him. He wasn't strong enough mentally
or physically to take any of it. Brian did everything to excess.'

As word of his illness leaked out, Jones found he had to fight against
rumours, perhaps from even within the organisation, that ill health
was forcing him to leave the group. 'I'm not on my last legs and I am
not leaving The Stones,' he said in a public statement. 'I fell ill during
our American tour and I have to take it easy for a while. The thought of
leaving The Stones has never entered my head.'

Just as The Stones' organisation perceived Brian to be getting a bit
out of hand, on to the scene came Tom Keylock, a hulking, Michael
Caine type. Hailing from a family of three sisters and one brother, Keylock served in WW II as a paratrooper with the First Airborne Division
where his polished skills in combat drew extended tours of duty in both
Ireland and Palestine.

'It changed my life all over,' remembered Keylock of his early days
with The Stones. 'I owned a car-hire company and got a call to pick
them up. I thought, The Rolling Stones, who are they? I sent one of my
chauffeurs over and he came back saying, "Never again!" and threatened to quit. So I turned up and it was a real hassle, but I got them
straightened out all right. I laid down a few ground rules: Keep your
feet off the windows and the upholstery and stop throwing cigarette

ends all over the place. So one thing led to another and Keith said, "Why don't you come and work with us?" I had a gut feeling I'm gonna do it. And I did it.'

Keylock recounts too his initial impressions of Jones: 'He was a genius. He could play anything. He really had a feeling for it, his whole body, his whole mind was into it. But Brian was a bit of a villain. You couldn't really trust him. He'd tell you he'd do something then he'd change his mind and tell you he wouldn't.'

One time, at a gig in Milan, Keylock recalls that Jones, after four or five numbers, complained, 'My amp's not working.' To which Ian Stewart dryly replied, 'No, you silly sod, it's not switched on!'

Keylock found that away from the business of being The Rolling Stones, the band members pretty much all went their separate ways. 'They were all friends, but they'd never phone up one another. Each one was into different things. None of them were alike.'

The Stones' new driver/minder meant business and was well equipped to deal with any eventuality. It was Keylock who later hired Brian Palastanga as Jones's personal chauffeur. According to Tom, Palastanga made the mistake of nicking a pair of expensive cameras from Jones's flat and promptly faced the unfortunate repercussions. 'If you don't tell me about those cameras I'll tear you to pieces,' threatened Keylock.

'I can get them back,' shivered a now terrified Palastanga.

Says Tom, 'I immediately filled him in, knocked all his teeth out, picked him up off the floor and slung him out the door. "You're sacked!" He wasn't looking too handsome when I last saw him.'

Bill Wyman once said Keylock was to be 'a key figure in the unfolding drama of life within The Stones.'

Meanwhile, a development that had tentatively begun to unfold in the early months of 1964 seriously threatened Jones's place in the band. Suddenly, in 1965, Jagger and Richards evolved into the songwriting powerhouse of The Stones. From penning Marianne Faithfull's top-ten hit, 'As Tears Go By', to a sequence of Stones' hits; 'Time Is On My Side', 'The Last Time' and the rock classic, 'Satisfaction', the Glimmer Twins, Jagger and Richards had all but completed their hostile takeover of the greatest rock 'n' roll band in history.

This was something Jones had not anticipated and it left him intimidated and badly shaken. Richards maintained he simply couldn't compose. 'Any musician who really wants to, can write. So far as I knew Brian never wrote a single finished song in his life. He wrote bits and pieces, but his paranoia was so great he could never bring himself to present them to us.'

According to Wyman, Jones did in fact pen several compositions for the band, but they were summarily dismissed out of hand with the kiss off, 'You can't write songs!' Only Keith and Mick, asserts Bill, were afforded the *opportunity* to compose.

Stewart, however, strongly disagrees. 'What really bothered Brian was knowing that the big rock money was in the writing and publishing, not the performing. He had a complete mental block against writing songs, he just could not do it. And because Mick and Keith wrote all the songs, which they were encouraged to do by Andrew Oldham, there was an unholy trinity of Mick, Keith and Andrew, and a very unholy trinity it was, I promise you. And Brian was just out of it. He would say, "They won't play my songs," but he couldn't write songs, he just couldn't. He would come to the studio with things he had written, but they were awful. Terrible.'

Added Jagger, 'Brian kept a lot of things to himself. I mean he never played me a song he'd written. He was very shy. But it was never a case of forcibly stifling him.'

If Jones did in fact compose, his inferiority complex and well defined fear of failure loomed so large he was unable to present them for consideration. Linda Lawrence recalls Jones frequently wrote lyrics on bits of paper and even sang them for her. 'They were like Donovan's, romantic, sort of spiritual, about his feelings. But Brian never said, "I'll show the boys this one," because he was insecure and thought his things too sentimental. I encouraged him to do his own things, but Brian would say, "They're not finished." That was his excuse all the time.'

Ultimately, Jones left some lyrics with New York journalist Al Aronowitz from a song entitled, 'Thank You For Being There':

> The maniacal choir that screamed out a warning
> Now sings a lullaby
> The walls that crashed to bury you and me
> Now shelter our hideaway

Mick and Keith, reportedly, soon began to hog the musical credits as well. Certainly, both Jones and Wyman were responsible for contributing key riffs and chord sequences to several high profile numbers, but when the records came out the credit went inevitably to Jagger/

Richards. Although Keith insists he came up with the riff for 'Satisfaction', many of Brian's peers privately suggest that it instead bears the indelible stamp of Jones.

Noel Redding went on record in *Golden Stone*, saying, 'It is said it was Brian who thought up the riff and played it to them. Then the lads said "Yeah right, thanks" and took it.'

That could shed some light on Jones's outward put-down of the song and his sarcastic breaking into 'Popeye the Sailor Man' during its performance on stage.

Bill Wyman now saw an exclusive club of Keith, Mick and Andrew, while 'the other three of us were secondary in Andrew's mind. He recognised that's where the talent was and the songwriting was necessary to carry us on. Suddenly we were being called "Mick Jagger and The Rolling Stones" and Brian took it personally that he wasn't the most popular member anymore, as far as the fans were concerned, because Mick started to get more mail than him.'

It was Jagger too, who was taking over as spokesman for the group, using his sarcastic wit to dazzle reporters at The Stones' press conferences. As a result, Jones was effectively shut out from interviews. The resulting frustration sometimes manifested itself in overt aggression.

Richards remembers one incident on tour where just prior to a performance the band had ordered some food. 'I'd gone out of the room for about ten minutes and when I came back Brian had eaten my piece of chicken! So there we were in the dressing-room, the announcer saying "Ladies and gentlemen . . . The Rolling Stones . . ." and Brian and I, with our guitars strapped around our necks, are just thumping each other. I gave him this incredible black eye which lasted for two months. All this because of a chicken-leg.'

Brian also began to lash out at his family. Despite Lewis Jones's claims of permanent reconciliation, Tom Keylock says they didn't visit Brian over a period of nearly nine years. He relates an incident when The Stones played a gig in Cheltenham and his parents showed up. Jones took Keylock aside and told him, 'Listen, my mum and dad are trying to get in the dressing-room. I don't want them here. I'll freak out.'

'But Brian, these are your parents . . .'

'I don't care.'

'Com'on, mate, you don't really mean . . .'

'*No*,' asserted Jones. 'I'll freak out. I don't want them in the dressing-room.'

Said Keylock, 'I had to face Brian's parents and tell them, "Sorry, Mr Jones, he doesn't want to see you.' I was very embarrassed over it.'

Over time, The Stones were slowly edging Brian out in the studio as well. Along with Wyman, Jones did some back-up vocals early on, but by 1965 they were cut off from that duty by Oldham's push to have Richards do more singing and thus promote Jagger and Richards as a one-two punch.

In *Stone Alone*, Wyman recounts Andrew's humiliating tactics, like switching off Brian's microphone in the middle of recording and then on playbacks fading out his instrument. 'He was made the outcast and it was terrible to watch,' recalls Bill. 'Brian would try to ingratiate himself to them by crawling first to Mick, then to Andrew, finally to Keith who he thought had the most empathy of the three. But that didn't work; it was a closed shop.'

Jones, however, found a way to cloud the pain through binging on drugs and alcohol. Not only did he find amphetamines a mood buster for his many bouts with depression, but also a boost to his inherent shyness, and now desperately sagging confidence. By early 1965, although friends warned him about the dangerous road he was travelling he insisted he needed them to cope. In fact, it was Jones's heavy drinking along with amphetamines that eventually caused his break-up with Linda.

Another offshoot of Jones's growing reputation as a druggie hit somewhat closer to home. Upon her graduation from teachers' college, Brian's sister, Barbara was virtually blacklisted in her search for a teaching position. Listing her school as a reference, Barbara, along with her family, learned that the headmistress had named Brian as a 'drug addict and an undesirable'. For the infuriated Lewis Jones, this development did little to bridge the widening gap with his son.

Former dancer, Ronni Money, the wife of rock musician Zoot Money, who'd befriended Jones in 1963 at the Crawdaddy Club, grew increasingly concerned over Brian's pill-popping: 'I recognised the weakness, knowing how easy it was to be sucked in, needing to take a drink before he went on or pop a pill. So I made him smoke marijuana. "If you need to take something, take something that isn't going to take you." So I turned him on.'

When Jones later met Bob Dylan and introduced him to Money he wryly quipped, 'This is the woman who straightened me out.'

But it wasn't to last. Jones began mixing whisky with prescription amphetamines, supplied by the so-called Dr Junkie of Chelsea, leaving him in no condition to work. In fact, when The Stones travelled to the States in May to record 'Satisfaction', Brian was in such terrible shape he spent several days in a Chicago hospital. Doctors warned Watts and Wyman, his only visitors, that continued drinking would kill him within a year.

'You'll never make thirty, cock,' Keith Richards compassionately warned him on several occasions. 'I know. I know,' Brian would answer wistfully. By now Jones was spinning hopelessly out of control.

Back in London, the guitarist once more immersed himself into the role of the rich and famous pop star by plunging into the social orbit dominated by upscale gallery owner Robert Fraser and Chelsea antique dealer Christopher Gibbs, along with a cliquish circle of trendy writers, photographers and film people. Whether a night out at the Scotch of St James, a pricey nightspot in London's chic West End, or greeting guests at the door of his elegant, newly purchased mews house at 7 Elm Park Lane, Jones was clearly acting out his self-fulfilling prophecy as the indefatigable sixties superstar.

Fortunately, the innocent public wasn't informed of all the malicious infighting surrounding The Stones, and the pulp press continued to churn out airy-fairy stories aimed at romanticising the personalities of the band. Case in point: this 1964 'Questionnaire' dedicated to Brian out of a typical British teen rag.

BRIAN JONES
REAL NAME: Lewis Brian Hopkin-Jones.
BIRTHPLACE: Cheltenham.
BIRTH DATE: 28.2.44.
HEIGHT: 5'8".
WEIGHT: 10st. 1lb.
COLOUR OF EYES: Greeny-blue.
COLOUR OF HAIR: Blond.
PARENTS' NAMES: Lewis and Louisa.
BROTHERS AND SISTERS: Barbara (17).
PRESENT HOME: London.
INSTRUMENTS PLAYED: Guitar. Harmonica.
WHERE EDUCATED: Cheltenham Grammar School.
MUSICAL EDUCATION: Self-taught.
ENTERED SHOW BUSINESS AT: 18.
FIRST PUBLIC APPEARANCE: Marquee, Oxford Street.
BIGGEST BREAK IN CAREER: Meeting the other Stones.

Paint It Black

TV DEBUT: 'Saturday Club'.
DISC LABEL: Decca.
HOBBIES: Women.
FAVOURITE SINGERS, ARTISTS: Johnny Cash, Bo Diddley, Jimmy Reed.
FAVOURITE ACTRESSES, ACTORS: Tony Perkins.
FAVOURITE COLOUR: Black/White/Grey.
FAVOURITE FOOD: Steaks.
FAVOURITE BAND: Muddy Waters.
FAVOURITE DRINK: Milk/Whisky.
FAVOURITE CLOTHES: 'Gear', 'Anello Boots'.
FAVOURITE COMPOSERS: Willy Dixon, Bach, Beatles.
MISCELLANEOUS LIKES: Having a shower.
MISCELLANEOUS DISLIKES: Public Transport.
TASTES IN MUSIC: Very catholic, but I hate brass bands.
ORIGIN OF STAGE NAME: Title of an old Muddy Waters Blues.
PERSONAL AMBITION: To stop smoking 60 fags a day.
PROFESSIONAL AMBITION: To tour the States. To get a number one.

As time went by Jones began exhibiting some rather bizarre behaviour. While on tour in France he would disappear in the middle of the night to climb the Eiffel Tower and phone friends at 3 a.m. to read aloud *Lady Chatterley's Lover*. Tony Kent recalls hanging out with The Stones in a restaurant in Pigalle when Jones had taken several downers. 'Brian took a spoon and dipped it into this sauce and tasted it and then he took another spoon and then another and all of a sudden he started saying, "Quick, quick, a match, a match!" So somebody got a match and he took it and started to breathe on it hard. His mouth was so on fire with this hot sauce that he was convinced his breath would light the match.'

His well-known indulgence in casual sex too provided an arena in which he could still dominate without the responsibilities of commitment. Kathy Etchingham, who was often at his flat observed, 'Sometimes there would be two or three chicks because Brian often liked more than one at a time. One time I went over there after he called and he was in bed with two chicks. He just threw their clothes on the bed and said to them, "Do you mind leaving?"'

Legend has it that while on tour Jones would sometimes pick up girls by ringing room service, thereby having his choice of any of a hundred luscious young ladies waiting down in the hotel lobby. One time Brian hustled a girl outside of a theatre in Hanley and asked her to accompany him back to London. 'He was all over her in the van on the way home. When we arrived in London we dropped Mick and Keith at their house then went to Brian's place. He leapt from the van, leaving the girl with us. He rushed into the house and barred the door.'

Jones left a baffled and angry Wyman and Watts to put her up for the night, give her some money and put her on a train back to Hanley the next morning.

Inevitably, some of these encounters turned nasty. On 6 May, on the road in Clearwater, Florida, a groupie who had spent the night with Jones limped down from the hotel room covered in bruises, saying Brian had beaten her up. When the feisty young lady met up with Jones later that morning she handed Jones two cracked ribs. Bill Wyman was forced to cover up the story in an interview for *New Musical Express*, saying Jones had fallen while doing some karate moves.

One of Brian's more memorable so-called casual encounters was with one Ms Joanne Alice Petrie, better known to the world as self-confessed super-groupie, Jo Jo Laine, the wife of ex-Moody Blues' founder and Wings' co-commander, Denny Laine. In an as-of-yet unpublished memoir written by this author, the inimitable redhead recalls a telling evening spent in the company of Mr Jones.

'The Rolling Stones were in town playing the Boston Garden. My friend Norma had met some of their entourage and told me we had a good chance of meeting the band before the show. Personally, I really wasn't all that keen on seeing Mick and the boys, I mean they weren't The Beatles were they?

'True to her word, Norma got us backstage and we stood there dressed in our most wild and provocative outfits, trying to look eighteen and cool. Our friend Jenny, a few years older, had driven us and she immediately set her sights on a tryst with Brian Jones. There were at least fifty girls mobbing the area and I could see The Stones' tour manager pacing the hallway scrutinising the night's pickings. Soon I saw one of the doors open and caught a glimpse of Brian himself peering out, perusing the crowd. He motioned in my direction to a roadie, who relayed the message to the tour manager.

' "Would you like to meet The Stones?"

'Norma nodded breathlessly, nudging me.

' "Right," he replied. "Stay right here while I thin out the crowd."

'Within minutes, only five of us remained, one for each Stone, I thought, plus a young man who was obviously gay. "Who's he for?" I playfully ribbed Norma. "Mick?"

'Before I knew it we were swept up in a circle of security officers and were running through the tunnel that joined the Garden to the adjacent Madison Hotel where The Beatles had stayed two years before. We clamoured on to an elevator passing secretaries, PR personnel and wives of the managers. Norma and I walked into one of the tiny rooms in the suite, hitting the jackpot. On a bed lay Mick Jagger on the phone, while Keith Richards lazily sprawled on the floor, one leg propped on a chair, smoking a huge joint. Norma started talking to him, but he was just staring at the ceiling, off somewhere in lala land.

'I stood there stiffly, self-conscious and tongue-tied, uncomfortable in such close quarters with rock's reigning superstars. I escaped to the hallway and wandered into another room. There was Brian lounging in the corner, head down, picking out random chords on an acoustic guitar. He looked up and smiled faintly in recognition when I came in. I knew he had picked me out downstairs.

' "Where did you get that lovely hair?" he asked.

'I felt instantly at ease with this sweet, feminine looking boy, who didn't seem to fit The Stones' rough 'n' tumble image at all.

' "Hey, do you want a beer?" he asked.

'I nodded even though I couldn't stomach the stuff, feeling the night suddenly full of great promise. Wherever Jenny was, she would be furious to know I was with her great love.

'At that moment Norma scurried in. "I want to go home," she stated sourly. Translation: I didn't make it with Keith.

'Brian moved toward the doorway saying, "There's no more beer in the room. Com'on, follow me."

'I picked up my purse and promised Norma, "I'll be no more than ten or fifteen minutes."

'As I tagged off after Brian down the hall, we passed one of the groupies I recognised from downstairs, a knockout blonde, arm in arm with Bill Wyman.

'When we got to Brian's room he left the door open which both surprised and impressed me. He switched on the TV and settled cosily on the bed as Johnny Carson came on.

' "What's it like being so famous?" I asked, helping myself to a sandwich on the buffet table.

' "It's not the bed of roses you'd think," he crossly denounced. "People mobbing you everywhere, girls hanging on you all the time clawing you."

' "I want to be a model and travel the world like you guys," I ventured.

'He looked at me hard, finally pronouncing, "You'll get sick of it, if you live long enough."

'I was to recall that comment only a few years later when on 3 July 1969, an emotionally deteriorating Brian was found dead in his swimming pool.

'He put his arm around me, very delicately and pointed derisively at Ed McMahon shooting the bull with Carson.

'"*Ho Ho Ho*!" He erupted mimicking the grisly sidekick. "What a wanker! Probably gets paid a million dollars to laugh like a fuckin' gorilla." We both cracked up so hard that Brian spat out his beer. "Tastes like cat piss anyway. American beer, what a fucking joke!" he said, adding softly, "but I do very much like you, Jo."

'Soon Brian began stroking my hair, planting light kisses all over my face. His hands slid up and down my arms and legs, raising goose bumps of pleasure. At that most inopportune moment, in popped Norma again.

'"Jo, I'm sorry, but we better get going. Jenny's downstairs in the car waiting."

'It was after midnight and I knew there'd be hell to play if I missed my ride. Only a couple of months back we'd been picked up by the cops for wandering the streets of downtown Boston barefoot at 2 a.m. Police were always on the lookout for underage flower children and enraged, our parents had grounded us for three weeks.

'Wistfully I bade farewell to Brian, wondering which girl he would choose in the next town tomorrow night. I couldn't help but think how sad it all was.'

It is not clear whether Jones's much rumoured bisexual tendencies were real or imagined. Brian did love to shock, as that was the quickest and surest way to capture attention. There had been talk that Jones had such an encounter with Jagger in the early days. The rumours have been almost unanimously denied by everyone in The Stones' circle except Anita Pallenberg, who claims Brian himself revealed to her the truth of the allegations.

'I only know that Brian did break up a lot of things by actually going to bed with Mick. And I think Mick always resented him for having fallen for it. In later years there have been rumours about Mick being gay, but then it was as if Brian violated Mick's privacy by revealing his weak side. So that was probably why he resented him.'

Nicholas Fitzgerald, Guinness Brewery heir and friend of Jones remembered Brian's telling pronouncements on the subject. 'I have a certain effect on women, and men too,' he would say. 'It's a pity we don't have a double bed; I rarely end up sleeping alone.' More direct, he told his young friend, 'A lot of people in rock are ambidextrous as far as sex is concerned. They're just too uptight to admit it or practise it.'

Author John Michael even suggested that perhaps another Guinness heir Tara Browne was more than just one of Jones's closest friends. In a veiled, nebulous comment, Michael said, 'The art of the time is always brewed up in a homoerotic atmosphere, isn't it?'

Of Jones's conjectured bisexuality even Pat Andrews concedes it was possible. 'Brian was very daring, very anti-establishment. You've got to remember that coming from a family where he'd been treated the way he was he had very low self-esteem. When you see all those pictures of him with his hair all blond it was possible.'

Or could Jones's sexual ambiguity be just another vain competition with Mick? According to Keith, Jagger's androgynous dress and on stage behaviour had its roots way back in Edith Grove. There Mick would parade about the flat in a shocking-blue linen housecoat as Richards describes it: 'Wavin' his hands everywhere, "*Oh! Don't!*" He was a real King's Road queen for about six months.'

Whether or not he would admit it, Jones desperately wanted to *be* Mick Jagger, an enduring vision of his own more confident and together self.

As 1965 wore on the bad blood between Jones and the 'unholy trinity' only escalated. On stage Brian still tried to upstage Jagger with his effeminate posturing and mischievous expressions. He once related an incident to Nicholas Fitzgerald whereby Jagger was allegedly threatening him with lyrics from The Stones' hit, 'The Last Time', during a performance.

Explained Jones, 'He had come to the lines about warning someone that they're going to have to pay a price. He sang them, snarled them directly at me. He wrote those words for me and I was really intimidated. I felt the sweat on my back turning cold.'

Oldham's increasing desire to squeeze out stodgy co-manager Eric Easton was viewed by Jones as the precursor to getting rid of him. Brian was close to Easton and looked up to him as a father-figure, confident in the knowledge that he was firmly on his side. 'It's obvious,' he confided to Fitzgerald, 'they are trying to get me out, so first they get rid of Eric then they get rid of me. Then The Stones become the property of Mr Bloody Oldham!'

There was some evidence to suggest it wasn't all in Jones's mind. Scottish film student and one time flatmate, Dave Thomson relates an incident where Jones was at a hotel in Glasgow listening at the door while Oldham and the other Stones were in conference. 'They're all in there trying to get rid of me,' Brian told him.

Thomson brushed it off as Jones's imagination until he shared a ride back to London with Andrew, Mick and Keith. 'Andrew was slagging off Brian: "We've got to get rid of him . . . how are we gonna get rid of him?" They mocked Brian, saying "Did you see what he was trying to do?" I said to Keith and Mick, "You can't seriously consider chucking Brian out of the group." Keith said no. Mick just shrugged. Andrew was the one who was always doing the slagging. It was jealousy.'

One particularly telling episode happened on the way to a gig in Bristol. Brian had taken a separate car, driving just ahead of the rest of The Stones when his vehicle broke down. As musician Phil May recalls, 'When the other Stones came along and saw him broken down on the side of the road they leaned out of the window, laughing, making faces at him and kept going, intending to play the gig without him. That was a bold rejection because there would be an awful lot missing from that night's performance without Brian and his slide guitar. So that shows you how strained the relationship had become.'

Ian Stewart tells of another time when he drove Jones to the recording studio, the guitarist believing he had a session. But when they reached the studio Jones found it deserted. Explained Stew, 'We had recorded the song, 'Little Red Rooster' the night before and all there was was a note from Mick telling Brian where he had to play, where not to play, like that. "I can't believe this," Brian said, "you guys had a session and now I'm just to fill in?"'

Things were quickly sliding downhill when Jones's prediction fatefully came to pass. On 14 August 1965, Allen Klein signed on to manage The Stones, effectively easing out Eric Easton and freeing up Oldham for more inventive publicity work. The aggressive, New York business mogul swept in by nailing a million dollar record deal and slapping up a one-hundred-foot Times Square billboard of the band in advance of a forty-two date tour that would net the group two million dollars.

But Klein would rule over The Stones' empire like a benevolent dictator. His Christmas cards revealingly read, 'Though I walk through the valley of the shadow of death I shall fear no evil, for I am the biggest bastard in the valley.' Klein channelled the band's money into an American company he controlled, thus firmly clutching the purse-strings.

Not only had Jones lost his trusted friend Easton, but he found himself up against another imposing character he was ill-equipped to deal with. By the autumn of 1965 Jones was reeling in a paralysing mindset, so much so, he told friends he was in genuine fear for his life. Often, he refused to leave his house until way after dark.

According to Dave Thomson Brian told him: 'They're out to get me, Dave, someone in America and someone over here. I don't know who they are, but they're out to get me.'

Fitzgerald tells of an anonymous phone call Jones once received from New York while on holiday in Tangier. 'Someone's planning my removal,' he insisted. 'And you know how they get rid of people in the States. You can take out a contract on most people for about ten thousand dollars. I think it could have been someone from the *New Musical Express*. Didn't recognise the voice. The hotel in Tangier told me it had come in from New York.'

As 1965 was winding down, Jones had taken up with French actress Zouzou of *Chloe in the Afternoon* fame. The relationship, which was promising despite the couple's language barrier, brought out the complexities of a man tortured by his own self-destructive tendencies and whose sense of self-worth had been effectively shattered. He was now exhibiting increasingly frequent bouts of depression exacerbated by constant drinking.

'Brian was trying to understand why he was famous, why he had money,' related Zouzou. 'I never met somebody who was so confused and wondering about himself. He loved people really, but I think most of the people took him for a clown. They played with him and destroyed him.'

Jones was 'going mad,' Zouzou alleged, smashing things and accusing her of not loving him, insisting he was too ugly. He phoned a hospital one day, desperate to have cosmetic surgery to change his face. 'One day I found him in the bathroom, trying to cut his wrists. He hated himself, felt he was a monster.'

Just at this time, when Jones was sinking desperately, cracking beneath unbearable pressures, into his life charged the woman who would both resurrect his capsizing life, and send him on a blinding free-fall from which he would never recover.

3 OBSESSION AND BETRAYAL
Brian Alone

WHEN BRIAN FIRST saw her, it was like gazing upon a sultry, sensual reflection of himself. The date was 14 September 1965, and the most extraordinary, sleek and tawny creature had just powered her way backstage at Munich's Oktoberfest Circus following The Stones' rowdy performance.

Jones was his usual frazzled self, this time reeling from his latest public hammering over the child support lawsuits slapped on him by both Pat Andrews and Linda Lawrence.

The stunning and statuesque mystery woman was a young model named Anita Pallenberg. She wasted no time in deciding upon which Stone to pounce. 'When I got backstage,' she relates, 'I went straight to Brian because he was the one I fancied. I tapped him on the shoulder and had a big smile ready for him when he turned around. I could hardly believe it, but he was on the verge of tears. For a weird moment I thought it was somehow my fault. He was the only one of The Stones who really bothered to talk to me. He could even speak a little German. There had been some kind of disagreement within The Stones, Brian against the others, and he was crying.'

'I don't know who you are, but I need you,' implored Jones. 'Please come and spend the night with me. I don't want to be alone.'

Pallenberg had an impressive pedigree worthy of her intriguing presence. She came from a long line of wealthy Swiss and German artists, including famed neoclassic painter Arnold Bocklin. Growing up in Rome, Anita was fluent in four languages and by the time she was twenty-one had studied art restoration, graphic design and even medicine.

Her striking, golden feline looks, however, garnered the attention of the fashion world and Pallenberg was soon appearing in top magazines as well as several avant-garde films by young West German director Volker Schlondorff.

Observed Christopher Gibbs: 'Anita in those days was absolutely electrifying. Whenever she came into a room every head would turn to look at her. There was something kittenish about her, a sense of mischief, of naughtiness. When I talked to her I discovered she was highly intelligent and extremely well-read. She'd read obscure German and Romantic novels like Hoffman, as well as all the usual Hermann Hessery.'

For Jones, the strong grip of the leggy blonde with a brain to match, was enough to lift him from his depression. That she could have had any one of The Stones, but chose him, significantly inflated his paper-thin ego.

As Richards remembered: 'The first time I saw Anita my obvious reaction was "What the fuck is a chick like that doing with Brian!" Anita's incredibly strong, a much stronger personality than Brian, more confident, whereas Brian was full of doubts. I just couldn't imagine that she didn't know better.'

But the liaison went far beyond sexual chemistry and their mutual interest in the arts and literature. Jones and Pallenberg shared a similar mindset of inexhaustible curiosity and caustic wit, as well as a sense of bold daring.

'Brian was very short, a head shorter than I. He could barely see over the steering wheel of his Rolls,' remembers Anita. 'He worried about the look of his teeth which were capped, but I made him forget his defects and just think about the positive side of Brian Jones.'

Within weeks of their meeting Pallenberg moved into his mews cottage with Jones. 'I fell in love with Brian all the way,' she declared. 'He was a great guy, you know. Talented, funny and with that instant quality of "Let's do it. Let's try anything." I knew I could just talk to him. I was his groupie really.'

Jones's motto of 'Let's try anything' was put to the test, the Acid Test, on the night of 5 December 1965. Following a concert in Los Angeles, Brian, along with Keith, attended the second Acid Test party thrown by notorious writer Ken Kesey. In those days, LSD was still so new it had not yet been declared illegal. Keith and Brian were among the first to sample this potent hallucinogen and found it deliciously to their liking. So much so that Jones would make it his drug of choice.

Back home in London Brian was eager to share his mind-altering adventures with Anita who predictably plunged right in. With the aid of a few imported hits of Augustus Owsley's fabled Orange Sunshine, the couple engaged in several highly-charged erotic fantasies, highlighted by sizzling role-reversals. 'The first time he took acid,' Anita pointed out, 'he saw creatures coming out of the ground, the walls, the floors. He was looking in the cupboards for people, "Where are they?" That's when he said to me, "Dress me up like singer François Hardy." He looked kind of like a girl in a funny kind of way; sexually I like women as well as men, and Brian seemed to combine both sexes for me.'

The dominating Pallenberg was also reportedly into S&M as Dave Thomson revealed: 'I actually saw her one night going into their room with a bloody great whip. I could hear her whipping Brian.'

As far as Ronni Money was concerned, however, Jones was yet again playing a role he felt others expected of him: 'Brian threw himself in at the deep end, he was out for as many kicks as he could get. Anita excited Brian; whatever young guys only read about he was getting on a plate. She was into the bisexual number and arranged scenes. Brian figured, "Right, this is what it's all about. This is what people want of me." Because Brian didn't know.'

By early 1966, Brian moved into a spacious apartment at 1 Courtfield Road, South Kensington, complete with vaunted thirty-foot ceilings, wrap-around windows, wine cellar and oak-panelled gallery bedroom, accessible only by a rope ladder. There the duo soon became London's most outrageous, sought-after couple. Pallenberg tinted and cut her hair in the same style as Jones's, who by this time was bleaching his already blond locks a lighter sun-kissed gold. Brian, who harboured a definite fetish about his silken mop, allowed only Anita to trim it.

'It was always such a big scene,' she sighed. 'He had to have three mirrors, and it was a nightmare for me, tiny little bits at a time. He'd get so pissed off and angry because he was so vain, very, very vain.'

Together they forged a revolutionary androgynous look, keeping their clothes together, mixing and matching not only fabrics and patterns, but cultures and even centuries. Jones would parade the streets of London wearing a Victorian lace shirt, floppy turn-of-the-century hat, Edwardian velvet frock coat, multi-coloured suede boots, accessorised scarves hanging from his neck, waist and legs along with lots of antique Berber jewellery.

According to journalist Al Aronowitz, 'Jones was the first man I ever knew to wear costume jewellery bought in the ladies' department at Saks.'

At Courtfield Road, Chelsea's power pair played host to a constant stream of beautiful people from John Lennon and George Harrison to

Sonny and Cher, Donovan and Jimi Hendrix. Trendy film maker Donald Cammell, heir Paul Getty, and Britain's bright young things would gather at the South Kensington flat to smoke dope, drop acid and discuss the issues of the day.

Observed Anita: 'Brian was very interesting socially. He dealt with the fame and all that. He picked out the best, the cream, Dylan, Terry Southern, Warhol. Brian set the pace.'

Jones's friendship with the equally quick-witted Bob Dylan, although honed on mutual admiration, turned on Brian's well-known insecurity. According to a former flatmate of Jones's, Dylan offered Brian a spot in his backup band, but Brian was too intimidated by his longtime idol to join up. 'Don't be so paranoid,' Dylan would chide. When Bob subsequently penned his 'Ballad of a Thin Man', widely believed to be about Jones, Brian saw it as a put-down and privately proclaimed to friends, 'Dylan is a fraud.' It was effectively the end of the relationship.

His liaison with The Beatles, however, bore sweeter fruit. Jones was invited to guest on a couple of Fab tracks as well as contributing hand-claps to 'Yellow Submarine' and 'All You Need Is Love'. He became good friends with both John and George though was vaguely shunned by the ever politically correct McCartney who probably sensed that Brian's days as a Stone were numbered.

Locked away in the flat for days at a time, Jones had not yet out-grown his childhood penchant for model trains. Covering the entire living-room floor was a miniature train with which Jones would stage spectacular crashes by dousing lighter fluid on the cars and setting fire to them while Pallenberg photographed the mayhem. The pair could be just as destructive in the outside world.

On a typical day at the beach they would often hire small power boats. Anita was particularly dangerous, ramming wickedly into any-thing in her path and often leaving a carnage of splinters in her wake. Jones, by contrast, would take the boat and drift aimlessly out to sea, so far that the coastguard had to be alerted. Asked what he was doing out that far Jones would simply sigh and say, 'I was following the seagulls.'

Jones began to spend his money on outlandish purchases, such as a double-decker bus. On a stoned whim Brian would ring the manufac-turers and order one of the monstrous vehicles. Secretaries at The Stones' office would then be obliged to explain to irate executives that, no, Mr Jones of The Rolling Stones had, indeed, ordered a bus!

Jones was a truly outrageous character. Stones' fan club secretary and future tour manager, Sally Arnold, recalls attending a dinner party thrown by Jagger in 1971 when he brought out some home movies of the band. One sequence shot during the Autumn of 1966 showed the famous photo session of The Stones dressed in drag to promote their single, 'Have You Seen Your Mother Baby Standing In The Shadow'. Following the shoot, Brian, who was dressed as an airline stewardess, plonked down on a chair, jacked up his skirt and began masturbating right on camera.

'I was shocked and embarrassed,' recalled Arnold in *Blown Away*, 'watching Brian playing with himself while everyone was laughing and joking, "Oh, isn't it enormous?" and "Oh, com'on Brian, hurry up!" Brian was loving all the attention, absolutely grinning away, quite pleased with himself. I was blushing so fiercely I had to leave the room so I didn't see the end, but I presume Brian obliged everyone with an orgasm. It seemed peculiar to me that Mick would show that film what with Brian long dead and buried.'

Jones's new Pallenberg-inspired confidence even reached into the studio. The sessions at RCA in Hollywood from 3 to 12 March 1966 resulted in the critically acclaimed, 'Aftermath', featuring some of Jones's most lauded work. He demonstrated an uncanny talent for infusing unprecedented instruments into a rock format, like the marimbas on 'Under My Thumb', haunting harpsichord on 'I Am Waiting', and the unforgettable dulcimer that showcases 'Lady Jane'. But there is no more stunning example of his brazen inventiveness than the clever incorporation of the sitar on 'Paint It Black'.

Said Keith: 'Brian would learn enough about an instrument, sometimes only for one song, to play what he wanted. This was his greatest gift. He would wander from instrument to instrument on each tape. He was one of those people who could pick up anything and get something nice out of it, even though he'd never played it before.'

'I've always been more interested in musical instruments than the others because I'm an instrumentalist,' affirmed Brian. 'Do you know, I don't know the words of most of our songs. That's why I play piano, sax and clarinet, because I don't sing.'

Even the usually uncomplimentary Andrew Oldham was impressed. 'His contributions can be heard on every track and what he didn't know how to play he went out and learned. You can hear his colour all over 'Lady Jane' and 'Paint It Black'. It was far more than a decorative effect. Sometimes Brian pulled the whole record together.'

As innovative as his moments of creative spark were, the constant partying became a distressing telltale sign of another, less endearing Brian. Jones wouldn't come into the studio for days and when he did finally show he strapped on a guitar only to laze about all day reading a book on botany as the record was being cut.

Even more revealing was Jones's eventual abandonment of the guitar, leaving Richard to overdub all his parts. Observed Ian Stewart: 'He enjoyed picking up these instruments and learning to do bits and pieces on them. And it got to the stage where he didn't want to play guitar at all. The only thing he wanted to do was to have Keith, Bill and Charlie put down a track and Brian would overdub his dulcimer, et cetera. They would start playing a song with Keith and Brian on guitar, then Brian would get fed up and say he wasn't getting the sound he wanted, his guitar was broken or his fingers were hurting.'

As one Stones insider put it, 'Once Brian put down the guitar, that was really the end.'

Typically Jones couldn't see it coming. After all, he was wealthy and famous, he had female fans waiting outside his house pleading for the privilege to make his bed. And he had one thing even the other Stones coveted, Anita. Although Keith's girlfriend was model Linda Keith and Mick's was Chrissie Shimpton (the stunning sister of mega-model Jean), frankly no woman could measure up physically or intellectually to the masterful Pallenberg.

According to insiders, she actually terrified the still painfully shy Richards, who admitted, 'We were falling all over ourselves because of her drop-dead beauty, but it was Brian she fancied and Brian who copped her.'

Jagger in particular viewed Pallenberg as a threat on several fronts. There were the smaller irritating things, such as Anita taking credit for the unisex look he believed he held claim to and her orbiting the high-society circles he always strived for.

Far more worrisome though was the apparent weakening of the Jagger/Richards tandem. Keith was hanging out at Courtfield Road where he and Jones were drawn together through their experiments with acid. As Tony Sanchez, the self-confessed dealer to The Stones pointed out, 'Mick was odd man out. Brian, especially, treated him with a thinly-veiled contempt and laughed at him because he was afraid of acid. Mick was guilty of the worst transgression of all: being straight. Brian and Keith started referring to him as Jagger rather than Mick and a rift began that looked as though it might even break up the band.'

The reality was that Jones, who only months before seemed about to crack, was fast rebounding and perhaps even ready to resume leadership of the band.

Anita was well aware of The Stones' disapproval of her, and Mick's in particular. 'They looked at me like I was some kind of threat,' she recalled in *Blown Away*. 'Mick really tried to put me down, thereby putting Brian down in the process, but there was no way this crude, lippy guy was going to do a number on me. I was always able to squelch him. I found out, you stand up to Mick and he crumbles. He tried to get Brian to stop seeing me, called me poison. He ordered Chrissie not to go near me. I figured he was jealous because I was the one close to Brian.'

Interestingly, Pallenberg might have protested a shade too fervently. 'I always got the feeling with Anita that Mick was the one she really wanted,' suggests Dave Thomson. 'I felt she was working her way through The Stones to get to Mick.'

Adds Stewart, 'Anita would come to sessions and things. She could be really funny. She'd make a suggestion that was half-serious and half-humorous and it would be a good one. You could just see the hairs on the back of Mick's neck rise. She was great.'

There was no question that Pallenberg's influence was instrumental in Richards moving away from Jagger and back to Jones. Keith recalls a pivotal incident during the 1966 American tour that drew them even closer. In Syracuse Jones tried to steal an American flag that was draped across a backstage chair. The police charged in, prepared to make an arrest, but Richards intervened, 'Fuck you, man, leave Brian alone!'

'To some extent, the hatchets were buried on that tour,' confirmed Keith. 'I went over to Brian's place a lot, mainly because we'd all started really blowing a lot of grass, freakin' out and getting into a relationship with him which I hadn't had for nearly two years, like it was all forgotten, almost. I had no ulterior motive for going round there except that was where everyone was hanging out.

'Brian knew I wasn't seeing Mick and saying "Oh, Brian's been smoking this or taking that." He knew I wasn't putting him down behind his back, that the other third of the triangle wasn't in play at that particular point. So he knew that whatever was going down was for real. Brian and I had a great time together. He was really a great friend, terrific to hang out with if he wasn't feeling paranoid towards you.'

That friendship, further rekindled by Richards's moving in with

Jones that September, was a development with ominous overtones. 'I moved in slowly,' says Keith. 'I still had to check myself as to whether I decided to become friends again with Brian because of Anita. I think it was fifty-fifty. Of course I fancied her then – everybody did the minute they saw her – but I wasn't about to fuck up my relationship with Brian. It was not the point for that. We were just good friends.'

Jones, however, naively pictured the trio as an incomparable power pyramid. But as one friend observed: 'The three of them were living in an incredibly chaste *ménage à trois*. Keith was very close to Brian at the time, but Anita was spinning her spell. She was a captivatingly attractive person and she completely bewitched both Brian and Keith.'

With Richards now in the mix, there were definite signs of a disturbing chink in the Jones/Pallenberg union. Brian never wanted Anita out of his sight and fashion assignments which took her to Munich or Paris would send the mercurial Jones into a rage of violence.

'He would pick up anything,' reveals Pallenberg, 'lamps, clocks, a whole table and just throw it. Then when the storm inside him died down he'd feel guilty and beg me to forgive him. His assaults were terrible. For days later I'd have lumps and bruises all over me.'

That summer Pallenberg and Jones accompanied Christopher Gibbs to Tangier, Morocco to purchase carpets and curios for his Chelsea shop. Brian found the exotic atmosphere both profound and ethereal as he wandered the bazaars collecting kaftans and tapestries for his studio flat, and smoking the strong north African hashish through a hookah. He was instictively drawn to the ancient, haunting Berber pipe and drum melodies that reminded him of the Welsh folk-sounds he'd grown up with.

Gibbs, however, remembers the trip for the daily bickering amongst his companions. 'They fought about everything; cars, prices, restaurant menus. Brian could never win an argument with Anita although he always made the mistake of trying. There would be terrible scenes with both of them screaming at each other.'

One night in their suite at the Minzah Hotel, the pair's verbal sparring erupted into unexpected violence. Jones raised his arm to strike Pallenberg and missed, striking it instead against an iron window-frame and fracturing his left wrist in two places. The incident, however, did not stop the dope-loving Jones from smuggling half a kilo of hash out of the country in the bases of two brass candlesticks. Brian was by now quite openly living on the edge.

Back in London, the ever-burgeoning Jones/Richards liaison had even spilled into the music. It was like the old days at Edith Grove, only this time the stakes were far more lucrative. Over the autumn, the pair collaborated on a future Stones classic, 'Ruby Tuesday', a song featuring Jones's greatest and most inspired influence. While Keith came up with the basic track, it was Brian's dedicated and brilliant musical layering that turned the gentle ballad into something special.

'Keith and I worked and worked on colouring, adding dramatic yet wispy touches here and there, altering the mix between lead voice and background harmonies, while creating an interplay of exotic instruments,' he later recalled.

Andrew Oldham then suggested that Keith Richards should become producer and director of a wimpy album called 'Today's Pop Orchestra' featuring the Aranbee Pop Orchestra. Said Wyman, 'I have always doubted Keith had anything to do with its production or instigation, I think it was probably Andrew's idea and execution, purely an Oldham projection of Keith to promote the album and to boost his public image, yet another round in Andrew's campaign to increase Keith's profile.'

At this time, interviews were arranged only with Richards and Jagger, in effect blocking Jones's access to the press. *Rave Magazine*'s Dawn James had been staunchly refused an interview with Brian on Oldham's orders: 'You cannot see him or phone him and he cannot give you any quotes.'

This prompted James to write, 'Brian Jones seems to have disappeared from the public eye. He doesn't feature very much in The Stones' present image. Once the rather weird, long-haired, almost mystical Brian was the most talked of and popular Stone, but nowadays people don't discuss him much.'

Meanwhile, Jones's wrist fracture had taken on even more serious consequences. His hand in plaster, having broken two bones, he was not able to play on The Stones' two-week British tour beginning 23 September. Accordingly, Oldham already had a substitute in mind and was set to have him accompany the band, until he considered the possibility of adverse publicity.

For the ever-fragile Jones, however, such backstage manoeuvring was enough to further unsettle his badly-rattled nerves.

'His arm was never put back together very well,' notes Stewart. 'He always said he couldn't play guitar and that he didn't want to play after that. He had no confidence on stage, he only played the odd solo here and there. Keith was quite happy to do all the guitar parts himself.'

Despite his own drug problems, which he responsibly kept out of the work place, Oldham detested the similar situation surrounding the band. 'I didn't like the drug thing because it got in the way. It interfered with business. I got impatient with all that courtier stuff, the chauffeurs and the bodyguards.'

Philip Norman too noted that Oldham grew eerily aware of the growing influence of Tom Keylock, 'A hulking Cockney whose eyes swam mistily behind thick bifocal glasses, who from chauffeur, had progressed to bodyguard, using muscles and combat techniques acquired in the army paratroopers.' Oldham noticed both his influence over Keith – who had an incurable weakness for tough guys – and Brian who was pathetically grateful even for so changeable an ally.

In another development which was to have monumental consequences for Brian, Oldham brought in Leslie Perrin, the wily middle-aged Fleet Street publicist, to handle The Stones' media.

Bill Wyman dubbed Perrin: 'The best operator in London, who wore a suit, seemed some distance from rock'n'roll and numbered Frank Sinatra among his many clients. Softly spoken and shy, but with brilliant tactics.'

Norman further remarked: 'He also used his extensive contacts in the borderland between Fleet Street and Parliament to enlist the sympathy of liberal-minded MPs.'

Brian, perhaps naively, looked to the publicist as another Eric Easton. 'Les is marvellous,' he confided to Nicholas Fitzgerald, calling Perrin a masterful manipulator who got the tabloids to dance to his tune. But all was apparently not what it seemed behind closed doors at The Stones' offices on Maddox Avenue.

Meanwhile, Jones embroiled himself in yet another controversy when in November 1966 he posed in full Nazi regalia for a cover of the West German magazine, *Stern*. There was Jones looking every bit the haughty, decadent SS officer, with a Chivalry Cross around his neck, squashing a doll beneath his polished boots while Anita knelt submissively at his feet.

Although the shot was discarded, copies somehow turned up back in Britain, erupting into a major media scandal.

Jones tried to allay criticism by insisting: 'I wear a Nazi uniform to show that I am anti-Nazi. The meaning of it all is there is no sense to it.' Privately he told Fitzgerald: 'That was her idea. It was meant as a send-up, to take the piss out of Fascism. But the stupid press deliberately turned it around the other way. I even heard talk in the States that the CIA were keeping an eye on us because they thought we were becoming a dangerous political influence.'

As for Pallenberg, she explained years later: 'It was naughty, but what the hell! He looked good in an SS uniform!'

From that murky manoeuvre Jones and Pallenberg rode boldly into the realm of the occult, says David Dalton, author of *The Rolling Stones: The First Twenty Years*. 'Brian was a dare-devil who liked to toy with the satanic; his insatiable appetite for drugs, Nazi uniforms, his unexpected outbreaks of cruelty all cast itself in his satyr-like grin. Perhaps, in his flirtation with dark powers, he let them sink their talons in rather too deeply.'

This was first noted by Marianne Faithfull in *Blown Away*, who adamantly claimed Pallenberg was into sorcery. 'She was sort of a dark queen, beautiful and wicked despite her blonde looks. Her smile was not like one you had ever seen before, it seemed to be a camouflage for some great, dark secret she was hoarding. The best way I can describe her is that she was like a snake to a bird and she could transfix you and hold you in place until she wanted to make her move.'

Photographer Gered Mankowitz concurred: 'Anita was manipulative, wicked, evil. I saw her as very frightening. I felt Anita and Brian were not beyond spiking drinks with acid to see what would happen. I did not trust them. In my view, Pallenberg and Brian were very manipulative, dangerous people.'

Film maker Kenneth Anger – a disciple of black magician, Aleister Crowley – alleged, 'The occult unit within The Stones was Keith, Anita and Brian. You see, Brian was a witch too. I'm convinced. He showed me his witch's tit. He had a supernumerary tit in a very sexy place on his inner thigh. Brian was the most psychic of The Stones. He saw the spirit world; for the others it was just the climate of the times. One gets the impression he just dissolved into it.'

At the height of his indulgence, Jones ordered special licence plates for his Silver Cloud Rolls Royce (purchased from George Harrison via Terry Doran) that read: 'DD 666' or 'Devil's Disciple 666', the symbol of the anti-Christ. 'In another age,' noted Jones, 'they would have burned me.'

The press predictably swooped down on these tawdry titbits. Said Pallenberg: 'One time Brian and I came back from Tangier and as we came through customs I happened to be carrying this little rose bowl we'd stolen from the hotel. Next morning the headlines read: "Brian Jones and girlfriend, Anita Pallenberg return from West Africa with more black magic artefacts for their satanic rituals." '

Paint It Black

Pallenberg admitted to casting a spell on Jones one night following an enormous blow-up that left her bloodied and fleeing to a friend's house. She moulded candle wax into an effigy of her lover and jabbed in a needle, piercing the stomach. 'The next morning I went back and found him suffering from severe stomach pains. He'd been up all night and was in agony, bottles of Milk of Magnesia and other medications all around him. The world of the occult fascinated me, as did witchcraft and the black magicians Anger introduced me to.'

The year wore down, taking a bitter toll. The second week of December, following a recording session in Los Angeles, Jones, Richards and Pallenberg spent a bizarre holiday in the dangerous drug-infested neighbourhood of Watts, feasting on a wide menu of illicit pharmaceuticals. Press agent, Tony Bramwell observed, 'They'd be totally under the influence of everything. They'd look like they were sixty, Brian and Keith. They were old men in their twenties.'

A fed up Jagger complained, 'I don't know where it's all going to end.'

One of the catalysts in Jones's further down-spiral was the tragic death of his best friend, Tara Browne, who'd wrapped his Lotus Elan around a lamppost on 18 December 1966. The loss left Jones inconsolable. Tony Sanchez remembers how Brian came to him, desperate and confused, droning on for hours about the meaninglessness of life and how he'd taken handfuls of Tuinols and Mandrax to blot out the pain. 'At first I understood his grief and shared it,' revealed Sanchez, 'but gradually it began to turn into something else. Brian seemed unbalanced, paranoid, eaten up by misery and loneliness.'

The mounting turmoil and frustration was manifest in the meeting of Jones's friend, Ronni Money and Anita Pallenberg. Money recalls being at the Scotch of St James club, talking with Jimi Hendrix and Eric Burdon when Brian and Anita walked in. Jones, delighted to see Money, came rushing up exuberantly screaming, 'Ronni!' giving her a huge bear hug.

Pallenberg, standing aside arrogantly, spat, 'So who's this one Brian? Another one of your one-nighters? I thought I'd met all of them by now.'

Jones immediately whirled around and smacked her in the face. 'Don't you dare talk to her like that, you fucking bitch!'

Anita's nose was streaming blood as the waiters buzzed around with napkins trying to wipe her dress. 'Afterwards, she played it very cleverly,' noted Money. 'She decided I wasn't too bad.'

56

'She didn't take care of him,' continued Ronni. 'Brian told me Anita was like a huge sponge that drained everything out of him. She didn't allow him any time to rest; she was all me, me, me. Nobody could live around that. People can get boundless energy when they shove amphetamines down their face all day.'

A few weeks later Jones rang Money, babbling on about how he needed her protection from people who dominated him, begging her to live with him, saying he would even pay her. Said Money, 'I don't think Brian could face whatever it was he'd become. And when you're on your own you have to face it.'

But that wasn't the end of it. A few days later Jones rang her at work, beside himself sobbing, 'Can you get me a girl? I just want somebody that's gonna be with me even if I've got to pay money. At least I know they're there because of the money. I don't know whether people want to be with me because I'm me or because I'm Brian Jones of The Rolling Stones.'

Money soon found a willing friend who called the next day and said, 'He was so nice. All he wanted to do was talk and I cuddled him a little.'

As the weeks passed Keith and Anita were fighting a growing mutual attraction, and it was eating away at Jones. As Keylock noted, 'Brian used to get pissed or stoned and he'd knock her about. I came in one day and said "Here, what's this?"

' "He gave me a good hiding," Pallenberg told me. "Look, a black eye."

'I said to him, "Don't do that, Brian. Anyone can hit a woman, that's not big. Do it again and I'll thump you!" He never got mean with the likes of me. I could control him. Brian knew I was around to look after him and I protected him quite a lot.'

As author Terry Southern once noted: 'Brian and Anita were like something out of an Arthurian legend, enchanted siblings who had been doomed to an idyllic and profane love.'

Tony Sanchez remembers once dropping by the flat to find Jones distraught, screaming, 'Anita's dead! I can't rouse her!' Sanchez raced to the bed where Pallenberg was stretched out unconscious from an overdose. They rushed her to the nearest hospital where she had her stomach pumped while an anguished Jones cried openly in despair. 'She started sobbing silently,' Sanchez remembered, 'with a terrible wounded look in her eyes.'

The year of 1967 delivered an exciting new project in the scoring of the German avant-garde film, *Mord und Totschlag (A Degree of*

Murder), which starred Pallenberg. For Jones, it represented a wonderful opportunity. Not only would he be able to keep an eye on Anita, but could now prove himself outside the narrow confines of The Stones. This marked the first time a rock star had composed a theatrical soundtrack, an avenue that perhaps most suited his talents.

Clearly Jones was in his element, recruiting Jimmy Page on lead guitar, Nicky Hopkins on piano, Kenny Jones on drums, and then plunging headlong into the project. Locking himself in his Courtfield Road flat he worked day and night on two tiny tape machines. Once in the studio, he refined the score with typically exotic flair, utilising instruments as diverse as flute, jazz piano, autoharp, sitar and even banjo.

Engineer Glyn Johns was initially sceptical. 'Frankly, I doubted Brian was capable of doing anything at all, including going to the loo by himself. I saw him as rather a lonely character and I actually felt sorry for him. But while he was working on it, Brian was extremely together and confident. He did very well and it came out amazingly.'

Director Volker Schlondorff often played nursemaid and confidant, hauling Brian out of bed and cajoling him after his latest row with Anita. But in the end his undeniable brilliance shone through. 'It wasn't just that his music was special, it was that the score was so spontaneous and vital. Only Brian could've done it. He had a tremendous feeling for the lyrical parts and knew perfectly the recording and mixing techniques to achieve the best sound.'

Even Richards admitted, 'For a project nobody ever tried before, to write a whole piece of music for a film, it was good.'

But Jones was about to take a huge fall. The *News of the World* had been running a series called 'Pop Stars and Drugs' and came out with a two-page exposé on 5 February entitled, 'The Secrets of the Pop Stars' Hideaways'.

The article pinpointed Jagger at the centre of its latest scandal: 'Another pop idol who admits he has sampled LSD and other drugs is Mick Jagger of The Rolling Stones . . . He too was a visitor at the Roehampton home of The Moody Blues. Investigators who saw Mick Jagger at the Blazes Club in Kensington, London, reported:

'He told us; "I don't go on it (LSD) now the cats (fans) have taken it up, it'll just get a dirty name. I remember the first time I took it on our first tour with Bo Diddley and Little Richard."

'During the time we were at Blazes Jagger took about six Benzedrine tablets, "I just wouldn't keep awake in a place like this if I didn't have them," he said.

'Jagger was at Roehampton when a pop star believed he was a historical character. He said of the incident, "We thought he'd gone starkers. He was charging around the room."

'Later, at Blazes Jagger showed a companion and two girls a small piece of hash (solid marijuana) and invited them to his flat for a smoke.'

It was a tragic case of mistaken identity. Although Jagger, Richards and Jones had all gone to Blazes, it appeared that Brian had somehow been confused with Mick.

The consequences were staggering. In an appearance on the Eamonn Andrews show the same night the story broke a furious Jagger announced he was issuing a writ of libel against the *News of the World*.

According to Trevor Kempson, chief crime reporter for the paper, recognising their grave error and facing the imposing Stones' empire, the tabloid had to find a quick way to allay the action.

Just a week later, on 12 February a nineteen-strong force of police officers, working on a tip, raided Redlands, Keith's Sussex home during a weekend party. The trio of Jagger, Richards and Robert Fraser were busted. Mick would subsequently be charged with possession of four Benzedrine tablets and Keith with allowing his home to be used for smoking cannabis. Fraser though got the worst of it, caught with heroin. According to his own account, the ever-resourceful Spanish Tony delivered £6,000 to a certain someone in the police department and the matter was seemingly resolved.

That is, until a week later when the *News of the World* came out with the story of the raid in minute detail. Said Fraser, 'It's almost as though they had a reporter sitting in the middle of the room taking notes.'

It didn't take The Stones long to discover there had been a traitor in their midst and suspicion fell on a very dubious character named David Schneidermann, the self-dubbed California 'Acid King' who had wormed his way inside the band's inner circle.

'It's obvious, isn't it?' piped Keith. 'The *News of the World* hired him to set us up, then tipped off the police so they could duck out of Mick's libel action.'

Schneidermann certainly had good connections. Not only had the police ignored an attaché case brimming with cocaine, cannabis and several hundred hits of White Lightning, but Mr Schneidermann mysteriously vanished from the country the very next day, never to be seen again.

Photographer and close friend Michael Cooper soon discovered the Acid King was something other than he appeared after coming across a collection of passports in Schneidermann's bag and learning he had a vast knowledge of firearms.

'I know it sounds fantastic,' he said, 'but I reckon he was much more than a creep hired by the *News of the World*. He was some kind of James Bond character. Someone right at the top put him in because The Stones were becoming too powerful. They were worried they might spark off fighting in the streets so they were going to try and break them. I'm sure the newspaper was in on it somewhere, but it was this guy using them, not the other way round.'

Nowadays, it seems there was no shortage of formidable enemies surrounding The Stones' camp.

As for Jones, who managed to squirm safely out of trouble, the *News of the World*'s Kempson observed: 'As far as I could find, he'd never shown any regret at getting Jagger into all that bother. He just thought it was all very funny.'

But it was far from a laughing matter. Jones had caused the star of the band major angst.

Incredibly, Jones cast off the situation with scarcely another thought, putting the finishing touches to his acclaimed film soundtrack and enjoying the rapid rise of 'Ruby Tuesday' in the charts. His alliance with Keith – as Jagger was busily courting Marianne Faithfull – seemed stronger than ever, and again the pair, with Anita in the turbulent centre, forged an unlikely band of three stoned-out musketeers.

Thus, when Richards suggested a motoring holiday to Morocco to escape the frenzied media circus surrounding the Redlands bust, Jones eagerly agreed. They set off on 25 February on the 2,000 mile journey in Richards's new Bentley, dubbed the Blue Lena after Lena Horne. Jones and Pallenberg snuggled in the back seat beneath a coverlet of black fur while Keith sat up front with chauffeur, Tom Keylock.

The journey began well. Stopping overnight in Paris to pick up film maker Donald Cammell's girlfriend, Deborah Dixon, they booked into a hotel. The following morning Keylock wrote out a cheque for the bill, but the clerk apologetically informed him that English money wasn't acceptable.

'How 'bout dollars?' suggested the chauffeur.

'Oh, dollars, yes, yes,' nodded the clerk.

Keylock signed the cheque and rushed upstairs, bellowing, 'Quick, let's split, there's gonna be trouble. I've just given them an English cheque made out in dollars!'

'So we get out the door,' relates Keylock, 'get in the car and I just threw the last bags in and I hear, "Mr Keylock! Mr Keylock!" and there he is standing in the street waving this cheque and I'm off.

'It was a hell of a laugh, but after all that we come back, we'd done a gig in Paris and they sent the cops downtown after me for bouncing a cheque.'

By the time the group reached the south of France in the Mediterranean port of Toulon, Jones became ill with a high fever and was admitted to hospital. 'You go on ahead without me,' he insisted, 'and I'll fly out as soon as I'm released.'

Driving southward through Spain it was now Keith who shared the back seat with Anita. All the smouldering looks and pent-up passion of the past several months could no longer be contained. 'Amazing things can happen in the back of a car and they did,' said Keith. Although the couple shared a torrid night in Valencia, Richards still viewed the liaison as only a temporary fling. 'I was still very wary and trying hard not to fuck up the new thing I had going with Brian.'

By the time Anita flew back to Toulon to accompany Jones on to Tangier the betrayal was clearly evident. Brian reacted in his usual ballistic manner, beating Anita in their hotel room until she was barely conscious. The following morning Brion Gysin observed his companion by the pool: 'It was a strange group; Brian with Anita, dirty white face, dirty blackened eyes, dirty canary drops of hair, barbaric jewellery and Keith Richards in eighteenth-century suit, long black velvet coat and the tightest pants.'

The group, now joined by Jagger and Faithfull, tried to act the part of carefree tourists on holiday, shopping in the Kasbah, sipping mint tea, puffing on Gauloises. But as Anita points out, 'Brian was suffering badly at this point from severe fits of paranoia. He started taking his clothes off on the street in Morocco. We'd have to hustle him into doorways and somehow get him back to the hotel.'

On the tenth floor of the Hotel Minzah, The Stones held a particularly lurid LSD session. Philip Norman describes the scene: 'Elmore James' music wailing, Keith strumming along on guitar, Mick pirouetting dementedly round the room and Brian Jones, "like a little celluloid Kewpie doll" with Tom Keylock murmuring intrigue into his ear. When trays of food were brought in everyone rode them around the floor like toboggans.'

That night, following another ugly row, Anita, who couldn't take any more, locked herself in her room. An infuriated Jones went berserk, storming into the streets of Marrakesh dragging back a pair of tattooed Berber whores with braided henna hair, insisting Anita participate in a wild orgy. 'My refusal caused Brian to go totally out of control,' recounts Pallenberg in the Hotchner book. 'He overturned a tray of sandwiches, spilling them all over the carpet and then he began to pick things up and throw them at me. He grabbed me and beat me, screaming senselessly, a tornado of violence.'

Pallenberg fled to Keith's room in genuine fear of her life.

'Fuck this,' Richards told her. 'I can't watch Brian do this shit to you anymore. Come on darlin', I'm taking you back to London.'

But Jones they knew would prove difficult, and to complicate matters, a plane load of reporters was due to arrive in Marrakesh to ferret out yet more sleaze in the aftermath of the bust. It was then that Richards, along with Gysin and Keylock hatched a dastardly plot to make their escape as told by Gysin in *Moroccan Mishaps with the Strolling Ruins*: 'I run into Tom with a message. Tom comes on strong like a Stone . . . "Right now," he says, "a small plane has just landed in Marrakesh, chockablock full of reporters come down to persecute us. The Stones are strong, they'll win, but we have one weak link. You know who it is. Brian. Brian talks 'is bloody head off to reporters . . . Brian must be kept away from them for his own good and ours. Why don't you take him out recording live music on this great public square like you said you would. Bring him back about six or a bit after."'

That afternoon, while Gysin kept Jones busy in the central square of Djomaa el Fna, Keylock drove Pallenberg and Richards back to Tangier where they planned to catch the ferry to Malaga. 'C'mon, we can't leave him here,' Keylock said to Keith.

'Yes we can! Keep going. Don't give me a hard time. Get going, we've done it, that's it!'

Meanwhile, Brian returned to the hotel after a pleasant afternoon recording the Moroccan musicians only to discover he'd been abruptly abandoned. He immediately erupted into a panic, frantically phoning Gysin. 'They've all gone and left me. I don't know where they've gone! No message, the hotel won't tell me. I'm here all alone, please help me!'

Jones then rang his trusted friend Ronni, back in London at 4 a.m. 'Anita's just fucked off and left me here,' he cried. 'She's taken all my money, my camera, my credit cards and she's gone off with Keith. Can you come over?'

Two days later Jones made his way back to London where Anita met up with him the following week. She told him it was over, but the humiliated, crushed Jones refused to believe it. Pallenberg later admitted, 'I'd already made my decision about him before this trip to Africa. I'd already been enchanted and swept up by Keith, Brian knew that.'

It was the ultimate betrayal, losing Anita, not to just anyone, but his band-mate and a person he trusted. A friend. Ian Stewart claimed Keith's actions were just another way of testing Brian. 'I think he pulled Anita on purpose,' divulged Stew. 'Brian became unglued when it happened. He really did. I mean he went fucking out of his brain. I think when Brian finally died, Keith felt very badly about it. He probably felt that he contributed towards it by pulling Anita the way he did, because he didn't do it in a very nice way.'

'It was a very cold-blooded affair,' Richards readily admitted. 'I know a lot of people blame me and Anita for that thing; Brian's father [for one].'

Upon seeing the haggard and shattered condition of his son, Lewis Jones stated: 'What I firmly believe was that when he lost the only girl he ever loved, this was a very severe blow to him. He changed suddenly and alarmingly, from a bright enthusiastic young man to a quiet and morose and inwardly-looking young man. When his mother and I saw him for the first time after this happened we were shocked by the change in his appearance and in my opinion he was never the same boy again. I am convinced that was the turning point in Brian's life rather than the pop scene generally.'

Dave Thomson put it even more strongly: 'I think the loss of Anita destroyed Brian. He was totally in love with her. It finished him. At the time he had no direction. He said, "They took my music; they took my band; now they've taken my love."'

The whole sordid affair promptly landed Jones in a west London Hospital, suffering from a breakdown. Nicholas Fitzgerald found his friend pale and despondent. 'Please don't talk to me about what's happened,' he whispered, 'except to say, if they think I'm going on the European tour in a fortnight's time with that bastard they must be crazy.'

But that's precisely what Brian did, as The Stones had an important tour beginning 25 March, including their first appearance behind the Iron Curtain in Poland. The shell-shocked guitarist found himself in the horribly awkward position of sharing the stage with the man who had just betrayed him. It was only a last-ditch effort by Anita, falsely promising she'd come back to him that put him back on the road. It was a dirty trick.

As it turned out, the tour was among the ugliest and most violent in the band's turbulent history, filled with the ransacking of hotel rooms, humiliating strip-searches and brutal riots where raging crowds were beaten down by water cannons. In some cities temporary cells were constructed at the sites of venues to contain the out-of-control teens.

As Ian Stewart remembers, the tour took on a negative tone for another reason. 'I didn't know anything about drugs until 1967, when we went on tour with an American road manager called Michael Gruber, who tried really hard to turn them on to everything. He did a good job. He's a bloody mess. There again, they thought the sun shined out of his arse.'

Tom Keylock would routinely search Jones before every border-crossing and then strong-arm him into flushing uppers and hash down the toilet. 'It was the only way to be safe,' he said. 'I used to tell him if he said he was clean and wasn't I'd chin him.'

One time Brian, however, wasn't clean and was subsequently busted in Milan, 'They didn't find anything,' revealed Keylock. 'He took six uppers all in one whack. You can imagine how he was flying.'

In Zurich a crazed fan scaled the thirteen-foot-high stage and began pummelling Jagger. Keylock, standing in the wings, rushed out with a show of fisticuffs launching a vicious upper-cut to the youth's jaw, a blow so explosive he broke his own hand. In Poland Keylock was nearly caught attempting to smuggle out a roll of film depicting the violent rioting. But it was Les Perrin who was ultimately detained for trying to smuggle Polish currency out of the country. In an ironic twist the authorities made him spend it in the airport gift shop. As for Jones, it was to be his final tour with The Rolling Stones.

In April, Brian attempted a reconciliation with Anita at the Cannes Film Festival where *A Degree of Murder* was nominated for an award. The resulting confrontation ended as usual, with Jones flailing away his frustration and pain, the relationship now irrevocably and permanently broken. This time, however, it finally sunk in; he'd lost Anita for good.

The loss caused repercussions far beyond a simple broken heart: 'I think the fact that Keith – a member of Brian's own group – took Anita away from him poisoned any possibility for the group to function the way it had before,' reveals Marianne. 'That was the beginning of the end. It tainted everything; there was no chance for Brian to survive in the group after that.'

Jones promptly dived head first into a reckless routine of drug abuse. A source the *New Musical Express* referred to as a 'bodyguard/nursemaid' to Jones, related a so-called typical day in the life of Brian: 'He'd wake up in the morning, take a couple of leapers, cocaine, maybe some morphine, a few tabs of acid and some Mandrax. Then he'd try and get dressed and end up with a lizard-skin boot on one foot and a pink shoe on the other. He could barely stand.' An only slightly exaggerated quote, one suspects.

Phil May, leader of The Pretty Things, who once shared a house with Jones, claimed Brian viewed his band as a threat to The Stones. One time he'd come off the road only to find that Jones had got hold of his group's tapes and records and burned the lot. On a subsequent occasion Phil and his band were listening to a Stones album when Brian stormed in, picked up a guitar and smashed it over the head of drummer, Viv Prince.

'Brian was so paranoid,' says May, 'he thought because we were laughing and smoking joints that we were pissing on the album.'

In this state Jones had to face the portentous events of 10 May 1967. The very day Richards and Jagger were brought up on indictments stemming from the Redlands bust, the Scotland Yard Drug Squad raided Jones's flat. A dazed Jones, who'd been up all night partying with Prince Stanislaus Klossowski De Rola Baron De Watteville, better known as Stash, watched in stunned confusion as a cadre of twelve police conducted a forty-minute search uncovering a paltry fifty grains of cannabis, enough to make up fewer than ten cigarettes.

Detective Sergeant Norman Pilcher then showed Jones a phial containing traces of cocaine. 'We do smoke hash,' he agreed nervously. 'But not the cocaine, man. That is not my scene. No, man, no. I am not a junkie. That is not mine at all.'

As Jones and Stash were whisked away to Kensington Police Station clearly something was amiss. The pair were befuddled by a purple leather wallet apparently found beneath a mattress containing the grass, an item neither of them had ever seen before. Then there were the crowds of reporters waiting outside the house and at the police station who obviously knew about the raid well in advance. Some people have asked why Scotland Yard were called out for such a relatively paltry bust.

It was undoubtedly because Brian's arrest coincided with the Jagger/Richards trial, which at the time was receiving a lot of media attention.

This was not just Scotland Yard, but the ruling establishment showing the world what they thought of The Rolling Stones.

For Jones this was of course the latest in a long line of scandals: his domestic abuse, drug problems, paternity suits and unreliability in the studio had earned him the tag 'Liability Jones' around the Stones office.

Much as the people who worked with him liked him, it was hard to empathise with Brian. His personal problems seemed much of his own making, and what could they do to help? Everyone must have surely felt that Brian would emerge smiling, as he always did, from his latest bout of depression.

For the first time since his childhood, Brian was truly alone. Courtfield Road, where he and Anita entertained the London elite was reduced to a crew of grubby hangers-on. Brian Palastanga recalls: 'We would have a party at Brian's place near enough every night, never musicians from other groups, just layabouts. They used to get in the Chelsea Potter Club and expect me to buy drinks with Brian's money. We would have it all put on a bill and I would pay for Brian in the end.

'From there, we would usually go on to a friend's flat where they would turn on and smoke pot. When we got back to Brian's flat there would be a bit of a ball. There'd be music – "Plenty of sounds," as Brian said – but there would be no sex, nothing in the open. They would just sit, smoke and talk.'

According to Mandy Aftel, Jones was ill-equipped to discern between his true friends and those who sought only to use him. 'His need for love and a demonstration of affection were too great to risk rejection from anyone. For Brian, "openness" was an involuntary response; he was like a fisherman who casts his line hoping it will make contact.'

An old school chum from Cheltenham, Peter Watson, recalls running into Brian once on the King's Road with a pair of heavily made-up dolly birds on each arm. Jones offered the girls to Watson like a condiment, 'Here, do you want one?'

On another occasion he took a woman friend to spend the night at London's swish Park Lane Hilton. On the way to the room Brian spotted rows of shoes lined up in the hall to be cleaned. He raced up and down swapping shoes and tossing others down the laundry chute. He later proceeded to order chips from room service only to stuff them in the waiter's mouth and hurl the rest out of the tenth-floor window. Before being kicked out by the manager, Jones left the water running in the bathtub.

Even more bizarre was the time he pulled up to a Chelsea record shop after having just washed his hair and demanded an employee find him a blow-dryer for his still-wet locks. A bewildered clerk produced one and Jones then fastidiously styled his hair for some fifteen minutes.

Palastanga himself often witnessed Jones's chameleon-like behaviour. 'Some people say there were two Brian Joneses, the drugged and the undrugged and they are wrong. There were a dozen baffling and wildly inconsistent sides to the character of this complex young chap. He could be charming one moment and boorish the next. He could be considerate to a point of being conned and then suddenly heave a brick through a window.

'I always knew he would be all right until he started to smoke pot, then he would change. He became violent and used to fight with people or punch a policeman or, as he did on one occasion, kick me in the stomach because I wouldn't let him have the key to the Rolls. Once he started smoking that was it, he couldn't stop until I eventually got him home and into bed.

'Sometimes, if we were in a pub I would try to make him drunk first by having whiskys put into his glass of bitter. That was the only way we could ever have an early night. I never saw him smoke unless there were some of his so-called friends with him. Sometimes he would say that he wanted to give up the drugs altogether, but it would be the same story as usual once he met up with people he knew.'

By now, Jagger and Richards had once again realigned; this time for good. The acquisition of Marianne Faithfull, the serenely lovely, former convent girl and daughter of a baroness, granted Mick entry into the high society he had always coveted.

'You could see it on Mick's face every time they were at a party,' says Donald Cammell. 'It was pure possession. "Look what I've got, isn't it fantastic!"'

Jagger was now making noise about wanting Oldham out of the organisation. The singer's initial loyalty to Andrew was fast dissipating in the wake of the legal problems which distanced the group from their co-manager. Also getting in the way was Oldham's well documented monstrous drug habit which rivalled even Jones's.

'Keith Richards has said the only time I hit it off with Brian was when we were both high and that's the truth,' affirmed Oldham. 'One time in New York, Brian took me to the offices of the notorious Dr Max Jacobson, known as Dr Feelgood because of his mysterious injections. We spent the night with some fabulous hookers who cruised in a Rolls Royce.'

Oldham meanwhile, was spending more time at the studio, where by all accounts he was sorely out of his element. 'Andrew learned record producing at the same time we did,' remembers Keith. 'He knew nothing about recording except what he wanted to hear, which may be the purest way of producing. But we started to learn more than Andrew and all of a sudden Mick and I figured we had more of an idea what this band could do than Andrew. Andrew just wanted hit records; we wanted great ones.'

June of 1967 ushered in the much heralded 'Summer of Love', inspired by The Beatles' revolutionary *Sergeant Pepper* album. Jagger became obsessed with the notion that The Stones too must evolve into a psychedelic band, which led to a showdown between him and Jones over the content of their next album. Brian rose up out of his drug-induced haze to lobby for a return to their R&B roots, warning Mick this new direction was a serious mistake.

'If he insists on recording that sort of crap,' he told Sanchez, 'The Stones are dead.' He even had Oldham on his side, finally realising the blues were the way to go.

Although Jagger prevailed, the dismal public showing of *Their Satanic Majesties Request* proved a personal humiliation and showed that Jones, like a punchy fighter who keeps coming back, refused to be quashed. His inventive Mellotron work on the album was about the only thing the critics liked. On top of that, Jagger and Richards's dabbling in the occult did little to help their image with Mick shown on the album in a witch's hat and black cloak.

In the biography, *Jagger*, author Carey Schofield writes: 'Anger's influence on The Stones was strong, particularly through Anita who enjoyed the spookery of demonism and according to some people spent a lot of time cooking up spells and muttering curses.'

Jagger then aped Jones by composing the music for Anger's film, *Lucifer Rising*, and was set to star in the lead until he backed off, letting his younger brother Chris take the role.

As Jones watched from the sidelines, no doubt sniggering at Jagger, he impudently quipped, 'Thank Christ for that. Now perhaps we can get back to playing music again.'

Taking a much needed break, Brian flew to the States to attend the three-day Monterey Pop Festival over 16, 17 and 18 June. Looking jaunty and dapper in silks and a gold beaded lamé coat ('his clothes were a kind of therapy' as Wyman put it), Jones was bolstered by the attention he still commanded, but praised R&B legend Otis Redding, declaring, 'The Stones think we're the greatest band in the world, but you couldn't give me a million pounds to follow Otis.'

Rumour had Jones taking a friendly trip with *Easy Rider* star Dennis Hopper, and STP with his close pal, Jimi Hendrix. This was, however, hotly refuted by Noel Redding who hung out with him the entire time and said he was in fine shape.

Upon his return Jones attended several sessions with psychiatrist Dr Leonard Henry, who admitted Brian to the Priory Nursing Home under the care of Dr Anthony Flood.

He made his first visit on 6 July 1967, accompanied by Tom Keylock, Les Perrin and Suki Potier, the former girlfriend of Tara Browne, who Jones caught on the rebound from Anita. Suki, with her blonde hair, sculpted cheekbones and fashion-model vocation reminded him of Pallenberg people said, but in fact she was more a female replica of Jones himself.

Even a mentally battered Brian could still demonstrate his keen wit. When Keylock took him to the hospital Jones said anxiously, 'You're not gonna leave me are you?'

'Brian, the doctor's not going to let me in there.'

The cockney minder then waited forty-five minutes before the door opened and the psychiatrist popped his head out. 'Would you do me a favour, Mr Keylock?' he asked in exasperation. 'Take him away because I have to make an appointment with *my* psychiatrist!'

Shuffling down the hallway Brian quipped, 'That's it! I done his brain in, didn't I?'

Dr Flood immediately pronounced his patient, 'anxious, depressed and perhaps even suicidal. I don't think Brian was living in a real world. He resented being ordinary or dressing like an ordinary person. He felt he never wanted to be part of the world in which he lived and when anything interfered, his reaction was to buy it off or pretend it didn't exist. He had the money and could be so different from 99.9 per cent of the population.

'I only got him on the outside of these things – which he didn't want to know about – and these things came back anyway. I think he was hoping to grow up within them and when he had grown up and had identified then he could step out and be a real big person. He wanted very much to be a big, important, famous person in some way, not in the pop way.

'This is why I was trying to encourage him to get out and record his Arab music, because he had to have something for himself, all his own.

He had very little. He didn't even have girlfriends that were all his own. He never really had a flat which was all his own. His musical instruments, the ones he became interested in, as his own, were the weird and wonderful ones, like the Kentucky violin thing with three strings.'

Jones managed to talk the doctor into releasing him overnight for a recording session at Olympic on 12 July 1967, but when he returned the next morning he was so loaded on pills and brandy he could barely stand. 'Without permission,' related Flood, 'he filled himself with Mandrax, which is a barbiturate sleeping tablet, and so I put him to bed and started all over again. I discovered that one of the reasons he had done this was that the chauffeur, who was not the best of men in these situations, had heard a rumour that while Jones was in the nursing home the police planned to plant more stuff in his flat. This threw him completely and he accepted it to be the truth.

'Two of the three psychiatrists who saw him felt he exhibited an incredible degree of paranoia. One wasn't sure whether his cries against the police were justifiable or if they were not quite as honest as I was brought to believe.'

Released on 24 July, Jones became convinced he had been targeted by the cops and the media. He and Suki became veritable vagabonds, moving from hotel to hotel in the West Country, or staying with friends in Marbella, Spain. As Suki later explained, 'After that first bust Brian was terrified to stay at the flat. He was certain the phone was tapped. Sometimes when the phone rang he wouldn't answer it; other times he'd pick it up and start yelling, "You looking to bust somebody? Well here I am, come and get me!"

'Every time we turned around there was an ambulance showing up outside or the fire department saying someone had called the police reporting a break-in or that Brian was about to commit suicide.'

'They won't be satisfied until they put me away for good, one way or another,' he told Suki.

Jones would frequently appear on his South Kensington balcony for spontaneous press conferences. 'It's all a hoax,' he remonstrated to reporters. One particular occasion, after police had broken into his flat following a report that Jones had taken ill, Brian, unshaven and naked beneath a fur-collared dressing gown shouted down to waiting journalists, 'I'm being constantly harassed by the police. See that van parked over there? It's an unmarked police car. It's been here every day. And you people, why are you always hassling me?'

Trevor Kempson shed some light on the situation alleging 'someone' in The Stones' organisation was deliberately leaking information about Jones, both to the police and the press. 'Of course Brian was being set up,' he claimed. 'All through 1967 and 1968, first the police would be tipped off he was holding, and a few minutes later the tip-off would come to me.'

Kempson even went so far as to name the source. 'I'm fairly sure those tips originated with Les Perrin. Also, one or two of The Stones' drivers who had criminal records and were therefore vulnerable to police pressure and saw Jones as being a threat. They didn't like him much anyway and weren't unhappy at earning a little pin money. There was good reason why Brian had to go, so far as [Les was] concerned, and that was the problems he caused Jagger which resulted in him suing the *News of the World*.'

Interestingly, Jones had grown exceedingly close to the Perrins. 'I think Brian suffered from pressures which were not necessarily from being a Stone,' ventured Les. 'I think he had private problems, like wanting to be loved tremendously. He needed to have an almost maternal love away from any other kind of love and he found a shoulder to cry on in my wife.'

According to Janie Perrin, to whom Jones affectionately identified himself as 'your other son', Brian twice phoned her threatening suicide. Each time she managed to cajole him out of it. When he called first from the Dorchester Hotel saying he was going to throw himself out of a window, Janie Perrin told him, 'Well, dear, go down a few floors before you do it. You don't want to make a mess on the pavement.'

Next, when he threatened to slash his wrists Janie told him to make sure he went into the bathroom so he wouldn't splatter blood on the carpet. 'I was ninety-nine per cent certain he wasn't going to do it,' she says in *Golden Stone*, 'but inside I was absolutely sick at heart he wouldn't respond to my tactics. I always tried to be light, but firm with him. Saying "I feel sorry for you" was not what he needed.'

Even the hardened Keith Richards could relate to Jones's plight. 'When the cops started leaning on Brian, the ones who ruled his area of London, they were vicious. They used to come for him regularly. Everything else he could have handled but with that kind of persecution on top, he was prone to a persecution complex anyway. But when it became a reality to him, Her Majesty's law coming through the door every day, he was so paranoid there wouldn't even be a bottle of booze around. The cops would walk in and immediately find some hash. He knew he didn't stand a chance.'

On 29 September, true to Jones's prediction, Andrew Oldham was effectively squeezed out by Mick and Keith who had now taken over producing as well. An interesting turn of events as Jones came to trial on 30 September.

Arriving in a natty charcoal-grey suit and polka-dot tie, Brian pleaded guilty to possession of cannabis and using his home for the consumption of unlawful substances, while entering a plea of not guilty to possession of methedrine and cocaine.

Despite the relatively minor nature of the offence the judge pronounced Jones guilty and sentenced him to a devastating nine months inside. Visibly shaken, Brian was led away in handcuffs, reportedly sobbing all the way to Wormwood Scrubs. Although he was let out the next day on bail to await appeal in December, the experience left a marked impression.

According to Richards, who described Wormwood as 'a medieval dungeon from the days of the Borgias', Jones had been roughed up pretty good.

The prison officers leered, 'We finally got one of those bloody longhairs' and threatened to give him a haircut.

In a 1974 interview with *Crawdaddy* magazine, Jagger remembered, 'Brian was so sensitive, that was what was so unfair about it, getting busted. It really brought him down. Brian came close to doing six months . . . He was followed all the time, but we all were. It was a systematic campaign of harassment which brought Brian down and destroyed the musical side of him as well.'

The lack of creative energy in Brian was hitting him hard. Whatever else was going on in his troubled life up to this point, he could always play an instrument, find escape and solace in the blues. He could always express himself extremely eloquently through music. Except now.

'I don't know what's happening to me,' he confessed to Sanchez. 'My mind won't even let me play music anymore.'

Gered Mankowitz reported, 'He was in such an awful state, falling into his food. He had to play a little recorder part. In a side-booth where they did the vocals he was propped up with chairs so that he couldn't fall over.'

Even the usually easy-going Richards showed signs of annoyance saying, 'If he keeps getting out of his box like this we'll have to find a new guitar player. Can't we find some woman to look after him?'

On 12 December Jones stood for an appeal on his September

conviction. Key in his defence was the following independent psychiatric profile submitted by Professor Walter Neustatter:

'His IQ is 133. Intellectual functioning shows assets in his range of general knowledge, abstract reasoning capacity, social awareness and vocabulary. He does not reveal signs of formal thought-disorder or psychotic disturbance of thought processes. However, Mr Jones's thought processes do reveal some weakening of his reality ties as a result of intense free-floating anxiety. He currently tends to feel very threatened by the world about him as a result of his increasingly inadequate control of aggressive instinctual impulses. This repressive control seems to be breaking down and he often resorts to conspicuous denial of the threat created by the breakthrough of these impulses into consciousness.

'At times he projects these aggressive feelings so that he feels a victim of his environment; at others he introjects them, resulting in significant depressive tendencies and associated suicidal risk.

'Mr Jones's sexual problems are closely inter-related to his difficulties of aggression; that is, he experiences very intense anxiety surrounding phallic and sadistic sexuality because of the implicit aggressive striving. However, these phallic strivings are also in conflict with his gross passive dependency needs. This conflict prevents any mature heterosexual adjustment, indeed, he withdraws from any genuine heterosexual involvement. These sexual difficulties reinforce Mr Jones's considerable emotional immaturity and effect gross confusion and identification. He vacillates between a passive, dependent child with a confused image of an adult on the one hand, and an idol of pop culture on the other.

'He is still very involved with Oedipal fixations. He is very confused about the maternal and paternal role in these. Part of his confusion would seem to be the very strong resentment he experiences toward his dominant and controlling mother who rejected him and blatantly favoured his sister.

'In conclusion, it is my considered opinion that Mr Jones is, at present, in an extremely precarious state of emotional adjustment as a result of his unresolved problems with aggressive impulses and sexual identification. His grasp on reality is fragile because of the debilitating effect of intense anxiety and conflicts surrounding these problems.

'Much of his anxiety is currently focussed on to his potential imprisonment, but its underlying sources are more deeply rooted. He thus urgently needs psychotherapy to assist in mustering his considerable personality resources and capacity for insight to contain his

Paint It Black

anxiety. Otherwise, his prognosis is very poor. Indeed, it is very likely that his imprisonment could precipitate a complete break with reality, a psychotic breakdown and significantly increase the suicidal risk for this man.'

That report, along with the testimony of two other psychiatrists, in effect stated that Brian could not mentally handle the prison sentence. The judge declared Jones's sentence set aside on three years' probation and a £1,000 fine plus continued medical treatment.

'I want to be left alone to get on with my life,' he told reporters before being whisked away in his Rolls.

Elated and relieved over his freedom, Jones had clearly only just been holding on. On 14 December he celebrated at a club by playing bass with the house band when suddenly he began kicking at the instrument until he bashed it to pieces. Later, Stones chauffeur John Coray found Brian collapsed in his new flat at 17 Chesham Street, Belgravia, and called an ambulance. After an hour's stay at St George's Hospital, Hyde Park Corner, the diagnosis was 'mental tiredness', along with a severe dental problem that required the extraction of two teeth.

Meanwhile, the stress Jones was under had now taken a significant turn for the worse. In October Detective Norman Pilcher – who arrested Jones – interviewed the long-suffering musician in the offices of Stones solicitors Joynson-Hicks in connection with a murder investigation. It seemed he had been at a club the same night the victim had last been seen alive. A shaken Jones, while not implicated, was forced to sign a statement before being released. Yet another nerve-wracking experience for the paranoid young man.

As 1968 unfolded, a certain London detective allegedly resorted to a relentless blackmail scheme. According to Tony Sanchez the same officer caught up with Jones on three separate occasions demanding payments of £1,000 or he'd bust him on dope charges. 'The third time I didn't even have any dope in the place,' Jones confided to Sanchez, 'so he just pulled some out of his pocket and told me he'd plant it on me if I didn't pay over the money.'

'I believed him implicitly,' says Sanchez. 'I knew the officer Brian was talking about had offered to give cannabis to people employed by The Stones in return for information about their whereabouts and their drug habits.'

Palastanga said that one night the two had just left a London club when a pair of policemen spotted Jones's unmistakable Rolls and

74

pulled him over to search the vehicle. 'We had some LSD wrapped in silver paper,' noted Palastanga, 'so I put it inside my mouth. We got away with it that time.' The stress went beyond Jones himself to others in his circle. Linda Lawrence, for instance, who'd briefly moved in with Brian, had to be rushed to hospital after she had collapsed under the pressure.

Then on 16 March, Linda Keith, Richards's former steady girlfriend, and casual girlfriend of Jones, was found in the Belgravia flat by police, the victim of an apparent suicide attempt. Keith removed her clothes, swallowed some pills and then proceeded to phone friends to inform them of what she'd done. Afterwards she locked the front door and was discovered splayed unconscious across the bed when police stormed in, breaking down the door to rescue her.

When Brian returned he was flabbergasted at the events as Linda had been sleeping when he left and there had been no hint of any problem. The following morning, as Keith left the hospital, apparently no worse for wear, headlines appeared in the tabloids: 'Stone Girl Naked in Drug Drama'.

For Brian it was devastating. Not only was the story potentially damaging in light of his probationary status, but his landlord promptly evicted him.

He told the press, 'I explained to the landlord that I rented the flat at £30 a week for my chauffeur. I only lived there when I was working in town. But he wouldn't listen to me. I have paid six months' rent in advance, but it didn't make any difference to him. He just wanted me out. I can't understand it. I have only the clothes I am wearing. All my other clothes and equipment are in the flat.

'I am very worried about her being so seriously ill. I have phoned the hospital, but they told me I couldn't see her as doctors were attending to her. They assured me there was nothing to worry about. I will go to the hospital tonight or tomorrow to see her. We are very close and I would hate to see anything happen to her. We both have the same interests and we have become inseparable. I am really cut up by this.'

With all his mounting trials even the studio no longer proved a reliable haven. Ironically, the stage had been set for a Jones comeback. The highly respected Jimmy Miller had been brought on board to produce a new album and had nothing but compliments for Jones's musical expertise, calling both his film score and work on bottleneck guitar 'brilliant'. Also in the wake of the *Satanic Majesties* debacle, The Stones were finally returning to rhythm and blues. Jones tossed aside his collection of exotic instruments and once more picked up bottleneck guitar, sounding better than ever. The resulting LP was the acclaimed *Beggars Banquet*.

But this time, looming larger was a rejuvenated Mick Jagger. He'd been effectively running the show for several years. According to Tony Sanchez, Jagger called a press conference in Les Perrin's office to announce, 'There is a tour coming up. There are obvious difficulties, one of them is with Brian, who can't leave the country. Brian's a junkie, he's burned out, we're gonna have to tour without him.' Even after the conference Jagger kept this up purportedly saying: 'Brian can't get into Tokyo because he's a druggie.'

The blatant cruelty drew its expected response from Jones. He began turning up at the studio so wasted on brandy and Mandrax he was in no condition to play. Sanchez later found the distraught Stone curled up in a pink velvet suit in a corner of Olympic Studios with a red guitar on top of him.

'They treat me like was a leper,' Brian despaired. 'I had a fight with Mick about it and he said I was a pain in the arse and I wasn't even a good enough musician to be in The Stones. Christ, it was my fucking band! The whole thing was my idea. They'd never have got there without me and now they have taken it all away from me.'

Sanchez came up with an intriguing insight about Jagger's view that the deteriorating Jones was a threat. 'It could only be because he knew what no one outside The Stones' immediate circle knew, that Brian really was what Jagger pretended to be. Brian was genuinely out of his skull on drugs most of the time, while Jagger used only minuscule quantities of dope. Brian was into orgies, lesbians and sadomasochism, while Jagger lived his prim, prissy bourgeois life with a baroness's daughter and worried in case someone spilled coffee on his Persian carpets. Keith felt guilty every time he saw him because he had stolen Anita and in doing so pushed Brian over the edge. And Jagger knew he could never really be the most beautiful, most glamorous Rolling Stone while Brian was around.

'I knew then that there could be no future for Brian with The Stones.'

On 21 May 1968, Jones was rudely awakened at 7.20 a.m. by a relentless pounding on the door of his temporary hideaway at Royal Avenue House on the King's Road.

Taking a peek through his spy-hole, he saw to his horror a trio of beefy police officers shouting through the letter box. Jones quickly grabbed the phone to call Les Perrin.

'Les, they're coming in through the windows, man!'

Actually, Detective Constable Brian Liddell was climbing in through the refuse chute to find Jones holding the phone dressed in a thin kimono sitting on the bedroom floor.

'Listen,' said one of the officers, 'I've been knocking on the door for ten minutes. Why didn't you open up?'

'You know the scene, man,' he replied indignantly. 'Why do I always get bugged?'

A regiment of police led by Detective Sergeant Robin Constable then scavenged about the flat. Finally a Detective Prentice ferreted through a bureau drawer and drew out a blue ball of wool encasing a lump of so-called Indian hemp. Brian's face went white. 'Oh no, this cannot happen again! Not when we're just getting back on our feet.'

'Is this your wool?'

'It might be. But I don't knit. I don't darn socks. I don't even have a girlfriend who darns. Listen officers, this isn't even my flat. I'm just staying here while the new place I have bought is being decorated.'

As Jones was once again carted off to the station and charged with possession of cannabis, the spectre of Les Perrin loomed at the heart of the incident. Had the publicist, as Kempson alleged, set up the tortured Jones?

According to friends, the police grilled Brian as to whether he had any wool – of all things – which might hide drugs. Jones, quite naturally, found the suggestion laughable.

One might draw the obvious conclusion that someone had already planted the dope and the cops were told where to find it. Could the instigator have been The Stones' publicist himself?

Perrin later categorically denied the charge saying, 'I remain convinced that Brian was innocent of that second bust. I phoned Brian from Chichester to tell him that a friend of mine at the newspaper had told me that he was going to be busted.

'Brian said, "There's nothing here for them to find."

'I said, "Well, if you have anything, get rid of it."

'He stressed: "There's nothing here for them to find."'

As Philip Norman has said: 'Unimpeachably respectable as he was, Les had shared in The Stones' notoriety, his telephone intermittently tapped, his wife Janie subject to disquieting police visits. At one point in the sixties, impressed by his PR job for pop music's make-believe criminals, some real bad guys approached Perrin and asked for his help getting better press.

'At times, the Chelsea police seemed only walk-on players in that long term conspiracy by so-called friends to steal Brian's stardom first, then his woman and finally to eject him from the band he had created.'

Once more, Jones fled London seeking refuge at Redlands while Richards was away in Spain with Anita. The country haven however, took on the air of a prison under the oppressive hold of Tom Keylock, whose rigid orders to keep Jones away from all drugs was carried out with the regimental doggedness of a drill sergeant.

During the research stage of this book I came across a very interesting photograph from this time. There was Tom Keylock, lying on a blanket on the front lawn of Redlands. It's a lovely summer's day and Tom's got his shirt off. A young lady's legs can be seen at the left hand edge of the picture, but to the right, on the grass, is a very real-looking leather holster with a big chrome-plated pistol sticking out. In Tom's hand, a shotgun.

'I didn't like Tom Keylock. Nobody did,' Derrick remembers. 'I kept away from him. He was the sort of person you didn't need. He'd drop Brian off and then split because in England servants are not welcome, and that's what he really was. But he was pushing his luck with Brian.'

Derrick remembers one occasion at the Chelsea Embankment home of wealthy young aristocrat, Mark Warman: 'Brian was particularly fucking raucous. It was one of those rare occasions when there was coke around and Brian was great, he was on top form. He was a little bit shaky 'cause he'd been through the busts. When Keylock rang the doorbell and came in, Brian changed. He got like scared.

' "Hey man, tell him to fuck off!" I said.

'But Keylock says, "C'mon, we're going!"

'Brian says, "No, no, no. Go down and wait in the car. Just wait man!"

'Everybody said, "Yeah, Tom get outta here, man. Fuck off!"

'He left us, he got really upset, clenching his fists and a tight jaw. He's a nasty man.'

The interminable four-month wait for trial was agony for Jones. His overwhelming fear of being alone caused him to phone up dozens of friends such as Jo Bergman and Janie Perrin in the middle of the night unable to turn off the kitchen tap or light the oven.

Derrick witnessed firsthand the final deterioration of Jones: 'At the end, he was a pain in the fucking ass, he really became more and more of a loon. He would drive by in Chelsea with that fucking Tom Keylock and fuck the cops off. Chelsea's a tight little part of the world and they didn't like it. They got the fucking needle for Brian. The cops knew he was getting high, but most people were around Chelsea. The cops didn't really give a shit. They somehow connected amongst themselves, the metropolitan police are like a clan. Detective Sergeant Constable, he singled out Brian and haunted him. He was the guy who instigated the bust.'

At the studio, The Stones were no longer even making an effort to acknowledge his musical presence. When he picked up a guitar and started to play a riff Jagger would stop him saying, 'No Brian, not that, that's no good.'

'What should I play, then?' asked Jones.

'Whatever you want,' sighed Jagger. But when Brian tried something else Mick again cut him off, 'No, that's no good either Brian.'

Finally Jones ended up in a corner drunkenly blowing a harmonica when Mick threw on his coat, gave him one last stare and left the studio.

Stones engineer George Chikiantz recalled how Jagger and Richards soon delegated only minor tasks to Jones, such as unimportant overdubs. 'It was a bit much the way they were going on at him. But Brian was no longer capable of fulfilling a real function in the group. It was difficult to contact him, like talking to a shadow. He just wasn't there, inside of his body. The saddest thing was to watch Brian spend three and a half hours trying to put a reed in a saxophone and nobody could stop him. We had to wait until he got thirsty and give him another Mandrax to send him to sleep.'

Even in those rare moments when he was quasi-coherent the guitarist was a target of his bandmates' derision. As Derrick observed, 'The Stones were having a right fucking go at Brian. They were all walking around doing naughty imitations of him, talking through their teeth. Because Brian used to get stoned on Mandrax and he'd talk really funny. They were all doing this impersonation of Brian down at Olympic Studios. To be honest, it was rather amusing.'

'They'd then get really fucking nasty to Brian, the worse they got, the worse he got. Mick and Keith ganged up on him because Brian was being a fucking asshole, man. It would have been the natural thing to happen anyway. He was working his way out of the band by being a fucking nonce.'

'It was quite ugly. Brian was out of his gourd, he had some demons.'

At this point, photographer Ethan Russell shot Messrs Jagger and Richards on a London rooftop and their mood reflected the grim atmosphere that hung over the band. He described the duo as: 'A scowling Mick; Keith apparently nodding out for the last time. The desire is for undigested meat, so people like carrion eaters can rise up on their hind legs and howl at the horror of it all. Sad, bad Brian Jones would soon be their supper.'

There lingers an ongoing controversy as to whether or not Jones ever indulged in heroin. While Anita Pallenberg and Ronni Money denied he ever once took the drug, testimony from others suggests otherwise.

Tony Sanchez, once said: 'He would shove anything that would stab or stroke his mind in through his mouth.'

Offered Tom Keylock: 'I think he did have some heroin near the end of it.'

Even Ian Stewart addressed the accusation: 'I knew he was probably on the hard stuff though I never actually saw Brian put a needle in himself. I never saw Brian with all the scars and things, but then I wasn't looking for it.'

Paul McCartney shares his own recollections: 'He was a nervous sort of guy, very shy, quite serious and I think maybe into drugs a little more than he should have been, because he used to shake a little bit. I remember being in a car with Chris Barber and somebody saying, "Bloody Brian, bloody on heroin." And we said, "Yeah, he is on heroin, but we're supposed to be his friends and you can't go around saying, bloody hell." '

Although the above recollections were, I'm sure, expressed in good faith, the facts indicate that Jones never even so much as dabbled in opiates, much less that he was any sort of junkie. Certainly Jones experimented with illicit substances, many drugs, but heroin did not appear to be one of them.

Brian's continuing drug use, along with his soul-stripping paranoia led to several aborted suicide attempts. Brian Palastanga claims to have witnessed two such incidents. The first took place at the Royal Garden Hotel when Jones climbed on to a window ledge and threatened to launch himself off the top of the building, only to be tackled and brought to the floor by the burly chauffeur. Another time he and Brian were driving along the Embankment and Jones raced from the car, scaled the wall and said he was going to jump into the Thames.

'Please help me!' he implored.

Marianne Faithfull recalls her attempt to try and mend fences between Jones and Jagger by inviting them both to Redlands for dinner along with Richards. In retrospect, a disastrous idea. Tensions that had been smouldering for months, years even, finally exploded when the two Stones exchanged heated, verbal abuse, that escalated into a shoving match. Suddenly, Brian grabbed a carving knife from the table and charged towards Mick just missing the lithe singer who darted out of the way.

He cried: 'I'm going to kill myself,' and ran blindly out of the house, across the garden, where he leapt into a moat.

'Shit, that water's twenty feet deep!' cried Keith as the three frantically followed.

Jagger plunged in after him and the two thrashed furiously in the water. Mick, livid, reportedly grabbed Jones's hair and dunked his head beneath the muddy water.

Afterwards, Jagger hauled Jones, caveman style, from the moat and pointed to his ruined velvet trousers.

'You stupid bastard, these cost me fifty quid. I hope you do go to jail and for a bloody long time!'

Back in London Brian appeared for his second trial on 24 September. Dressed in a grey pinstripe suit under orders from Les Perrin, before a gallery of fifty teenage fans, along with Mick and Keith, he took the stand. First he submitted to questioning by his counsel, Michael Havers: 'You said that you never take cannabis because it makes you so paranoid? What do you mean?'

Jones: That refers back to the events of last year. The effect of the drug for me was a heightening of experience that I found most unpleasant. That made me very frightened of it.
Havers: Were you advised what would be the consequences of breaking probation by using drugs?
Jones: Yes sir, I have taken no chances.
Havers: Had you the slightest knowledge that there was cannabis resin in that wool?
Jones: No, absolutely not.

Under cross-examination, Prosecutor Roger Frisby asked why he didn't open the door to police.

Jones: I was afraid. Well, the events of last year and there had been so many drug raids in the Chelsea area, I was just worried, I wanted advice.
Frisby: Mr Jones, who, if not you, put the cannabis in the bureau?

Jones: A lot of people had come and gone while I was living in the flat, but I have no reason to suspect any one person. I have no idea how cannabis got there and I've denied it ever since cannabis has been found.

Frisby: What I am suggesting is that the cannabis was yours, that you knew it all along and that you are now lying to us.

Jones: I am not guilty, sir. I believe that my whole conduct, while the police were in the flat, points to a denial.

Although the jury returned a guilty verdict, certain factors were taken into consideration before sentencing. Testimony from the psychiatrists strongly suggested Jones was terrified of prison and thus wouldn't go near the drug again.

'If I put a reefer cigarette by this young man he would run a mile,' stated Dr Flood.

The flat's previous tenant, actress Joanna Pettet, had been interviewed in America by the FBI and admitted the wool was probably hers, though she denied any knowledge of the cannabis.

Lastly, Brian had sufficient time to ditch the dope if he in fact knowingly harboured it, which weighed heavily in light of his lenient £50 fine.

Afterwards, an elated Jones proclaimed, 'I'm so relieved and happy to be free. I'll state till my death that I did not commit this crime.'

Seconding that motion was, surprisingly, Lewis Jones. 'I am absolutely convinced, and shall always remain so, that Brian was unjustly convicted of the second of his drug charges. Brian was innocent of that charge and I base this mainly on the fact that the very night it happened he rang me up in a state of great distress because he was deeply concerned about how his affairs were affecting the family and he swore to me that he was innocent of it and he hoped I'd always believe him. I promised him on that occasion I believed him and nothing has ever, or will ever, change my mind.'

In October Brian returned to his lone sanctuary, his beloved Morocco where he was recording the musicians of Joujouka, whose hypnotic brand of folk music combined flute with polyrhythmic drum sounds. Brion Gysin recalls an incident that took place during the recording. Two musicians were walking along with a goat when Jones, watching in fascination, leapt up imitating the sound and proclaimed, 'That's me!'

'About twenty minutes later,' recalled Gysin, 'we were eating this goat's liver on shish-kebab sticks!'

The album resulting from that excursion, *Brian Jones Presents The Pipes Of Pan At Joujouka*, was released posthumously on Rolling Stones Records in October of 1971. Nearly two decades later its ethnic influences resurfaced on The Stones' 1989 smash, *Steel Wheels*.

Jones returned from the satisfying journey wanting to put the past behind him and get away from London. On 21 November he purchased a centuries-old property for £30,000 near Hartfield, East Sussex, known as Cotchford Farm, former home of *Winnie-the-Pooh* author A. A. Milne. Here he could sink comfortably into the role of country squire, raise animals, maybe even settle down and have kids one day. The place was as solid and impenetrable as the hills around him.

Back in London, however, he had to face reality. Although Jagger and Richards had by now completely wrenched away the band, Jones was still staunchly clinging to his lifeline.

'I think Brian was very, very scared. I don't think he realised how ruthless Mick Jagger was,' said Marianne. 'I think Mick wanted to get rid of him very early on, but he couldn't make a move as long as Brian and Keith were so close. Of course, when Keith ran off with Anita that fixed it.'

Added journalist Ellen Grehen: 'He felt if he was no longer a Rolling Stone then he was nothing; without his music there was no other reason for him to be.'

By the year's end, the ambitious and unprecedented *Rolling Stones Rock And Roll Circus* came to town. The proposed BBC TV special filmed over 11 and 12 December 1968, was a free flowing extravaganza of rock under the big top. Performances by John Lennon and Yoko Ono, The Who, Jethro Tull and, of course The Stones themselves were bizarrely interspersed with acrobats, fire-eaters and midgets, capped by ringmaster Jagger posing with a tiger. Even the audience were participants, in their fluorescent ponchos and felt hats, gathered about the centre ring to enjoy the festivities, highlighted by a supergroup performance comprised of Lennon, Richards, Eric Clapton and Hendrix drummer, Mitch Mitchell.

In the midst of the mayhem, Jones, attired in a purple velvet jacket, gold trousers and top hat seemed to be trying a bit too hard. A quiet desperation lay just below the surface, his voice showing strain as he barely whispered, 'Here come the clowns!'

Whether cavorting with the midgets and the strongman or furiously whipping the maracas on 'Sympathy For The Devil,' Jones appeared isolated, displaced, breaking on the inside. How bitterly ironic that this, his final performance as a Rolling Stone, has yet to be seen.

In an exclusive interview conducted for this book by author Dave Thompson, Ian Anderson, the respected flautist of Jethro Tull, reflects on the tragedy that was Brian Jones: 'The footage for the *Rock and Roll Circus* definitely exists, I don't think it's been destroyed, but The Rolling Stones, and Mick Jagger in particular, don't want it shown because of Brian Jones not really being a part of what was going on at the time and the fact that he died shortly after. It is the end of the Brian Jones era and very close to the end of his life. At the time Brian was a perfectly charming guy, perfectly nice, but he was out there just barely in contact with the known universe and was completely unprepared to be able to play and perform. Very neurotic, a bag of nerves. He was cheerful and friendly to us, but completely ignored by his bandmates. They were going through a bad time anyway, trying to get back on the road. They'd just recorded a new album which turned out to be a great record. But they desperately wanted to go back out and perform and Brian was a real embarrassment to them because of the problems with his health. His psychological state was very bad and the band couldn't relate to him. It was a very uncomfortable situation for everybody in the studio at the time and the end result is a bad memory for The Stones who feel rightly or wrongly just a little bit of discomfort. I wouldn't use the word guilt; but discomfort about the way it all ended for Brian.'

4 STRAW DOGS
Treachery At Cotchford

AS THE LONG country days wore on, Brian slowly began to keep to the beat of Cotchford's languid shuffle. For the first time in years he'd found the presence of mind to be alone and think deeply. Suddenly there was no pressure to perform, or indeed do anything at all. Like the dreamy Christopher Robin walking the dew covered fields of Pooh Corner, Jones spent days wandering the self-same spaces as the former master of the house. Pitching stones into the jagged stream from Pooh's bridge, ambling silently amidst the stoic rows of firs that presumably once hid Eeyore and Owl from all but young Christopher Robin, or simply sitting quietly with his beloved dogs on the curved wooden bench at the end of the garden watching the sky. Brian Jones was home, and at home, for the first time in his long, errant, disconnected life.

'This place is me, man,' he told a journalist chum shortly after moving in. 'I don't really know how to say it exactly, but there is magic about. A definite feeling. A force. It's something to do with what Milne created here I'm sure, but even more to do with me and my life. I feel as though I've always been here and always will be. I'll never leave here I'm sure.'

For the ever-restless Jones, finding a home was only the beginning. There was much to do at Cotchford and Jones was committed to its full revival. For to work on the ageing fifteenth century house was to work on himself. It was a proposition that both excited and scared the confused, sensitive young man. As it was, both had been neglected for a long, long time.

Although a mere half-mile from the tawny outskirts of Hartfield, East Sussex, the lush ten-acre estate, bordering the expansive Ashdown Forest was a world away from the cramped, debris-strewn hotel suites and solitary panelled rooms the twenty-six-year-old guitarist had called home since leaving the shady indifference of his father's china-filled house in suburban Cheltenham.

Constructed originally from a jumble of rustic farmers' cottages knocked together around the turn of the century, Cotchford first said hello to the Milne family in 1924 when they too sought refuge from the bustle and strain of London, some forty miles down the road. After a full year of concentrated construction the esteemed author and his family were using the house as a weekend retreat, later moving there permanently to pen the single greatest children's fable of the twentieth century, *Winnie-the-Pooh*.

For several years, Milne and his faithful wife, Daphne, directed a complicated series of renovations to the estate, carving out a lovely terraced garden behind the house and ultimately a series of winding stone paths. There in a lush opening at the side of the house, a comely statue of the family fortune, Christopher Robin was installed, deity-like on a pedestal and nearby a sundial with the carved images of Pooh, Piglet, Tigger and Eeyore endlessly racing round and round. Inscribed on top is, 'This warm and sunny spot belongs to Pooh, and here he wonders what to do.'

All in all, a fitting spot for the grown-up Christopher Robin of the Woodstock generation to seek refuge from the unremitting pressures of commerce and adulation that made and then unmade The Stones' golden-haired guitarist.

For all its pastoral loveliness and upper-crust isolation, Cotchford Farm had a very definite dark side as well. For it was there, somewhere inside the sturdy brick-lined walls of the rambling L-shaped domicile that author Milne and his beloved 'Billy Moon' (as he sometimes called the tow-headed Christopher Robin) quietly drifted apart forever. In what was to be Milne's final encounter with the written word he wrote to a friend, 'Did you read Moon's article on me in the *Sunday Dispatch*, when I was supposed to be dying? You'd have been disgusted. Oh well, I lost him years ago . . .'

After Milne died in 1956, the old man's famous son put the premises up for sale, ultimately assuming an anonymous life in Brighton as an antiques dealer. Years later, when Cotchford's current owner, millionaire developer Alistair C. H. Johns wrote to invite Christopher back home for an anniversary celebration of Pooh's creation, he reportedly received a terse note stating that Milne's only son and heir would not be able to make it. End of story.

The Milne family weren't the only ones to find heartbreak amongst the shady wonder of Cotchford however. Mary Hallet, the farm's longtime housekeeper and latter day confidante to Jones lost her first husband to meningitis. The poor fellow dropped dead suddenly while making the rounds in his postal van, only to have his pockets picked clean by thieves as he breathed his last. Tragically, years later, her only son was run over and killed in a nearby lane.

By 1956 Cotchford was sold to wealthy American businessman Stewart Taylor, who, along with his exotic, chatty Spanish wife, Margarita, carried out a series of costly, extended modifications to the, by now, rather architecturally confused property. Foremost amongst them was the addition of a large oblong-shaped swimming pool surrounded by a patio of inlaid field stone in the sprawling back garden – a curious accoutrement considering the almost perpetually damp and rainy country climate of Cotchford.

Mary Hallet remembers: 'I went to work for them rather reluctantly as I was born in that house and it did seem odd cleaning up for strangers in my own former bedroom. Before long they had a little girl called Linda who I helped look after. The Taylors were at Cotchford for about thirteen years, but eventually split up. Margarita simply announced one evening that the house was to be sold and she had promised the new owner I would carry on doing my old job for him.

'The first time I actually saw Brian was when he came to meet the Taylors. He was walking down the drive and I was going up with Linda and that's when I met him. He was dressed in a fur coat and had shoulder-length hair. I thought it was a woman! He was very nice when I spoke to him. He looked rather like Pooh Bear coming home again. But he didn't move in straight away.

'He was very kind. He always made you feel at home. He was full of life. The only time he was not good was when he got the asthma. Sometimes he'd try to talk and he'd only get a word at a time out. He sort of gasped between words. I'd lost my son only a little while before he came. He was twenty-three and Brian was just a bit older and I think that's what made us friendly. He'd often come up to our place, have a cup of tea with us and chatter. He was definitely lonely. I went down most days, not weekends as a rule, unless he'd ring up and ask. I had my own home and children so I didn't have all that much spare time. I do want to say, however, that I never saw *anything* I thought could be drugs there. He didn't even look as if he took drugs. There was loud music at times though.'

Brian's day-to-day life as the re-born squire of Cotchford was both idyllic and profoundly out of character for the apparent rebel who had spent the last decade wreaking more havoc on the world than virtually any of the other sixties bad-boy pop stars. And yet here he was; playing darts down at his friendly local, the Haywaggon, watching sport on the telly with the villagers, working side-by-side in the garden with his grounds' keeper, teetotaller Michael Martin (who Brian affectionately called 'Artichoke'), and somewhat improbably spending quiet evenings studying the Bible.

Once again, Mary Hallet: 'We used to talk a lot. We often discussed the Bible. He said he thought living on earth was the hell and that heaven would come after. At times I think he was very unhappy. Fame and money didn't really bring him any good things. He certainly wasn't crazy as people often say, he was a lovely boy.'

Michael Martin, himself a lay preacher at a nearby church, says that Brian knew the Good Book back to front, often peppering his speech with Biblical references. Things eventually went so far that Jones expressed a desire to take to the pulpit, preaching the gospel to the errant youth of the neighbouring countryside.

'I'd like to come one Sunday,' he once told Martin, 'to talk to your kids, to tell them that it might look like I've got all the money I want, that I can go anywhere and do anything, but my life till now has been rotten. I know it seems to them a world of complete pleasure, but they should know what it's really like.'

Although it's true that near the end of his life Brian did come to appreciate the teachings of Christ, he was still a long, long way from seriously embracing the rather narrow perimeters of the Christian lifestyle. As a matter of fact, from all accounts, despite his recent reclamation, he still had quite a bit of the old devil in him.

Case in point; the degradation of one Mary Hallet. 'It was one Saturday morning, she says. 'Brian was down there all alone and he said, "There isn't much doing, will you sit and talk to me?" So we sat at the table and were having a chat when he asked, "Would you have a drink with me?" I said, "I don't really drink."

' "Oh, please do. Just one."

' "Well, I'll have just a quarter of a glass."

'He said, "If I get a quarter of a glass, do you promise you'll drink it?" I said, "Yes."

' "You really promise?"

' "Yes I do."

'So off he goes into the dining room and comes back grinning with a pint glass which is a quarter filled. Well, I'd given my promise, hadn't I? It was delicious! I sat there talking, sipping, I was perfectly all right, but when I went to get up, I hadn't got any legs. He laughed and offered to bring me home in the van, but I said no. I crawled up the vegetable garden path and came out on to the lane, creeping close to the hedge-row hoping no one would see me.'

Accompanying Brian on his new life at Cotchford was his girlfriend Suki Potier. Although the couple first met when Brian's great friend Tara Browne invited him to a party at the Guinness ancestral home in Ireland in 1966, they didn't really start dating until the balmy Summer of 1967, when Suki joined Brian and Tara's widow, Nicky Browne, for a holiday in Marbella, Spain, towards the end of July. She had stood by him during his two harrowing drug busts, put up with his generally reprehensible behaviour, his drinking, blatant womanising and even took care of him when either his questionable constitution, or his asthma, got the better of him. Despite her loyalty, however, Brian still pined quite openly for Anita Pallenberg, causing every bit as much trouble as one might expect. Suki loved the inherent glamour and prestige of bedding the rich and famous and consciously cultivated her role as the swinging, carefree, pop stars' consort.

Wild woman that she was, Potier too, soon surrendered to the seductive charm of the country, apparently taking seriously her role as Brian's protector and conduit to the outside world. 'I loved him deeply,' she confided in a rare interview shortly after Brian's death. 'He was so much more than people ever knew or saw. He could be a right bastard at times, lashing our irrationally at the people who loved him, but all of that was only on the surface. He'd been hurt by his parents as a child and was wounded. All he ever wanted was the simple love and comfort of a home and family, but like an old dog, he had been kicked so long and so hard all of that was buried underneath years of hurt and resentment.'

Brian was close to Suki, but not particularly affectionate, or ever really committed. 'Believe me, *Brian* was the only woman he ever really loved,' said Suki in a telling remark. 'Sometimes he would look right through me, staring off into space. I used to just make myself busy when he was like that as trying to get through to him was all but impossible.'

The truth is, Brian was far too concerned with getting himself straight, mentally and physically, to have an awful lot of himself left over to give to anyone. 'Someday . . .' Potier remembers him saying softly, 'Someday, I'll be better and it won't have to be this way anymore.' So Suki waited – just like poor Pat Andrews, Linda Lawrence, Linda Keith and plenty more willing young women whose names history fails to record. And, of course, sadly, 'someday' never came.

One of the most spectacular changes in Jones during his tenure at Cotchford however was his sudden and totally unexpected re-immersion in his music. For some time Brian had only really played at being a musician. Strumming along at sessions and at home with friends like Jimi Hendrix, Denny Laine, or John Lennon, his heart really wasn't in it. But now, suddenly he was on fire to make his own music, and according to those around him, it made him very happy.

'He often used to play and sing,' says Mrs Hallet. 'He'd be there practising while I was working. He'd often say, "What do you think of that?" and I always said, "Very nice." I know there were a lot of musicians down there because we used to hear the noise. I had to tell him if it was too much so as not to trouble the neighbours. One night there was a great deal of music down there and it roared all through the neighbourhood. Oh dreadful! I told him it sounded like the end of the world was about to come.'

Another local, Dennis Burke, the confident, nineteen-year-old publican at the Haywaggon, recalls the often ecstatic music that sometimes erupted from his world famous friend down the road. 'I used to go into his music room with him, I'd never seen a synthesizer before and he'd got one. It was absolutely fantastic. He'd play it for me. He hadn't given up by any means. I can also remember him strolling the grounds at the back of his house playing the saxophone. This big husky sound used to just well up and roll through the valley. I'll never forget seeing him standing there under the blue sky, birds flying overhead and him playing his heart out. He was a wonderful guy.'

It is important to remember that Brian, so long deliberately out to shock and cause distress, now wanted nothing more than to become part of the close-knit rural community he called home. Well known for his outrageous, gender-bending costumes, eye make-up and effeminate manner, by the time he moved to Cotchford he consciously rejected all of that in favour of a more confident, less dramatic, conservative look. Brian knew well the simple, unaffected people he was dealing with and went out of his way not to antagonise them or cause offence.

'You've got to remember that Hartfield is a small, sleepy village,' says Burke. 'Brian felt pressured and decided to move from town. He was just Brian Jones who lived up the road at Cotchford Farm. He wasn't a hippie or anything. He was quiet, neat and tidy. No smoking joints, nothing like that. He was nothing but charming. He was a man with problems. He was a man who needed the support of other people. I went to his house many times. He was very proud of it. You know we have this big race every year called the Grand National. And it's traditional that pubs hold a lottery. You come in, pay a pound or two and draw a horse. If you actually draw out the winner you're going to get something like £50 or £100. Anyway, Brian wanted to go for that so I went up to his place with a few tickets. He said, "Oh, great, it's on telly this afternoon. You've got to stay and watch it with me." And he made me. Actually, I was only too pleased to be with him. He was so thrilled with such a simple thing as someone coming round with a lottery ticket. He was so unpretentious, so genuine. He was really pleased to see me, just a bit of company. There weren't any females around that weekend and I think he just liked being with other people.'

Rising to the challenge of establishing Cotchford as one of the most elegant, eye-catching country homes around, Brian sought to decorate his prize with the finest furnishings his often sporadic income might allow. Towards this end, he and Suki painstakingly searched the antique markets off the King's Road for pieces that would distinguish Cotchford, and its owner, as being at the very pinnacle of good taste and refinement. Brian's middle-class sensibilities, it seemed, were about to be shamelessly indulged.

One of the first things they bought was an obscenely expensive William Morris tapestry of the Elfin King, cavorting with his wee subjects in the wood. Another was a large Edwardian woven screen of a long-haired little boy sitting pensively in a garden gazing at his reflection in a deep pool. Brian used to like to think it looked rather like him. Today it is leaning against a wall in the newspaper strewn parlour at Mary Hallet's. Lewis Jones gave it to her after Brian died. Another prize is an intricately carved, teak inlaid Moroccan end-table, presented to her by Brian himself, which she proudly shows off to each and every visitor.

Brian's love of all things Moroccan was very much in evidence throughout Cotchford. The result of careful buying trips to the back streets of Tangier and Marrakesh with his old friend, Chelsea antique dealer Christopher Gibbs. Gibbs, a dashing, intensely sophisticated pop star type himself, saw Brian as a brilliant, though supremely selfish character who revelled in his seemingly inborn propensity to piss people off. Gibbs knew too well that when Jones's rather well-defined dark side got the better of him, the only intelligent course was to run for cover and wait for things to blow over. And God help those who got in the way.

'We were all holed up in a hotel in Tangier once,' says Gibbs. 'Brian and I used to swan about the local cafés and markets smoking joints and generally enjoying ourselves. The problem was that Brian was always so supremely paranoid he was convinced that people were somehow out to get him. Even there in Tangier! I told him he was mad and that no one even knew who he was, but he wouldn't have it. "No, I'm sure they're watching me," he would whisper. In the end, I just let him have his way.'

During the same trip, Jones went well over the top several times, culminating in a very ugly scene one evening following a particularly sweltering afternoon's merry-making amidst the steamy, exotic music bars of Marrakesh. Gibbs was relaxing in his suite when Brian, obviously in a panic, called him to his room.

On entering, the laid-back young man was horrified to find the entire premises trashed beyond recognition. Glass was everywhere, as evidenced by the total lack of any intact windows, mirrors or crockery.

'You've got to help me, man!' Brian screamed as he stumbled through the debris littering the room. 'It's Suki!'

Scanning the suite, Gibbs's eye settled upon a dishevelled heap atop the bed, covered, like everything else, in shards of jagged glass. Unconscious, Suki was badly bruised and bleeding from a deep gash on her forehead. Gibbs looked over at Brian. 'Well,' called the totally out of it Stone. 'What are we gonna do about it?'

'What are *you* going to do about it, you mean!' Gibbs countered angrily. 'You've got to phone the bloody doctor, man.'

'You know I can't do that,' Jones cried pathetically.

In the end, Gibbs made the call, and before long an ambulance arrived and bundled up the poor girl in what looked like an old beat-up bread truck. 'You go with her,' Brian demanded as they carried her away on a stretcher.

'Sorry mate,' said Gibbs, grabbing him forcibly and pushing him into the van. 'It's about time you took a bit of responsibility for yourself.'

The next day, remarkably, it was as if nothing had ever happened and the shopping spree continued virtually unabated. Another Brian Jones masterpiece of human carnage.

After a time Brian realised that the old farmhouse needed much more than new curtains and furnishings and so got in touch with The Stones' office on Maddox Street in London, requesting help in organising some serious interior/exterior renovations.

Senior Stones minder Tom Keylock quickly filled the bill, calling in his old school mate, builder Frank Thorogood to outline and price the work Brian wanted doing. Thorogood, a highly-suspect character, had previously done work at Keith's thatched cottage, Redlands, as well as chic photographer, David Bailey's posh London digs. Neither client, it seemed, were particularly pleased with the result.

Among the many stories relating to Thorogood was a charge made by Keith that several people in Thorogood's employ were steadily and gleefully ripping him off. When Thorogood went to work for Brian, Richards apparently warned the errant builder about attempting any such liberties with his new employer and was thus assured that Brian would be well looked after. 'That's what I'm afraid of,' Richards reportedly replied.

Within days, Thorogood and a trio of his regular labourers from nearby West Withering, recorded as only Johnny, Mo and Dave, went to work. It seems an initial quote of around £11,000 was made by Frank for the work which Brian, knowing less than nothing about the ins and outs of negotiating any sort of contract, readily accepted. Being a good friend Keylock, long a trusted member of The Stones' inner circle, gave Thorogood the kind of instant clout and personal carte blanche to enable him to get away with just about anything he wanted.

The unworldly, ethereal, eternally preoccupied Jones was therefore a prime target for the full gambit of fraud, theft and deception the shifty Thorogood carried around in his hip-pocket. 'Like lambs to the slaughter,' one Stones intimate later remembered. 'Frank had Brian marked as easy pickings from the day he moved in.'

And move in he did. Almost immediately Thorogood hit Brian with the proposition that as he was based way up in London, it only made sense he take up residence at Cotchford, so that Jones's work might be more readily accomplished. Sceptical from the very beginning, Brian reluctantly went along with the idea, instructing Mrs Hallet to tidy up the Milne's old guest-flat above the small garage, stationed at the left-hand side of the drive, just off the lane. Before the dust had settled Frank Thorogood was permanently ensconced at Cotchford. And from that day on Brian's life was quickly turned upside down.

'Frank was a right bastard,' recalls Dennis Burke. 'I thought he was a rip off. He was taking Brian for a ride and he knew it. I didn't get the impression Brian liked him one little bit. When Frank was at the pub it was always, "Oh, give me a large Napoleon brandy." It was either on Brian's account or Frank would settle it with Jones's money. I always got the impression that, "Yeah, okay, Brian's account this month is £300. I bet there's another £100 on there for you somehow." I took Frank home once in my car. I had a Spitfire at the time and he said, "You've got a crap radio in here. Brian's got some radio cassettes in his garage. I'll give you one, no problem!" Of course, I never heard another word. I was doing him a favour and just for the sake of it, he'd promise you something. Brian never did that. He didn't need to.'

As virtually everyone interviewed for this book (other than his close friend Tom Keylock) had little good to say about the builder, it becomes clear that not only was Frank Thorogood a crook, but was also sorely incompetent when it came to his chosen field of endeavour.

Mary Hallet remembers: 'The house was occasionally given to some slight flooding after a big rain, so the Taylors put in a very clever drainage system in the kitchen with the tile floors sloping in just a bit so that any water could be sucked down a drain in the middle of the floor. Well, Frank ripped all this out and replaced it with a fitted stone floor which, of course, held the water, making a terrible mess every time it rained.'

Still, the so-called work carried on with Brian footing the bill through his personal account at the Stones' office. Thorogood simply submitted an invoice and it was paid, later to be deducted from Jones's holdings. Exactly what old Frank figured into those bills is anybody's guess, but after Alistair Johns bought the place in 1970 he estimated that no more than three or four thousand pounds worth of work had been done. One bill found after Brian's death was for more than £18,000. So where did all the money go?

On 4 January 1969, Brian and Suki jetted to the isle of Ceylon (now Sri Lanka) off the southern-most tip of India, for a holiday. Although Jones was harassed by a couple of anti-hippie hotel managers in the resort town of Kandy, he soon recovered and the couple had a terrific time.

Suki remembers: 'Brian was very different in Ceylon. He got himself together. He even played with a local group on stage. He fought two fights for me, which I was amazed at. These men had been fancying me and Brian got really jealous.'

While there, they visited famed science fiction writer Arthur C. Clarke and travelled to a remote village to meet a man who claimed to have been Hitler's personal astrologer. In the course of Brian's reading, the old man stopped short and with a serious look, admonished the young musician not to 'go swimming without a friend' throughout the coming year.

'The water holds much danger for you,' he warned.

'Only when I drink it!' Brian countered laughingly.

He also told Jones to beware of false friends and people who posed themselves as being caring and loyal. 'But most of all,' he drilled home, 'mind the water'. Several days later the happy couple flew back home to Cotchford.

The minute Brian stepped inside the house he sensed something was wrong. There was no one about in the middle of the day – a work day – and the place was a mess. Wine bottles littered the kitchen and dirty dishes filled the sink. Someone, it seemed, was taking liberties while the boss was away. What was worse was that a new wooden fence Jones had wanted put up while he was gone lay on the front lawn exactly where it was when he left. Suki didn't dare say a word and quietly went about clearing up the kitchen.

Brian meanwhile, was fuming. Intent that his fence would be put up one way or the other he rang his mate Dennis. 'Look,' he said, 'I want a fence around my house. I've had it here for ages and the builders have really pissed me off. Can you and some of your guys get together and do it for me?' With that, young Burke rang up a few of his buddies and set out for Cotchford.

'It wasn't a major fence,' recalls Dennis, 'we're not talking Hollywood here. He'd just got it into his head that he wanted it up. Not for security reasons. I think he just wanted to make the neighbours aware that he was a genuine guy and didn't want his land unfenced. Anyway, I got the guys together and they did the job. He was totally amazed. There he is paying these expensive builders and here was a bunch of villagers prepared to do it. They were getting good money and yet they weren't doing what he wanted.'

A little water on the kitchen floor and a fence, of course, are small potatoes when stacked against the kind of serious claims levelled against Frank Thorogood over the years. But the fact is, there was a great deal of real import that Brian, always terrifically unsure how to react to weighty matters, kept behind the closed doors of Cotchford.

'On my last visit to the farm,' remembers Jones's longtime friend, Nicholas Fitzgerald, 'when Brian was still a member of The Stones, he told me that he had between $60,000 and $75,000 hidden round the house as well as some $15,000 in Swiss francs. He hadn't been under any pressure to pay bills, most of that was done by The Stones' management, who also paid the servants in cash. And all the drugs he had ever bought had been paid for in cash. But when I asked Brian what had become of the rest of the money, he simply shrugged and said, "Gone. Ripped off." '

Gardener Michael Martin also confirmed in *Golden Stone* that large amounts of cash went missing during Thorogood's reign at Cotchford. 'You used to have to go up to Brian sometimes when he was in bed, because he often slept till noon. By his bed there were always piles of money, just lying there, tall piles. If I wanted something, I'd explain to Brian and he would stretch out, peel off notes and give them to me. All I can tell you is when the police searched the house they couldn't find a single note. Not one.'

One may argue that if Brian Jones was, as the evidence suggests, so acutely aware that he was being systematically ripped off by Mr Thorogood then why didn't he take immediate steps to either let him go, or in the case of the outright thefts which occurred, call in the police. The simple answer was that Brian was interminably weak. If there was one fatal flaw to the man that was it.

As George Harrison once said, 'Just because you're paranoid doesn't mean something bad isn't going to happen to you.'

And Brian was definitely paranoid. The more bad things that happened to him the more paranoid he became. The wider the web of conspiracy in his mind the tighter the grip on his psyche. When someone fucked him over it simply validated his suspicions.

It's not that Brian didn't reach out for help. He did. As a matter of fact, he approached just about everyone he knew with his problems. Constantly. After years of hearing him go on and on about everyone that was out to do him in, people got so sick of it they folded up. As a result, Brian was now very much alone. Alone in the green hell of Cotchford surrounded by the only people he had for support. No matter what bastards they were.

'Brian alienated himself from many former friends, like John Lennon,' says Nicholas Fitzgerald, 'who avoided his phone calls because he knew they meant trouble. Brian couldn't seem to comprehend that other people had their own problems, and when they hinted as much he was hurt, assuming they didn't care about him.'

In a 1970 interview Lennon confirmed his feelings about Brian. 'Well, he was different over the years as he disintegrated. He ended up the kind of guy that you dread calling you on the phone. He was really in a lot of pain. But in the early days he was all right, because he was young and confident. He was one of those guys that disintegrated right in front of you. He wasn't brilliant or anything, he was just a nice guy.'

'I know you think I'm paranoid,' Jones told Fitzgerald. 'Maybe I am, but not about this. I know how much they're ripping me off. For Christ's sake, Nicholas, it's like one of those bad movies, where everybody's trying to convince a guy he's bananas.'

To top things off, Jones was having big problems with the band. Despite their phenomenal success, the truth is The Rolling Stones never really sold that many records, not at that point anyway. Pete Bennett, the group's flamboyant promotional manager, confirms that during the mid-to-late-sixties The Stones owed a great deal more to hype than monumental record sales. It was their personal appearances, he says, that really brought in the big bucks. The reality that Brian was unable to travel to the US due to his recent drug convictions went a long way towards convincing the band to give Brian the sack.

'Jones was very much the star of the group you know,' recalls Bennett. 'The girls went nuts for him and it drove Mick crazy. While Jagger was jumpin' around on stage Brian just stood there really cool and aloof. I'm the guy who sold The Stones to the world and I'm tellin' you, Brian Jones was definitely the star attraction.'

The fact was that Brian and Mick, in particular, had a long history of not really getting on. When Brian held the reins in the beginning it was he that wanted Jagger turfed out and now that Mick was on top, that's exactly what he had in mind for his old chum. Ian Stewart remembers, 'Mick was very forceful about Jones. He said it was imperative we get rid of Brian and replace him with someone who could perform.'

Stone's intimate, Ronni Money, wife of eccentric performer Zoot Money, knew Brian and the situation very well. 'Mick was relentless in his pressure to get Jones out of the band,' she related in *Blown Away*. 'He played on all of Brian's weaknesses, his paranoic insecurity, his alcohol dependency, his fears and his self-destructive impulses.'

Brian's role within the volatile infra-structure of The Rolling Stones had a great deal more to do with his personal charisma than his virtuoso guitar playing. Jones was certainly competent on the guitar, but he was no Jimi Hendrix. He was, however, just what The Stones needed to get over their own peculiar brand of rough-hewn, outlaw rhythm and blues. Certain people close to the band, though, apparently had other ideas.

One of the greatest stumbling blocks to Brian's future in The Rolling Stones was the fact that Anita Pallenberg was now linked so inextricably to Keith. While Richards and Jones were close, it would have been difficult for anyone to successfully oust Brian from the group. But now that he and Anita had parted, and parted so badly, emotions ran high and both sides ardently resented the other.

Troubling too was the fact that despite his immense talent as a musician Jones just couldn't seem to write. He tried certainly, but the end result was inevitably never quite up to par. The alliance between Mick and Keith grew ever stronger and Brian, who was often catty about his colleagues' writing, was slowly eased even further out.

'The thing that bothered Brian,' remembers Marianne Faithfull, 'was they never used his songs in any of their sessions. But then again he never really submitted a song that was ready to be recorded. Bill Wyman did, and he accomplished the unheard of by getting them to record one of his tunes ['In Another Land'] on the 'Satanic Majesties' album. That showed that if Brian hadn't been so paranoid about their having ganged up against him, and if Brian had actually presented them with a good song, they would have recorded it. So much of his resentment of Keith and Mick was in Brian's head. What Brian said was, "I can't play them my songs, because they'll never, never record them, so I won't play any for them," thus avoiding the humiliation of rejection. Of course, that was pure paranoia.'

All of this weighed heavily on Brian's mind as he tried to work his way through his troubles at home with the renegade builders and his always volatile relationship with Suki. Added together, the fragile peace of mind Jones first experienced when moving to Cotchford was shattered, allowing much of the old flotsam and jetsam of his convoluted psyche to once again rise to the surface. One of the most worrisome manifestations of Brian's interminable stress and anxiety was his hard-hitting return to the bottle.

While he had successfully quit drugs forever (friends were routinely searched before entering the house), the easy lure of the black-hole high of drink proved irresistible to the undeniably addictive young man. 'With Brian, I'm afraid it was always silly drinking, but not embarrassingly so,' recalls Dennis Burke. 'I mean the guy could hold his alcohol. He used to drink a lot of vodka. He was never an embarrassment to me as a publican. He never picked a fight. If anything, he got silly when he drank instead of aggressive.

'I remember he drove down one lunch-time on his little motor-bike and had a lot to drink. When he got on to go home, however, he crashed into the window of the sweet shop across the road. He didn't go right through though. In retrospect, I should have driven him home, but he wasn't legless. He just went out of control, crossed the road and went straight into the shop. Anyway, he's on his side and us guys are yelling. "Christ, did you see that? Come on!" He wasn't particularly injured, but he needed treatment. He said, "Look, get me to the hospital, but don't tell anyone my name." And we said, "Okay, right, no problem."

'Fortunately, they didn't know who he was. He wasn't badly hurt, just scratches and bruises, and we took him home again. Now he was eternally grateful for that, for obvious reasons. You could imagine what the media would've made of that had they got hold of it, but he was always nice to us so why should we want to screw him? I would say in retrospect, that he was *potentially* alcoholic. He wasn't to my knowledge, on drugs, however. I was in his house and at the pub with him many, many hours and I *never* saw any drugs whatsoever. It was vodka, vodka, vodka! I mean our sales of vodka went up from one case a week to five.'

Brian's current state of mind, of course, didn't exactly make it difficult for anyone to rip him off. After a time, local residents say that Jones and Thorogood actually switched roles, with Frank literally ordering the unhappy young man around in his own home. He also brought in a friend to live at Cotchford, presumably telling his wife up in town he was snowed under at work and couldn't get home anytime soon. The workmen too, it seemed, made liberal use of the farm as a clandestine knocking-shop for their extramarital adventures and Mary Hallet for one didn't like it.

'It was dreadful,' she said, 'every time you turned round they were there with these awful women. Brian used to say, "It's all right for me, Mrs Hallet, I'm still single. But these blighters all have wives and families." He was terribly embarrassed that I had to see it all. That's the kind of considerate boy he was.'

Trying as the times were for Brian he still had Suki. These days, however, he had taken to once again occasionally going up to London for an evening of clubbing, Potier waiting patiently at home playing the long-suffering rock star's lady. Although the lovely young woman agonised over Thorogood's maniacal hold over her troubled boyfriend, she felt typically powerless to do anything much about it.

'Before long Frank controlled everything,' she complained. 'Where we went, what we did, even how much milk we should give the cats. He was there on the pretext of helping Brian, but all he ever cared about was himself. When all that money went missing from the house Brian was sure it was Frank, but what could we do? Frank was paid directly by The Stones' office and as such, was loyal to them, not Brian.

'For the moment anyway, Brian was dependent on The Stones for his income and all of our expenses. I'm sure he felt he couldn't rock the boat.'

Strangely, Mrs Hallet feels strongly that the provocative Suki herself had something to hide: 'I saw Suki sitting there, talking to Thorogood one day. I was working close to them and I couldn't help but hear it. She was saying, "Brian won't know anything about it. We'll do that." I don't know what it was, but it was something they were up to the next day. I didn't trust her. I think she was out for what she could get.'

One lifeline for Brian during that time was his psychiatrist Dr A. L. Greenburgh who saw him semi-regularly in London. Interestingly, Greenburgh was one of the few people who wasn't all that sure Brian's purchase of Cotchford was entirely positive. 'It was never his, I'm sure. It wasn't a creative thing buying Winnie the Pooh's house. If he had gone up to the Pyrenees or the whatchamacallit Mountains where he went to record his Arabs, and found himself a broken-down castle or fort and turned it into the best goddamned, most luxurious place then that would have been his. But he wasn't ready for it. He was scared . . . he really wasn't breaking out.

'I'm talking about things which were his, of his own "outside" the sort of fantasy world in which he, perforce, lived as a pop star. I'm sure a large number of people in the pop world are capable of being two people at the same time if their entourage, their followers, would allow them to be. Some of them have more personality than Brian did, in that sense, but surely it's possible for someone in that world, if he has some real identity in the sense of a formed personality, to go home at night and have something else, and not be dependent all the time on the Milky Way.'

Brian's tenuous link with the everyday reality shared by millions notwithstanding, he forged ahead with the work at Cotchford and did his best to try and unravel the complicated relationship between himself and the rest of the band.

Unfortunately, by then the writing was already pretty much on the wall. Brian Jones's days as a Rolling Stone were numbered and what's more he knew it. It was now only a matter of trying to bow out as gracefully as possible, and more importantly, figure out what he would do next.

'I can understand how the guys are feeling,' he told friends, trying to make some sense out of the continuing blood feud. 'I can't really tour very easily these days. It's Keith I don't understand. First he takes my love and then my band. How the hell am I supposed to fight that?'

'Brian, in many ways, was a right cunt,' counters Keith. 'He was a bastard. Mean, generous, *anything*. You say one thing, give it the opposite too. Up to a point you could put up with it. When you were put under the pressures of the road, either you took it seriously or as a joke. Which meant that eventually – it was a very slow process – it shifted and changed. It is impossible to describe – but in the last year or so, when Brian was almost totally incapacitated all of the time, he became a joke to the band. It was the only way we could deal with it without getting mad at him. So then it became that very cruel, piss-taking thing behind his back all the time.'

One of the great dichotomies relating to Brian Jones is the apparent contradiction of those who insist that during his last year he was almost totally debilitated against those, like Mary Hallet and Dennis Burke, who say that despite his drinking, he was pretty much in the peak of health.

When Mick Jagger says blithely, 'We felt like we had a wooden leg,' one must temper acceptance of that remark with the notion that Jagger very much wanted him out of the group and had to justify his actions with both the fans, the press and the complex business machinery that surrounded The Stones.

And yet, when Stones management executive, Jo Bergman remarks that 'Brian was six years old all the time,' one intuitively knows what she means and can accept it. He was very much the naughty boy. But that, of course, was half of his enduring charm. The fact is that nothing in life is absolute, much less a soul as complicated and compelling as Brian Jones.

By the dawn of 1969 Jones had travelled a hard road and he showed it. He had good days and bad days, but he very much *wanted* to get better and that was the main thing. It was also the thing that some people obviously didn't want him to do. 'He was looking for affection and love anywhere he could get it,' says Burke. 'From me, the house-keeper, from anybody and that's why he was getting ripped off.

'What I want to convey is the warmth of the man. He was lonely, but that is not a characteristic which is necessarily bad. He was very much concerned with, "I'm in a new place now. I'm part of the community and I must behave in the right way." He was totally knocking the image. Trying to correct the image that the media and living in London occasioned him. And he was a good boy. He just wanted to be part of the community. He used to stop in the local store and chat to the old boys who hung about outside. What more can one say?'

As the inevitable split with the group drew nearer, Frank Thorogood systematically turned up the heat at home. He saw to it that Brian's life was made as consistently uncomfortable as possible. Whether it was hiding his motorbike in the shrubbery, jumping up to intercept his phone calls, mercilessly ordering him about or even shadowing his superstar prey, Thorogood's petty campaign of terror kept Jones so on edge he found it impossible to concentrate on his career, to the point that eventually he simply caved-in and hid inside the bottle.

'He was drunk most of the time,' said Dennis sadly. 'He used to come down to the pub at lunch and in the evening on a pretty regular basis. He needed to go away. He wanted to start a new project. He didn't want to sit at home all day, he wasn't at that stage. He didn't ever get to that stage. He had plans.'

Bill Wyman remembers a Brian sometimes battered beyond all recognition: 'For some two years, not only had he been physically vulnerable and battered by his drug busts, but within The Stones he was sad, isolated and obviously unhappy.

'He loved his new rural home where he bought an Afghan hound; but his inner trauma, aggravated by the loss of Anita and the assumption of band leadership by Mick and Keith, found Brian totally marooned. Towards the end of May, during a recording session, Brian intimated he was thinking of leaving to pursue his own career. Nobody was particularly surprised. Intoxicated by fame and success, he paradoxically had no empathy with the direction in which Mick and Keith's commercial songs had taken us.

'He felt we had deserted our roots. The purist bluesman and instrumental experimenter inside Brian clashed with the hard-headed songwriting machine of Mick and Keith, who knew how to steer The Stones upward. A split was inevitable. It had been mooted as a possibility two years earlier, but Mick was said to have been against Brian's departure, since it might destroy our image. Whatever Brian's debits, he was a great visual attraction; now, though, we were securely established and it seemed to me Mick and Keith felt we could afford to lose him. He had become unreliable.'

Even as Brian was desperately trying to figure out how to handle his problems with the group, life at Cotchford became more and more intolerable. After a time he couldn't even think straight which only made Frank's work that much easier.

That Thorogood was intent on making Brian look and feel as bad as possible is now clear, as are the ways in which he accomplished his vile task.

And what was behind Thorogood's actions? He simply took it upon himself to discredit and disorientate Brian of his own volition. He was making money hand-over-fist, but that's not all people of his sort are after.

All the humiliation, degradation, subterfuge and mind games point to Thorogood being a sadistic tormentor of Jones. That Frank was thoroughly enjoying Brian's uncomfortable position was not lost on Brian's ever-faithful housekeeper.

'I didn't like him at all!' recalls Mrs Hallet. 'He was rude. You'd think he owned the house. He was the boss of the lot. He was always saying what was to be done. He ordered Brian around quite a bit. Brian was very easy going, too easy, wasn't he? I'm sure some of the other builders were also in league with Frank Thorogood, to get as much as they could out of Brian. I've seen them go in the cupboards and they'd take things and put them in their coats. I didn't say anything to them or to Brian, I minded my own business. One of them, Dave, I would say was a very nice chap.'

'Frank was like someone from the Bronx who's on the wrong side of the law,' says Dennis, 'An opportunist. Brian was nothing but a charming, confused young man with too much money and too much success. He'd been rejected by his band and his parents and he was just lonely. He wasn't bitter though. He wasn't saying, "Those fucking assholes". But it was strange that he would come in the pub regularly and no one else from The Stones would ever come in with him. They didn't ever visit him as far as I know. It was a total rejection.'

By the mid-spring of 1969 it was time to consider serious action. Brian had to be cut from the band once-and-for-all. The Stones were hotter than ever and in the minds, of some people anyway, there wasn't enough glory to go around.

'Brian started changing and getting much better,' Suki remembers. 'He was off the sleeping pills and tranquillisers. Then The Stones' situation would come back to him like, "My God, am I leaving or not?" He started drinking, getting worse and worse and that's when I split. I said that I'd come back when he wasn't a pop star anymore.' By the beginning of April she had packed her few things and was gone forever.

Now that Suki had bailed out Brian was well and truly on his own. Although he still indulged his late evening ritual of extended phone calls to just about anyone who would listen, there was no one left to look out for him. When the receiver went down, there he was standing in his kitchen in the middle of the night, drunk, alone and scared. For Brian it was a hell like no other.

'He would often call me at three or four in the morning,' Stones employee Sally Arnold recalls. 'He would sound as high as a kite and would say sorry to disturb you, what time is it and when I told him, he would say, "Oh, it's not that late. Sorry, but you must listen." He needed constant attention.'

And so it was, that on a mild summer's eve on Saturday 9 June 1969, at around 7.30, Mick Jagger, Keith Richards and Charlie Watts climbed into their chauffeur driven cars and made for Cotchford.

Arriving a couple of hours later the three paused in the lane to confer before walking the few final yards down the sloping drive to do the deed. Almost immediately Jones's dogs noisily announced their arrival and Brian slowly opened his heavy oak front-door.

'Hey man!' Keith called out merrily, all right?'

'Yeah . . . hey, how ya doin' guys,' Brian quietly intoned, fully expecting the worst, 'great to see you. Come on in.' At the threshold Jagger only nodded while Charlie gave Brian a friendly slap on the back.

Once inside Brian busied himself getting everyone a drink while ushering them all to find a seat in his cosy parlour just off the kitchen. Steadying himself at the sink Brian poured himself a tall whisky and Coke then, putting on a wide smile, made his way inside the lion's den.

After a few uneventful minutes of small-talk there was a painful lull in the conversation into which Richards inserted, 'Brian, you're out of the band, cock. You're fired.'

Jones smiled weakly saying nothing.

'Hey, man,' Mick threw in, leaning forward, 'we've got to do a US tour behind the new record and you know damn well they'll never let you in.'

'Mick Taylor of The Bluesbreakers is already on tap to step in man,' Keith continued.

Looking slowly around the room Brian finally spoke, 'Well, to be honest, man, I really don't want to go back on the road. Those fuckin' one nighters are just too goddamned rough, you know? Maybe it's best . . . for right now anyway.' Leaving the door open ever so slightly was a way for Brian to save face. Something always very important to the wildly insecure musician.

Jagger saw his opportunity and dived right in. 'Sure man . . . and in the meantime we'll still take care of you. The office is still at your disposal. Just let them know what you need, you know. Just like before. As far as a, well . . . settlement, I guess you'd call it, I think we could break free about £100,000. But we can talk about it.'

'What about the press though?' asked Jones. 'They'll all be after me for sure.'

'Why don't you say that you're resigning because of musical differences. I mean, it's actually true in a way isn't it?'

'Okay then,' Brian said gathering himself together to stand. 'That sounds okay. We'll do it that way.'

Within a few minutes the three men filed out after an awkward, tense tour of the downstairs. The whole thing only took about thirty minutes. Charlie Watts never said a word.

After they left Brian bolted the door and beckoning his dogs to his side he wept bitterly for the next four hours.

'It was very important to us,' Keith later explained, 'as we were going back out on the road behind a new record, that we resolve this thing with Brian. The fact that he was expecting it made it easier I guess. He wasn't surprised. I don't even think he took it all in. He was already up in the stratosphere. There was no serious way we could consider going on the road with Brian . . .'

'He was just gone,' said Mick. 'He wouldn't turn up half the time, when he did he was not in any condition to do anything. We had to baby him – it was really sad.'

To many who knew them, the only really sad thing was the way Jagger and Richards treated their old colleague. Marianne Faithfull's ex-husband John Dunbar remembers: 'It was a really terrible thing they did to Brian. They had a lot of other options than to sack him as cruelly as that. That took away whatever last reserves Brian had. It was Mick being the Godfather.'

That very evening The Stones office, via Les Perrin, issued a terse press release, attributed to Brian, to all the local media. It read simply: 'I no longer see eye-to-eye with the others over the discs we are cutting, we no longer communicate musically. The Stones' music is not to my taste anymore. The work of Mick and Keith has progressed at a tangent, at least to my way of thinking. I have a desire to play my own brand of music rather than that of others, no matter how I appreciate their musical concepts. We had a friendly meeting and agreed that an amicable termination, temporary or permanent, was the only answer. The only solution was to go our separate ways, but we shall still remain friends, I love those fellows.'

Shortly thereafter, Mick too issued a statement full of all the sincerity and affection he never showed Brian: 'The only solution to our problem was for Brian to leave us. He wants to play music which is more his own rather than always playing ours. We have decided that it is best for him be to free to follow his own inclinations. We have parted on the best of terms. We will continue to be friends and we're certainly going to meet socially in future. There's no question of us breaking up a friendship. Friendships like ours just don't break up like that.'

Obviously Brian couldn't now be alone. Jim Carter-Fea, manager of the trendy Revolution club, moved in for a couple of weeks following the big coup to keep him company. Not surprisingly, the Brian he found was emotionally frail and in great pain. Night after night he would sit in the garden drinking from a small silver flask of vodka firing-off rounds from his old shotgun into the outer reaches of his property. 'Fuck it,' he would say under his breath every few minutes. 'Fuck it . . .'

On one occasion, after their ritual round of drinking and partying up in town, Jones and Carter-Fea rolled up in front of Olympic Studios at about 4.30 a.m. Inside, Brian's old band was rocking away the small hours cutting their new album. Brian stared straight ahead, his arms limp by his side.

'They're in there making music,' he finally whispered, 'and they don't want me.' For a full forty minutes the two sat there in the biting cold, neither saying a word. Then Brian started the engine of his silver-grey Roller and squinting in the first brash light of the new day drove off slowly down the road in the direction of Cotchford.

5 BLOOD FROM A STONE
The Crime

B
Y THE MIDDLE of June things had reached a crisis point at Cotchford. While Jones was physically in good shape and emotionally still quite optimistic, the pressure was on to keep Brian under wraps and preoccupied, away from the media and out of the music business. The last thing The Stones needed now was competition from their most popular member.

The transition from Brian Jones to Mick Taylor had to be a smooth one. The success of both their new single, 'Honky Tonk Women', and their forthcoming US tour depended on it. At this point The Stones desperately needed both, as the group coffers were running dangerously low.

The question, however, arises as to Thorogood's motive in all this. It's likely Frank may have taken it upon himself to oppress Brian as a means of anticipating what he somehow *thought* his famous employers wanted. A move which precludes the participation of anyone other than the builder in the alleged plot.

Some people over the years have suggested that perhaps The Rolling Stones themselves were possibly involved in Brian's death. But other than the obvious very public feuding amongst the band and Brian during those last turbulent years, there is absolutely *nothing* to suggest that Jones's steady decline and ultimate death was anything other than a terrible blow to Messrs Jagger, Richards, Wyman and Watts.

After Brian left The Stones it was made immediately clear to him that although he was no longer technically part of the group, he was still very much a 'member of the family'. As such, he should feel free to keep in close contact with the group's London office and let them know if he needed anything.

Les Perrin's press office, in particular, would be available to Jones in anticipation of any new projects with which he might be associated or, conversely, any concerns he had regarding the press, his role in The Stones, or his public profile.

Mostly for his own protection at this time, Les Perrin considered it a good idea to keep Brian away from the media. Les had taken note of how Brian had a nasty habit of getting into difficult positions when allowed free access to the press.

Brian was of course happy to have someone to talk to. A rock'n'roll emperor with no clothes, he was made to feel special and sought after.

Exactly what he needed, as many have stated.

Charlie Watts considers that The Stones' dealings with Brian were perhaps too perfunctory. 'He got much nicer just before he died,' remembers Watts poignantly. 'But I felt even sorrier for him, for what we did to him. We took his one thing away, which was being in a band. That's my opinion anyway.'

During the final year of his life Jones was very much under the direct control of Frank Thorogood, and the effect was catastrophic. A fact confirmed by virtually every major player in this drama; from Keith Richards, to Mary Hallet and her family, Dennis Burke, Janie Perrin, Ronni Money, Dick Hattrell, Nicholas Fitzgerald, Jim Carter-Fea, Ian Stewart, Michael Martin, Suki Potier, Bob Forrester, Alexis Korner, Helen Spittal, Anita Pallenberg, Tony Sanchez and literally dozens more people who knew Brian. Everyone, that is, except, Tom Keylock.

'I will challenge anyone on television,' Mr Keylock boldly pronounced during my interview with him in December 1993, 'to show me evidence of *anything*. There is no way that is possible. No way! . . . I know everybody that worked for Frank. Unfortunately, Frank's dead now. He died a couple of weeks ago. Everyone he employed he trusted. They kept their mouths shut. Brian used to make them at home, have a drink and whatever, sure. But when they went away you'd never hear any of them talk about him. He got along with them famously. He got along with them. They done their jobs during the day.'

On 17 June, Anna Wohlin joined Brian at Cotchford Farm, moving in at Brian's suggestion. Keylock, say some, was dead against it, but in this instance, at least, Brian's wishes prevailed. Jones met the 22-year-old student at a party in town, introduced by newspaper photographer, Jan Olofsson.

Mrs Hallet reckoned Anna was very good for Brian although she doesn't really remember them being together much. According to other sources, the couple weren't particularly close. Some have even hinted their relationship was pretty much platonic, reasoning that Brian only wanted her around him for some sympathetic company. In truth, Brian still had a lot of unresolved feelings for Suki and of course for Anita Pallenberg, whom many think was in fact his one true love. At any rate Wohlin bounced in on the rebound and there she stayed right to the bitter end.

On 3 July, the day after Jones's death. Alexis Korner commented on Brian's mood around this time. 'I saw him ten days ago [23 June] at his country home when we played together for fourteen hours. We worked out some musical tracks and listened to music Brian had compiled recently in Morocco.

'We also went through a list of possible musicians for his new group. He was very keen to start up again, in a style more involved with jazz. He was very content living in the country and talked to my wife about settling down, though his present friend, Anna Wohlin, was not a girlfriend in the usual sense; she was a good companion.'

Interestingly, Dennis Burke dropped by that same afternoon. 'I did go there one day when Alexis Korner was there and Brian introduced me,' says Burke. 'We had a chat and he was trying to set something up with him.'

Tom Keylock too, recalls Brian's association with Korner. 'Alexis Korner, he was very good to [Brian]. A close friend, Alexis was. He came down to Cotchford and he was trying to set up something for Brian and I'm sure it was John Mayall of The Bluesbreakers helping as well. He had some people try to help him. I've never said it, but in my opinion he was too far gone. He was really screwed by then.'

This whole question of Brian's post-Stones musical career offers the fascinating possibility that Jones had somehow linked up with both John Lennon and Jimi Hendrix with the intention of forming what would have obviously been quite a group. As far back as *The Rock 'n' Roll Circus*, Lennon had discussed the possibility, meeting with eager approval from Jones. At this point, John's position within The Beatles' sagging empire was no longer giving him what he wanted from his art and he was anxious to move on. Hendrix too, was well known to be desperately unhappy with both his manipulative manager, Michael Jeffries, and the narrow, pop-oriented limits of his band, The Experience.

Going back to the spring of 1969, while Brian was still with Suki, he confided to Nicholas Fitzgerald the truth behind the rumours. The two friends were sitting in the Haywaggon polishing off a couple of vodka and Cokes when the provocative subject arose. At first Brian was vaguely reticent to discuss the matter according to Fitzgerald, but then went on, swearing Nicholas to secrecy.

'Listen, man, you can't tell a soul,' Jones began.

'You know me better than that,' countered Fitzgerald drily.

'In December of last year John and I recorded a tune, "Go To The Mountains", for Apple. We called ourselves Balls for some reason. It's not really a bad name I guess. Denny Laine played lead and we had another guy on drums. I can't say who. The track though turned out really great.'

'So, are you getting together or what?' inquired Nicholas.

'It's still too early to say. I've got loads of options. Dylan invited me to team up with him and Jimi is keen to work with me as well. The problem is I'm not sure they'll let me into the States which obviously would make things difficult if we ever felt like touring.'

With that the subject turned to Brian's rocky relationship with Suki and ended up with the two men taking a leisurely walk from the village back up to Cotchford.

When Jones next mentioned the potential union it was over the phone to Fitzgerald at home in London. 'Listen, mate,' he began, 'I've been advised by Alexis that this whole matter of me starting a group with John and Jimi could be quite dangerous if it ever got out.'

'How so?' Fitzgerald inquired.

'Don't you see, this could split up not only The Stones, but The Beatles and Jimi's group. The three biggest acts in the world, for Christ's sake. A lot of people would stand to lose if that ever went down.'

Tom Keylock remembers several encounters with Hendrix over the years: 'Jimi used to be around Brian's place in King's Road, you know, playing. In actual fact, Brian said, "Get some bread for him, 'cause he's broke. He's got no money." He'd had a few number ones out, but he never had any bread. Nobody ever give him any bread! So I give him some. I don't know if he ate a lot, but he was always smoking! [He was] very hard to speak to, very . . . what's the word, "introverted"? Very shut and quiet. But when he was on stage ah, he was wild, man.'

The fact is, if Lennon left The Beatles it would have meant a loss of untold millions to Apple. Merchandising, recording contracts, performance rights, the Apple companies; everything would be seriously affected.

Other popular musicians linked to Jones during this period were Steve Winwood, Mitch Mitchell and John Mayall.

That Jones was very much dependent on Rolling Stones Ltd for his livelihood is certain. After he left the band, virtually the only money he could expect was his 'severance pay' of £100,000 yearly (payable for as long as The Stones survived as a group) as well as any royalties due for his former work with the band.

Allen Klein reportedly thought the amount too generous but was overruled by Mick and Keith.

At this point, Rolling Stones Ltd was still very much holding the purse-strings at Cotchford, which granted them an undeniable hold over both Brian and his employees.

Mary Hallet recalls the group's accountants kicking up a fuss over Jones paying her modest telephone bills and even moaning about Brian having too many pets: 'What with the high price of cat food and all.' When Jones's on-call chauffeur, John Corey, was sacked early that summer and Mrs Hallet was similarly threatened, even Frank Thorogood began to worry.

As usual, 'Mr Keep It Together Man' Tom Keylock was there to smooth everyone's ruffled feathers and maintain the status quo. 'Don't worry, Frank,' Keylock told him. 'We need *you* man.'

'Before I went to work for Brian,' recalled driver Corey after Brian's death, 'I couldn't stand him. I thought he was a long-haired, ignorant, arrogant twit. Like most of the public, I thought of The Stones as a dirty, filthy [group] who hadn't had a bath for months.

'But I was surprised to find that he was in and out of the bath twice a day every day. As a person he was very quiet, shy, nervous and sensitive, but very friendly. He was a brilliant, talented musician, music was his whole life. But he was also a very unhappy person.'

After Corey was fired, Brian went from a chauffeur-driven Rolls Royce to a battered mini-cab, driven by Joan Fitzsimmons.

'Another wonderful example of The Stones looking after their own,' Suki Potier has said. 'I'm sure Mick and the rest of the boys didn't begrudge Brian anything, but there were people around who were watching the pennies. People with an axe to grind. Brian once told me they kicked up a fuss when he happened to mention to someone in the office that he was thinking of buying a little motor scooter. And this, from the man who not only founded the group but was also responsible for a great deal of their multi-million-pound international success.'

Interestingly, after Brian died and plans for this prototype super-group fell through, Denny Laine commandeered the name Balls for another band formed briefly by the singer. As for the original demo cut by Lennon and Jones, during the research stage of the work a very bad cassette copy was procured from a former employee of John's in New York. Not surprisingly, the piece is very interesting, combining a tough reggae-style rhythm with an exuberant rock'n'roll vocal by Lennon. Jones's playing, incidentally, is predictably flawless.

Alexis Korner recalls Brian's resolve finally to get something together on his own and the terrible price he paid for his musical free-dom: 'I didn't see Brian until the last few months and that was because Keith and Mick rang me and said, "Would you please go down and see the man, he needs to talk to someone." He'd just quit the group. We were talking about him getting a band together.

'From this point of view, it was exactly the right time to die. It was only from our point of view it wasn't the right time to die. It was his life and if he died at the right time from his point of view, he did it right. He was up when he died and not down. You should always die on the day you're feeling up. During that last couple of weeks he was really up because he was into that band.

'He really believed that eventually he would get it going. I think it would have been disastrous if he had, because he would have had to, by nature, compete immediately with The Stones. It would have been a disaster. At least he didn't get that far and I'm pleased he didn't get that far. And I'm pleased he died on an up. It's our problem he died, not his. So I really felt glad for him for that.

'I'd seen Brian every now and then, but not to speak to, because for several years he could hardly put two words together anyway. That time when he was looking like a disintegrating version of Louis XIV. What are you going to say to him? Absolutely nothing! He would have just about recognised me, thought of nothing to say and we'd've stood there.

'I went down to see him when Mick and Keith rung me and said, "Would you?" So I went down with the family. We made a family thing of it. Which I thought was the best thing to do. They said very simply, "He won't really trust any of us. So he has to speak to some-body he has known for a long time, who he has no reason to distrust. Could you talk to him?" So I said, "Yeah, sure." And that's why me, because they knew he wouldn't trust them.'

There is no question that Korner was totally sincere in both his desire to assist Jagger and Richards in dealing successfully with Jones, and indeed, wanting to help Brian as best he could.

Brian being Brian, he did his best to keep his friends fairly close during this trying time. Dick Hatrell remembers his last visit to his old mate in Hotchner's *Blown Away*. 'After he and The Stones broke up, I went to see him and he seemed to have pulled himself together. The house was stuffed with priceless antiques. Brian did complain about the workmen doing the restoration, charging him for work that was not done. He also said that he was paying for food and drink for a large group of workers.

'Brian also restored all the little stone statues around the pool that Milne had fashioned after the characters in his book. Brian loved that house because *Winnie-the-Pooh* had been one of his favourite books and he used to read passages from it out loud. Brian seemed in pretty good spirits the last time I saw him.'

One amusing incident relating to Brian's great love of A. A. Milne's fanciful creations was Tom Keylock's story about Brian getting pissed one night and rushing off into the garden to fetch a sledgehammer from a garden shed.

'What the hell are you doing with that?' a bemused Keylock shouted after him.

'I'm gonna find out once and for all if Milne's original manuscript is buried inside the sculpture of all the characters like they say.'

'No, you're bloody not!' screamed Keylock, racing to stop Brian as he raised the great hammer high over the delicate garden art.

'I only just made it in time,' laughs Tom today. 'That boy was a real piece of work sometimes, let me tell you.'

Another guest to Cotchford, Helen Spittal, an ardent Stones/Jones fan from Hampton Court, recalls Jones's desperation over Thorogood's continued presence at the Farm: 'At one point Brian and I were up in his bedroom,' she says. 'He was looking out of the window at Frank swanning about, acting as if he owned the place, and he began talking to me about him, saying that he just wasn't doing anything he was supposed to. I said surely he must have a contract he was tied to and couldn't he get his solicitor to do something about breach of contract to get Frank off the premises. But it was no use. I guess it was for the sake of peace and quiet, but Brian just let things carry on as they were.'

The fact is, Jones recognised the time was drawing near when he had to take a stand against Frank Thorogood. He discussed it with several people including Les Perrin's wife, Janie, who frankly refused to set foot on the property until things had changed significantly. 'He asked us to come down to see the house,' she says in Jackson's book, 'and I said yes, I'd love to, but I'm not coming if those cowboys are there. Brian said definitely that he'd had enough and was going to clear the place, clear the whole place of everyone for good, "It'll just be you and Les – bring Steph – and Mrs Hallet and me." He said, "I'm going to get rid of this lot. I've made up my mind this time."'

Brian's power to make good on his promise, however, was effectively stalled by his seemingly utter inability to stand up to controversy. Especially when that controversy emanated from a towering, aggressive East Ender like Frank Thorogood.

Says Eden Phillips, a London based writer and editor: 'The Stones long had a fascination with the thugs, tearaways and minor villains of London's East End, who they employed as chauffeurs, minders and general gofers . . . the presence of "hard-men" in their entourage gave The Stones a fashionably street-wise edge to their image. And while Keith Richards had few, if any, problems in controlling the band's drivers, who became known as The Stones' Mafia, Brian Jones was never mentally strong enough to stand up to them. He was, at heart, a middle-class boy from Cheltenham who could dominate people who played by society's rules, but not people who never knew those rules in the first place.'

Even Keith Richards admitted that several of The Stones' so-called chauffeurs wielded an unhealthy 'influence' over Brian.

Still, if he really cared to, Jones could have got rid of these guys. At his disposal were several high-powered solicitors, his worldly-wise, tenacious father, public opinion, the international media, and quite simply, the innate clout that came with having once been a Rolling Stone. So why didn't he?

Reg Pippet, a charming part-time actor and lifelong Brian Jones aficionado may have put his finger on it in a 1993 interview conducted for this book. 'He had to have people around him as Tom Keylock would say. He felt lonely I assume. He must have felt insecure. He had to be adored, have people around, be the centre of attention. People who I've talked to however, say he wasn't happy.'

The duality of Jones's nature, desiring to be loved but fearing the attention, is illustrated earlier that same year, when Dick Hatrell heard that Brian had returned to Cheltenham for an evening out and immediately set about finding his old friend. What he found profoundly shocked him. 'I searched all over town and eventually found him in a club frequented by musicians, called the Waikiki,' he remembered in *Blown Away*. 'He was literally hiding in a dark corner. He didn't want anybody to see him, which I thought was very, very sad.

'He put his arm around me and said, "Great to see you, man," and all that, but I sensed a change in him, he was beginning to be a wreck. I can't say that he was mentally ill, but he was certainly beginning to show rather odd mental behaviour, paranoiac, afraid that there were people after him, pursuing him, out to get him. I said, "Brian, what the hell are you doing to yourself?" He said, "That's the way it goes, man," or something to that effect. Very sad.'

The fact is, Brian's paranoid disposition would have been very handy for anyone intent upon causing him harm. After all, who is ever going to believe a guy with Jones's reputation when he starts going on about people trying to kill him? It's a classic Hitchcockian device. If you want to do someone in, first convince him and everyone else he's mad, and from there it's a fairly simple matter to in and do the evil deed. Such tactics obviously wouldn't work against everyone, but for an insecure young man like Jones it seemed perfect.

As June drew to a close, both Brian and Anna were increasingly concerned with what a friend later described as, 'the terrible tricks played by Frank.' One afternoon after Mrs Hallet went home for the day, Brian went to a cupboard for a glass and found a large dead cat lying there stiff as a board. According to Brian, who later confided the incident to a local friend, it was no accident. 'The builders insisted it somehow crawled up in there and died, but I don't believe it,' said Brian. 'Since when do animals mutilate themselves? Its fuckin' eyes were poked out.'

Other friends remarked that Anna had complained about Frank on several occasions putting his hands down her shirt. She informed Brian, who just looked at her and didn't say anything. He was apparently very upset about it, but felt powerless to do anything. The catalogue of tricks played by Frank on Brian grew longer every day.

'When I'm on the phone,' Brian told his friend Nicholas Fitzgerald, 'the line will suddenly go dead. Then when I get the engineers in, they say there's nothing wrong. They're always leaping up to answer the phone and then they tell me it was a wrong number. I just can't trust anybody. I know they're up to something.'

One person spending time with Brian at this juncture was a young designer called Elan. He'd come on to the scene via model Penelope

Tree's crowd and gravitated to Jones. A fast-talking gay American from East LA, Elan wasn't especially attracted to the self-obsessed Jones. Today, he claims more of an understanding with Anna, and speaks with assurance of her feelings about the relationship with her famous lover.

'Anna cared deeply for Brian, but she used to get very frustrated by his behaviour. He often used to shut people out. But he could be very chummy as well. With Brian it was pretty much pot luck. You could never really be sure what you were getting.'

On Monday, 30 June, Brian rang his psychiatrist, Dr A. L. Greenburgh, in the mid-afternoon, urgently requesting a prescription of Durophet (known on the street as Black Bombers). Although reluctant, knowing Brian's background well, Greenburgh finally relented and wrote out a prescription for just ten capsules. How, or even if, Jones actually collected them is not known.

Although within 72 hours Brian Jones would be dead and the world fed the myth that drugs played a major role, the truth was otherwise. 'Spanish' Tony Sanchez recalls visiting Brian at Cotchford and offering the superstar Stone a hefty line of coke. 'No thanks,' Jones told him sharply, 'I'm a boozer now, man. Just like the old days.'

As the two men chatted in the garden the conversation turned unexpectedly into a tirade against Thorogood and Brian's current state of desperation. 'We had a few more glasses of wine,' Sanchez has said, 'And then Brian leaned across to me: "Want to work for me Tony?" he whispered. "That bastard Keith gave me is taking outrageous liberties. I mean he cooks for me all right and everything but he treats me as though he's my boss. I sent him out to buy some furniture a few weeks ago and I only discovered quite by accident that he had brought two sets of everything – one for his house, one for mine – but when I mentioned it to him he just told me not to be so petty.

' "Everyone seems to think I'm a millionaire or something but I'm not. Mick and Keith get all the money for writing the songs and they take a larger share of the profits from the records and concerts as well. They're not going to pay me that first £100,000 for some time and I'm really worried about how I'm going to pay for everything until then and I don't trust anybody. I know it sounds as though I'm getting paranoid again, but I'm not. It's just that there are a lot of people around who seem to think I'm still so out of my skull that I don't know what's going on. But I'm not blind. I've got a pretty good idea who's ripping me off and how much they are ripping me off for.'

Indeed, testimony that Jones had successfully given up all illicit

Brian Lewis Hopkin-Jones: victim first of his loveless middle-class upbringing and later of the success he fought so hard to achieve. Seen here at London Airport in December 1966 with Anita Pallenberg – the one woman he loved above all others? (*Hulton Deutsch Collection Ltd*)

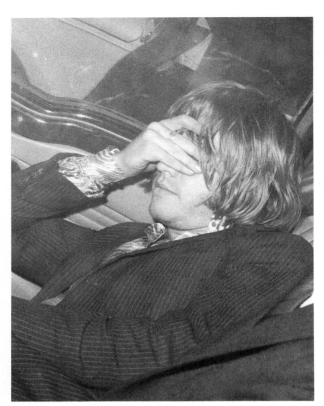

Left On 21 May 1968, Brian leaves Chelsea police station after being charged once again with possession of cannabis (*Hulton Deutsch Collection Ltd*)

Below Brian with the two most important figures in his professional life: Mick Jagger (whom he initially tried to oust from the group) and Keith Richards (who waltzed away with Anita Pallenberg) (*Square Circle Archives*)

Right Brian arriving at a Harley Street clinic on 15 December 1967. Although he required dental treatment, this was also one of many voluntary attempts throughout the 1960s to overcome self-destructive drug abuse (*Syndication International*)

Below Brian (second from left) leaving court in London on 26 September 1968 after another drugs charge. Shown here (left to right): Stones road manager Tom Keylock, Brian, minicab driver Joan Fitzsimmons, girlfriend Suki Potier, and Brian's lawyer (*Syndication International*)

Above   The pool at Cotchford Farm where Brian Jones was murdered (*Sesa Giuliano*)

Below   Tom Keylock fends off the press who flocked to Cotchford on 3 July 1969, the day of Brian's death (*Syndication International*)

Above Brian's funeral procession at Cheltenham, amidst all the pomp befitting the town's most famous son (*Hulton Deutsch Collection Ltd*)

Below Making their way to Brian's grave are (left to right) Brian's parents, Louisa and Lewis Jones; his sister Barbara; Suki Potier; and Tom Keylock (*Square Circle Archives*)

Above Mick Jagger eulogising The Stones' fallen comrade during the band's Hyde Park gig on 5 July 1969 – only two days after Brian's death. Three weeks earlier, Mick and Keith had ejected Brian from the group . . . (*Square Circle Archives*)

Opposite top Mick and Marianne Faithfull run the media gauntlet on 23 June 1969, near the end of their turbulent relationship (*Square Circle Archives*)

Opposite bottom Keith Richards and Anita Pallenberg enjoying the high life together. Their relationship did Brian no good, though: he mourned the loss of Anita and was estranged from his former best friend Keith until the day he died (*Square Circle Archives*)

Above Brian's local, the Haywaggon, in Hartfield. Publican Dennis Burke insists that on several occasions here, Frank Thorogood displayed his 'sinister' hold over the emotionally insecure Stone (*Sesa Giuliano*)

Left Frank Thorogood and Anna Wohlin on 7 July 1969, arriving at the official inquiry at East Grinstead into Brian's death. Was Thorogood Brian's killer? . . . (*Syndication International*) drugs is well documented and believable. When I asked Mary Hallet about the presence of drugs at Cotchford she told me emphatically that Brian was far too afraid of being busted ever to fool around again. 'A lot of times [The Rolling Stones] had them planted on them, hadn't they? Brian told me that Mick Jagger had drugs planted on him. He was very unhappy one day and said that Jagger had drugs planted and he said, "I haven't got a bit of brandy in the house." So I said to him, "Well, I do have a wee bit in a bottle at home. I'll go and get it for you." I came up and got the little bit of brandy we'd got and he was that grateful. It helped.'

Anna too, often told friends she was literally frisked by Jones before he allowed her inside after a day trip to London. Suki Potier says the same.

Helen Spittal recalls taxi driver Joan Fitzsimmons delivering a prescription to Jones during her visit to Cotchford on 12 June and Brian going to great pains to prove to her that the pills were strictly legal. 'Brian was most insistent that I saw the bottle with him,' Helen said to Laura Jackson. 'Read the details on the label of what the tablets were, the dosage and everything so that I knew there was nothing untoward about them . . . Earlier, Brian had been talking about the *Rock'n'Roll Circus* and how he'd never seen Keith as high on drugs before as he had been that day. And he was worried about it. He was really genuinely concerned about it. From experience I guess, seeing the way Keith could go if he wasn't careful.'

In *Golden Stone*, Ronni Money similarly recalls a Brian far removed from the raunchy druggie history has portrayed: 'All this talk about Brian being crushed is a load of shit! I was in LA by this time, but Brian and I used to ring each other practically every week . . . and the truth is, he was strong . . . We used to have some real long talks and even on the telephone I knew he really was off drugs. The high he was on was the real him, the way only Brian could be when he was excited and fired up about something. Believe me, I could tell the difference. He was his old self, all right. I was delighted for him.'

Even Frank Thorogood himself seems to support this view with the remarkable comment: 'While Brian was at Cotchford, he didn't touch drugs. He had had enough of living dangerously.'

By the early evening of that last day of June 1969, all was quiet at Cotchford. There was a light breeze blowing and the summer night sky was flushed with the pastel colours and billowing clouds that define the pastoral Sussex countryside.

117

Inside the house Brian sat quietly strumming his guitar while Anna busied herself in the kitchen.

'It's nice tonight, isn't it?' he called out softly across the music room to no one in particular. 'I feel really good.'

Meanwhile, up in the flat Frank Thorogood was on the phone to his friend, nurse Janet Lawson, making arrangements to pick her up at nearby East Grinstead station a little later on. Thorogood then drove the van into Hartfield where he met one of the casual builders known to us only as 'Frank'. They sat together in a corner of the Haywaggon and talked quietly over drinks for some time. As they rose to leave the two men smiled slightly and shook hands. Without Brian knowing it, the stage was being set for his final exit from the life he found so exacting and difficult.

The morning of 1 July too was unusually quiet. Although the pollen count was a disturbing 335, Brian and Anna slept peacefully while Mrs Hallet tidied up the house, setting aside a tray of muffins and toast for their breakfast.

Rising well after noon, Brian by all accounts was in high spirits, joking with Anna and even running in the garden with the dogs. By mid-afternoon Jones retreated to his downstairs studio to work out some arrangements and sipped a glass or two of white wine.

Anna joined him around five to hear some of the finished music. A little later, an unattributed source claims Brian spoke defiantly about his problem with Thorogood.

He told of having to make a move to sack 'this bastard' before things went too far. His money was coming through from the Stones office soon, and then he could hire whoever he wanted. He said he was scared, but that 'it has to be done'. Apparently during the course of that fateful day, several people told Brian to be careful about how to handle the situation, not to make Thorogood angry.

His reply was strange: 'I've got someone on my side that's going to help with any problems. They won't dare fuck with anyone when they see what I've got on them.'

Unfortunately, just what Jones meant by this cryptic remark has never been discovered as that was the last time he mentioned it to anyone. It was enough though to bolster his resolve and push him to the point of actually telling them all to clear off late that next evening. A move we now know to have been a deadly mistake.

Other than Jones's surprise declaration of independence, the day was uneventful until the early evening when an unsettling change was noticed in Brian. He became edgy and worried, but refused to talk about it with anyone. Perhaps he was anticipating the difficult situation of sacking Frank. At seven o'clock, he left the communal areas of the house. It is thought that he went to his bedroom in order to make a private phone call where he wouldn't be disturbed.

Unbeknownst to anyone, Jones was talking to Suki Potier, who listened anxiously as Brian discussed his plans to get rid of Thorogood. After ringing off, Brian made his way downstairs only to find both Frank and Janet having a drink in the dining room.

'Oh, hello, Brian,' Lawson called out happily.

'Come join us, cock,' Frank intoned. 'How goes it?'

'Very well,' Jones answered thoughtfully, obviously taken aback to see the very person he'd just been discussing with such passion sitting there in his house.

Meanwhile, back in the city Suki was desperately concerned about Brian. Exactly what the two talked about is not known, but it was obviously very upsetting to them both. Around 8.30 p.m. Potier phoned Nicholas Fitzgerald, quite distraught. In his 1985 memoir of his life with Jones, *Brian Jones: The Inside Story Of The Original Rolling Stone*, he recalled the conversation.

'There was a great deal of strain in Suki's voice as she said, "Nicholas, when did you last see Brian?"

' "Last week. He was here in London. Why, Suki?"

' "I'm very worried about him. Something's going on. He's called me three times. He thinks he's in some kind of danger. Says he's being watched. Followed even. What's wrong, Nicholas? D'you know anything?" . . .

' "When he called me this morning, he seemed quite cheerful."

' "He's all right in the daytime," Suki said, "when Mrs Hallet's there. It's in the evenings when she's gone that he calls."

' "Come on, Suki. You know as well as anybody that he likes making mountains out of molehills. In town last week I thought he looked more relaxed than he's been for years."

' "I'm still worried about him. I don't like the kind of people he's been hanging around with down there at the farmhouse. What d'you know about the girl who's moved in?" . . .

'I told Suki I had met Brian's girl only a few times and I didn't know a lot about her. "At least," I added, "she can keep an eye on the help."

' "I really am worried to death. Go to Cotchford Farm and see; don't

119

tell him you're coming. Just see if everything's all right. Just to put my mind at rest. I can't go myself for obvious reasons. We'll just get back to square one, and that won't solve anything." '

After calming her down by saying he'd think about it, Fitzgerald decided against running right down there. He knew both parties well and figured it was just possible one or both of them were exaggerating. He was concerned enough, however, to dial Brian's number at 11.00 p.m. just to make sure everything was okay.

After about the fourth ring someone picked up the receiver but wouldn't say anything. Fitzgerald figured maybe he'd got the wrong number so he called back, but the line was engaged. He waited a few minutes and then tried again. And again. Every time it was the same story. Eventually, he gave up and went to bed.

In her witness statement to the police given some 36 hours later Janet Lawson offers her version of the evening's events. 'I saw Brian that Tuesday evening when I dined with him and friends at the farm.

'We had wine with the meal and Brian attempted to persuade us to use the outdoor pool. We all declined, but he swam and we took drinks out to the side of the pool. It was 9.00 p.m. and the floodlighting was on.

'He was a good swimmer and was acrobatic in the water.

'I think we watched him for about two hours and then I left to return to the flat.' Nicholas Fitzgerald however swears the floodlights over the pool weren't installed until the next afternoon when he visited Cotchford, a fact later confirmed in an interview given by Frank Thorogood. Just one in a long line of so-called facts that don't match in this case.

Anna Wohlin too sticks pretty close to this same story in her affidavit, stating, 'On Tuesday evening the 1st July, 1969, Janet Lawson came to stay for a couple of days. On that evening we all had dinner together and then had some drinks. After that Brian had a swim in the pool for a couple of hours. Frank, Janet and myself did not go in the pool that evening: we sat with our drinks and watched Brian. While he was in the pool Brian came to the edge and asked me for his squirter, which he used as a name for his inhaler. He often used it and I didn't think anything about it. He used the inhaler and then went on swimming. He suffered from asthma. On Tuesday night I told Brian I wouldn't go in the pool because I was too cold. I think that the temperature of the water that night was about 80 degrees.'

Strangely, at 10.30 a.m. that next morning, Nicholas Fitzgerald received a call from a man called Ralph Hampton, who said he'd met Brian in the Haywaggon the night before and Jones had given him the number, asking him to ring and advise Fitzerald to phone Brian at home that morning. And to keep on ringing until he got through.

Now rather worried himself, Fitzgerald and a friend nineteen-year-old Richard Cadbury, left London for Hartfield by car around 11.00 a.m.

On Brian's last day on earth, Mrs Hallet went to work as usual, meeting Jones in the dining room about noon. Rising about an hour earlier, Brian and Anna came downstairs and after a quick cup of tea and some brown toast settled down to watch a tennis match on telly.

'There was nothing at all different to any other day,' Mary remembers, 'except he'd got a very bad attack of asthma. He had a job talking. It was just a word at a time. I wouldn't say he was weak. I wouldn't say he was extraordinarily strong either. He was just normal. He was full of life. The only time he wasn't was when he got the asthma. He had quite a few attacks. I remember that morning he'd try and talk to you and he'd only get a word at a time out. He'd sort of gasp between words.'

Difficult as it was, Mrs Hallet stood by patiently as Brian told her he was planning a party that evening. According to Suki, that was her idea to ensure there were plenty of people around when Brian gave Thorogood the sack. Just to be on the safe side. 'He told me people were coming that evening,' Mary recalls. 'He'd got quite a few coming.'

It was around this time too that Tom Keylock states in his witness statement he rang Brian and spoke to him regarding Jones's plans to go on holiday to Morocco and afterwards form his new group.

By this time another possible superstar union had been mooted. Brian was scheduled to go to see Humble Pie founder Steve Marriott the very next afternoon to begin rehearsing with him in expectation of perhaps working with the group for a while. In those days Humble Pie were almost as big as The Stones in the US and it would pump them up even further with the presence of a personality like Brian.

In an exclusive interview conducted only two weeks prior to his tragic, mysterious death from fire in April of 1991, Marriott spoke for the first time regarding his professional involvement with Jones: 'You ask if Brian was murdered and in all honesty I have to say . . . yes, he was. Most definitely. If it were an accident, tell me why my fuckin' phone rang three days before Brian was due to come down: I was warned off working with him, telling me it "wouldn't be good for your career to get mixed up with someone like Jones". "Not good for my career or not good for my fuckin' health, you bastard!" I screamed down the phone. "That's entirely up to you," the voice stated calmly. "This is just a friendly warning, that's all."'

Marriott went on to say he was pretty sure he knew the identity of the man on the phone and that he was still living up in London somewhere, but he was reticent to name him for fear of reprisals to his family. 'These are very serious people,' he warned me over our shaky transatlantic line. 'You better be careful yourself, man. I'm not kidding. Just look at what they did to Brian, and he was one of The Rolling Stones, for fuck's sake!' Two very real death threats later, I know what he means.

Steve also commented that when Jones didn't show up as scheduled that next day his heart sank. 'I knew then, man,' he told me. 'I sent out one of the roadies for a paper and afterwards we all just broke down and cried. He was such a beautiful cat. What ruthless bastards! I hope they fuckin' rot for what they did.'

Around 1.00 p.m., Mrs Hallet finished her work and was saying goodbye to Brian as she started out of the front door. 'See you tomorrow, luv!' Jones called out, giving a gentle wave. 'Alright then,' replied Mary happily. It would be the last time she would ever see him.

One very important point is that Mrs Hallet distinctly recalls seeing Frank Thorogood hovering about outside as she ambled up the drive the two hundred yards or so to her cottage. Thorogood, however, stated to police that he had gone to London to see his wife early that morning.

'On Wednesday, 2 July 1969, I went to London during the day and came back to Hartfield between six and six-thirty,' said Thorogood. 'I saw Brian on my return and he was his usual self, watching television. We talked for a while and he asked that I go to the public house to get some drink. I went in a taxi to the Dorest Arms, Hartfield, and bought a bottle of vodka, bottle of wine, Blue Nun, half bottle of brandy and half bottle of whisky.

'I left the bottles with Brian after having a drink with him. I had vodka, he, brandy. His girlfriend, Anna was there. I think she had wine.

'I left them and went to my flat which is close by.

'I stayed in my flat talking to Janet who was staying at the farm for a few days.'

Interesting how Thorogood could drive up to London leaving Hartfield at around 1.00 p.m. and be back at Cotchford (after cutting through rush-hour traffic) at 6.00 p.m. The driving time from Hartfield to London is about two hours, which would have landed him there just about 3.00 p.m. To reach Brian's place at the time he said, he would have had to turn around almost as soon as he arrived. Hardly worth the trip, was it?

At 1.30 p.m. that afternoon, Fitzgerald and Cadbury arrived at Hartfield and made straight for the Haywaggon for a bite of lunch. To their surprise Brian was already there, drinking at the bar with one of the occasional builders from Cotchford. After a few minutes of polite chat Fitzgerald excused himself to go to the gents. A couple of minutes later, Brian rushed in and excitedly began telling his friend he was being held hostage by Thorogood and begged Nicholas for help.

'You've got to help me man,' said Jones. 'These bastards are after me every second. I feel like a prisoner. I've rigged up an intercom system downstairs so I can hear what they're up to from my room, but they're very clever. I'm sure someone's put them up to it. I plan to give them all the boot this evening.

'Anyway, let's talk about it later. If I'm gone too long they'll have a go at me. I do hope you can spend the night.'

With that, Jones, Fitzgerald and Cadbury drove to Cotchford, arriving around 2.30 p.m. Walking through the back garden, past the pool, Nicholas noticed two young casual workmen – later identified only as 'Joe' and 'Frank' – erecting a pair of powerful spotlights directly over the pool.

'What for?' asked Fitzgerald.

Brian, seemingly ignoring him, didn't answer, so the young man let it go.

Settling down in some lawn chairs placed haphazardly in the middle of a long strip of grass to the side of the house, Cadbury and Fitzgerald were bombarded by Jones with the situation between him and the builders. Eventually, though, Brian ran out of steam and wandered back inside the house with Cadbury while Fitzgerald dozed in the hot July sun.

One very puzzling bit of information gleaned from my research was the persistent rumour that Jones was aware of strange lights flashing in the hedgerows and around his house. When asked, Mary Hallet knew nothing about it, but as she was virtually never around at night this is not surprising.

He did, however, mention it to Nicholas who commented on the fact in 1985. 'Brian had complained that there had been lights shining into his house and on the bushes continually for weeks before he died. Everybody thought he was paranoid about someone trying to get him. But I found a strobe light in the grounds after his death. So perhaps he really was under close scrutiny.'

Another continued point of contention is Tom Keylock's presence at Cotchford on the date in question. In his signed statement of 3 July, he clearly states that he 'last spoke to [Brian] by telephone at midday on Wednesday, 2 July 1969, when he was his normal self . . .' No mention is made of the so-called tour manager being physically present *at any time* throughout the day or evening. Beyond that, he has insisted to many over the years that he was not there and only *heard* about Brian's death after the fact. The problem is, that concept is contradicted by both the man himself and the London-based company with which he is currently associated, Excel Productions.

During my interview with Mr Keylock in the bar at the Gloucester Hotel in Kensington on Sunday, 5 December 1993 he said this concerning his whereabouts that day:

Geoffrey: The taxi driver [Joan Fitzsimmons] had been around that day, right?
Tom: Yeah, and she'd left.
Geoffrey: Where were you? You weren't there?
Tom: No, I was at . . . well, I'd been there in the morning and gone, and I went down, I was down at Redlands with Keith. We'd run him up to Olympic Studios where he was recording . . .

Also, in the proposal for a forthcoming video documentary (controlled by Excel) on Brian called *Who Killed Christopher Robin* by Terry Rawlings (on which Tom Keylock is a consultant), there is an interesting passage on the third page. It reads: 'We will examine closely just what happened on the night of his death. This will take shape in interviews, conducted amongst others with the three people who are still alive and were present that night in 1969:

Frank Thorogood – Brian's live-in builder;
Janet Lawson – (Nurse) and Brian's guest that night;
Tom Keylock – Rolling Stone tour manager.
For the first time since that night almost twenty-five years ago, all

three have been quite sensationally taken back to the very spot where he died.'

It's hard to believe that someone who must have had regular contact with Excel wouldn't have seen this proposal before it went out.

Further, on Sunday afternoon, 17 October 1993 in the lounge of my London hotel, The Cranley Gardens, Tom Keylock told me (in the presence of my seventeen-year-old daughter, Sesa) that he had indeed been at Brian's on the night of 3 July. But more on that later.

By 6.00 p.m., Nicholas had awoken, joining Brian and Cadbury in the house. They then retired to the music room where Jones was anxious to play them some demos of his solo work with the likes of Jimi Hendrix and John Lennon.

'I'm missing some very important tapes, you know,' Brian confided in hushed tones. 'I worked for days on one of them and it just disappeared. I'm certain it's that bastard Thorogood. Anna's caught him going through my things several times.'

Strangely, Wohlin's version of the events of that last afternoon make no mention of Fitzgerald's visit to Cotchford, or, indeed, Brian's brief appearance at the Haywaggon. In fact, some parts of her police statement do not tally with other peoples' recollections, though everyone agrees that Brian was indeed at home. '[We] watched the tennis on television for most of the day,' she says. 'We had a salad for lunch and another snack later. During the evening of that day Brian and I were watching television.'

Remember though, that Frank Thorogood stated he had taken a cab into town to buy some booze at Brian's request. Upon his return he sat around with Jones and Wohlin who both shared a drink with the builder. Why was there no mention of this by Wohlin?

At 7.00 p.m. the telephone rang and Brian spoke to a young girl he'd supposedly met in London with the extravagant name of Luciana Martinez Delarosa. Although he was a little foggy on the particulars, she claimed he had invited her up to the house and then boldly announced that she had arrived. She was at Hayward's Heath Station and needed to be picked up. Brian laughed to himself as he hung up the phone. 'Well, I guess tonight's as good a night as any. At least there'll be some people about.' Pretty young girls suddenly turning up out of nowhere was obviously nothing new to Mr Jones.

At this point, Jones seemed happy enough knowing that there were several people who were 'on his side' around and once again confirmed to Nicholas that tonight he would definitely lower the boom on the

Thorogood contingent. Fitzgerald, too, felt things were pretty much under control and so volunteered to ride into town with Cadbury and pick up Ms Delarosa. They left Cotchford Farm at 7.15 p.m. or thereabouts.

Within minutes of their departure, Brian's flamboyant mate Elan pulled up in his dilapidated purple Mini. 'Hey, man!' the young friend called out to Brian, who happened to be standing at the window of the music room looking out towards the drive.

Jones nodded happily. That same funny way he does in all the old film clips. More like Prince Philip or someone than a naughty Rolling Stone. Within minutes Brian and Elan were laughing away as Jones banged away on his old twelve-string acoustic. The party had begun.

Nicholas and his mate had meanwhile made it to the Hayward's Heath Hotel and walked into the bar in hopes of spying the young lady. She had told Brian that's where she would be. It was now 7.40 p.m.

After a couple of embarrassing encounters with the wrong young women, the two men sat down to wait, ordering some dinner to pass the time. The girl, however, never showed. At 9.55 p.m. Nicholas went to the pay phone and dialled Brian's. 'A girl's voice said, "Hello?"' Fitzgerald wrote in his now hard-to-find book. 'I asked to speak to Brian. There was no answer. In the background I could hear a lot of noise and loud music, as if a party was going on . . . Could Luciana have arrived with a bunch of friends?

'I said, "Hello?" There was still no reply, only the sound of revelry. After no one answered about three minutes later, someone put the phone down at the other end . . . Had someone taken the handset from her?'

Obviously, something was very much awry. Back at Cotchford things were happening very fast. But what? An explanation of the various official witness statements doesn't really help due to the contradictory nature of the remarks contained therein. Take for example Frank Thorogood's version of the evening's events: 'About 9.30 p.m. Brian came to the flat and asked that we join him for a drink. I think it was nearer 10.00 p.m. because it was dark and Brian had a torch. Janet and I went with Brian to the farmhouse where Brian and I had more to drink. I had vodka and he was drinking brandy.

'We watched the *Rowan and Martin* TV programme and when it finished at 9.50 p.m., Brian suggested a swim in the pool. By this time we had quite enough to drink. We got our costumes which were in the farmhouse and went to the pool.'

Janet Lawson, however, offers a somewhat different story: 'Brian Jones visited the flat about 10.30 p.m. on Wednesday evening and invited my friend and I to join him at the house. We did so and Brian guided us back to the house with a hand torch. It was clear that he was unsteady on his feet as the light was unreliable. He seemed to be talking quite sensibly, I believe about the drainage scheme. Nevertheless, it was obvious that he had been drinking.

'My friend and I sat at the dining-room table and drinks were there, but I did not take it. Brian and my friend were drinking spirits.

'Brian attempted conversation, but it was a little garbled and he excused it by saying, "I've had my sleepers," or some such phrase. From this I gathered he had taken sleeping tablets.

'At about this point in time, Anna, Brian's friend, joined us and she, Frank and Brian decided to swim. I declined because I considered that Frank and Brian were in no fit condition to swim. I felt sufficiently strongly about this that I mentioned it to both the men. They disregarded my warning and it was obvious that they were drunk.

'The men went upstairs to search for costumes and Anna took the dogs to the side of the pool. I followed her and watched her go into the water. She had been drinking, but appeared capable to care for herself.'

There are several points here that are at the very least questionable. Firstly, Frank makes no mention of Brian being in any way intoxicated when he first shows up at the flat. As far as he knew, the only thing Jones had was *one drink* a couple of hours ago, after Thorogood returned from the pub.

Lawson, however, obviously strongly disagrees. She has him 'unsteady on his feet' on the way back to the house, but in her next breath blames that not on Brian's state of mind, but on the quality of the torch. She further states that he was talking 'quite sensibly' about Cotchford's 'drainage scheme'. A rather involved and technical topic of conversation at the best of times. Still, she somehow comes to the conclusion that 'it was obvious he had been drinking.' Based on what? Especially when weighed against the fact that Anna made no mention of anyone drinking at this point.

Still, from Wohlin yet another scenario arises. 'At about 10.15 p.m. we were going to bed and then Brian said that he wanted to go for a swim. I wasn't very keen and he went over to Frank's flat and came back with Frank and Janet. I came downstairs and they were sitting at the dining table with drinks. Brian put the garden floodlights on and put the drinks on a tray to take out. Then he and Frank changed into swimming trunks. They were laughing about with each other.'

Here Anna seems to maintain that no one had been drinking, or indeed, doing *anything* to excess. All she says is that Frank and Brian were 'laughing'. Lawson mentions that Brian's speech is slurred from the 'sleepers' he had taken. Why does no one else make note of this phenomenon? In fact *no sleeping tablets* were found in Jones's body at the autopsy.

Somehow, by the time everyone ambles out to the pool for a swim, Thorogood says that while Brian was 'staggering' he was still remarkably able to 'swim safely'.

Lawson, however, once again disagrees. She calls the whole swimming adventure an 'escapade' of which she seems to highly disapprove and even *hides* so that no one will press her into joining in the revelry. She says that Brian needs to be held up on the diving board and then 'flops' into the water. His swimming she then describes as 'sluggish'.

Perhaps it might be prudent here actually to chart some of the many conflicts inherent in the three official statements.

BRIAN VISITS THE GARAGE FLAT
1) Frank Thorogood says it was 9.30 p.m. or 10.00 p.m.
2) Janet Lawson says it was 10.30 p.m.
3) Anna Wohlin says it was 10.15 p.m.

One could argue that in the normal course of events people might not be expected to recall exact times during a typical evening's entertainment. But what of Thorogood's statement that they were all at Brian's watching *Rowan and Martin's Laugh-In*, which finished at 9.50 p.m.? It's a little tough to watch a show somewhere before you even arrive. Besides, the times vary so greatly, that surely, this fact, irrespective of anything else, should have alerted police that the witness statements didn't match. A fairly elementary tip-off in any investigation.

What supposedly happened next is also fraught with contradictions. Once again, Frank Thorogood: 'Brian was staggering, but I was not too concerned because I had seen him in a worse condition and he was able to swim safely. He was a good swimmer, but he was an asthmatic and used an inhaler. He had some difficulty in balancing on the diving board and I helped to steady him, but this was not unusual for him. He went in off the board and I went in the shallow end. He was swimming quite normally. Anna was in the pool with us for some of the time, then she went indoors leaving us in the pool. Janet also went indoors.

'After we had been in the pool for about twenty minutes or so, I got out and went to the house for a cigarette leaving Brian in the pool.

'I honestly don't remember asking Janet for a towel, but if she said I did, then I accept it. I know I got a cigarette and lit it and when I went back to the pool, Anna appeared from the house about the same time. She said to me, "He is lying on the bottom," or something like that. I saw Brian face down in the deep end on the bottom of the pool. Anna and I got in the water and, after a struggle, got him out. His body was limp and as we got him to the side, Janet joined us and helped get him out.'

And now Janet Lawson: 'A few minutes later the men joined in the water. I wanted to disassociate myself with the escapade and in order to keep an eye on the trio I partly hid myself in an effort to avoid their requests to join them.

'I say that Brian had great difficulty in holding his balance on the spring board. Frank was doing his best to assist him, but not very successfully.

'Eventually Brian flopped into the water and yet despite his condition seemed to be able to cope and made his strokes in the deep end. His movements were sluggish, but I felt reasonably assured that they all were able to look after each other.

'I returned to the music room in the house and played a guitar.

'I heard Anna return to the house and talk to the dogs as she went upstairs.

'I went to the garden and saw that the two men were still in the pool. I returned to the house.

'About ten minutes later Frank returned to the house and asked for a towel. I went out to the pool and on the bottom I saw Brian. He was face down in the deep end. He was motionless and I sensed the worst straight away.

'I shouted under the open window of the bedroom to Anna who was speaking on the telephone. I ran into the house and shouted to Frank. Both joined me, I was by then in the water, but realised I couldn't manage him alone and I shouted to Frank to get into the pool to get Brian out.

'I returned to the house to use the phone, but I had difficulty as the line was engaged and there were several telephones in the house, but I was not sure of the location of them all.

129

'I returned to the pool to get Frank to use the phone and he and Anna were struggling to get Brian out of the water. I helped and we eventually got him out.'

Finally, Anna Wohlin remembers: 'I went into the pool before they came out and stayed there awhile after they were both in there. They were both a bit drunk. Janet didn't go in the water. After a while I went up to my room to get dressed leaving the two men in the water and Janet at the side. While I was in the house the phone rang, I answered it. It was for me. I heard Frank come in then and he picked up the phone in the kitchen. I told him the call was for me and he put the phone down. Then I heard Janet shout, "Something has happened to Brian." I rushed out about the same time as Frank. Janet was there and I saw Brian lying on the bottom of the pool. I dived in and got him off the bottom and Frank came in and helped me to pull him out.'

Once again let's take a closer look:

WHO ALERTS THE OTHERS THAT BRIAN IS IN TROUBLE?
1) Frank says it was *Anna*. ('She said to me, "He is laying on the bottom."')
2) Janet says it was *her*: ('I shouted . . . to Anna . . .'; 'I shouted to Frank.')
3) Anna also says it was *Janet*. ('. . . I heard Janet shout . . .')

WHO FIRST PULLED BRIAN FROM THE POOL?
1) Frank says it was *him* and *Anna*. ('Anna and I got in the water . . .') Then, says Thorogood, Janet assisted them. ('Janet joined us and helped get him out.')
2) Janet says it was *her*. ('I was by then in the water . . .') Then, says Lawson, she returned to the house, thereafter coming back to the pool to help Frank and Anna. (. . . He and Anna were struggling . . . I helped . . .')
3) Anna says it was *her*. ('I dived in . . .') Then, says Wohlin, Frank assisted her. ('Frank came in and helped . . .')

Frank Thorogood: 'Janet said that she had difficulty with the phone and I went to the house and dialled 999.

'I returned to the pool and the girls were trying to revive him. When the ambulance men came they took over. The doctor came and said he was dead.'

Janet Lawson: 'He lay on his back and as Frank went to the house to phone I turned the body over and attempted to pump the water out of him. It was obvious to me he was dead, but I turned the body back and I told Anna how to apply mouth-to-mouth resuscitation as I applied external cardiac massage.

'I carried on for at least fifteen minutes, but there was no pulse.'

Anna Wohlin: 'Janet went to phone for help. Then she came back and said she couldn't get through. I think I must have left the phone off the hook. Then Frank went to phone and Janet and I applied artificial respiration. While we were doing this I felt Brian's hand grip mine. We were still trying when the ambulance men came. Then they took over. Then the doctor came and said Brian was dead.'

In the end one is left with far more nagging questions than answers. Still, sometimes questions alone help point the way. Questions, perhaps, the police should have been asking at the time. Consider these final nuggets:

Janet Lawson noted that Brian 'seemed anxious' when everyone was sitting together having a drink at the dining-room table. Was it at that point he told Frank everyone was fired? And if so was Thorogood's reaction somehow tied to Brian's 'problem' in the pool?

Why if Janet Lawson was so concerned that her three friends had all been drinking to excess and might be in some peril did she disappear into the house to 'play the guitar'?

Anna Wohlin says that just prior to the tragedy she left the pool on her own leaving Janet 'at the side'. But Lawson insists it was she that initially left the pool as she clearly remembers hearing Anna enter the house and speak to the dogs. Frank, however, says that both Janet and Anna left together.

Who was Anna Wohlin talking to on the phone so nonchalantly at such an unusual hour? Nicholas Fitzgerald says he rang the house at 9.55 p.m., but the girl who answered 'didn't sound foreign' so it's difficult to believe it was Anna. Besides, this call would have presumably come in much later than Fitzgerald's. Still, if Anna first heard Lawson's

131

cry for help while she was chatting away, why didn't she alert the caller to hang up and aid her by ringing the police?

Why didn't officials seek to discover the identity of this mysterious caller?

Why does Anna recall Frank Thorogood getting out of the pool and walking into the house to answer the phone when he makes no mention of it? And why didn't Lawson, who was then just a few feet away, pick it up rather than making Frank, soaking wet, walk all the way back inside?

Why doesn't Janet Lawson mention anything about this strange incoming phone call happening at almost the exact second Jones was drowning?

One also wonders why Brian would ever consider being alone in the pool with Frank Thorogood in the first place if he distrusted and hated him so much? It seems a little out of context. Especially if Jones meant to fire him that night.

Where were Brian's ever-present dogs during all this? Other than Janet implying that they followed Anna into the house no mention is made of their whereabouts during the period of the actual drowning. Surely all the attendant commotion of Brian lying there dying would have brought them outside again barking wildly?

Janet Lawson, an experienced professional nurse ran back inside the house after seeing Brian's body lying at the bottom of the pool. Surely she, more than anyone present, realised how important seconds are when the brain is deprived of air?

Lawson, having leapt into the pool (fully clothed) trying desperately to save Brian, climbed out and again rushed inside to phone for help, leaving the potential resuscitation of Jones to two totally untrained people she had already stated she felt were at least mildly intoxicated.

Janet said when she tried to ring for help there was some problem with the phones, but Frank apparently had no trouble at all getting out. At least he didn't mention anything about any such difficulties in his statement.

All things considered, the 'official' version of the events of Wednesday, 3 July 1969, seem confused to say the least. Perhaps there are other potentially more credible explanations of Brian's last moments. Possibilities that have escaped scrutiny all these years. A single, silent truth patiently waiting to be uncovered. A truth that might, at last, clear Brian's name.

Confirming much that has been speculated about over the last two or more decades is one of the part-time builders working at Cotchford Farm during this time, who, for reasons which will soon become obvious, prefers to preserve his identity. For the purposes of this work I have called him simply 'Joe'. Even I have no idea what his real name is. He first approached me in the lobby of the Kensington Park Hotel in London, while I was there promoting my book *Blackbird: The Unauthorised Biography of Paul McCartney*.

As I was returning late one afternoon from a round of television and radio interviews, he stopped me near the lifts and asked if I were indeed, 'the writer'. I laughed and told him I was certainly one of them, and continued waiting for the lift.

'I'd like to talk with you, mate,' he began tentatively.

For a moment I thought he was yet another journalist staking out my hotel for a quick, unscheduled interview. At this point though, I was tired and told him so.

'It's important. Really. I've read all your books.'

'Well, at least you're not a journalist,' I joked, 'they never read anything. Okay, let's find some place out in the lobby. But I've only got a few minutes.'

The man I met that day was well over six feet tall, with a full head of greying, shoulder length hair. He was massively built, and more than a little intimidating. After listening to him for a little while I decided he was for real, probably not immediately dangerous, and so invited him up to my room where we could speak privately and maybe even record our talk. He took some convincing, but when I assured him the only reason I wanted to tape the conversation was so that I could be certain of being absolutely correct in everything he told me he finally relented.

'Okay,' he whispered menacingly. 'You can have my words, but *not* my identity. *Never my identity!*'

I assured him we had a deal and he relaxed appreciably. What follows then, is a transcript of most of our discussion that evening. There were a couple of times he got a little edgy and either reached over and turned off the recorder or requested me to pause the tape. In view of the harrowing stuff he was telling me I wasn't about to argue.

Geoffrey: So for the record maybe I should explain a little bit about what's happening. I met this guy . . . [BREAK IN TAPE] . . . in association with Brian Jones, you might say. A couple of preliminaries; first of all, could you tell me your name please?

Joe: No, if you don't mind, I'd rather leave that out.

Geoffrey: I'll tell you right now, I'm not going to fuck about with you. If you have something to say, I'll listen. If you want to come clean I need to know who I'm dealing with. You could be anybody.

Joe: Well, so could you by the same token. I've known about this for twenty-three, twenty-four years now so I'd rather keep out of it meself 'cause I wasn't really involved. I was there, I saw it all, I know who done it, but I don't want to get involved. I mean . . .

Geoffrey: Hold on a minute. You weren't that innocent, were you?

Joe: You can't see anybody killed and just write it off, just forget it.

Geoffrey: And you can't *kill* anybody and write it off either, can you?

Joe: Well I didn't kill anybody, so I don't know. I mean I saw somebody killed. Okay, maybe I was involved in it, but I don't think I was responsible entirely for his death.

Geoffrey: Tell me why you're talking to me today, first of all.

Joe: I want it off me shoulders. That's basically what it is. It's been getting me down. I'm a married man now and I've got kids as old as what I was then.

Geoffrey: Does your wife know about it?

Joe: No. I've never told *anybody* about this. And believe me, it fucking weighs you down. You've got to live it to know.

Geoffrey: How did you get hooked up with Brian Jones to begin with?

Joe: Well, I never knew Brian Jones, did I? 1969 it was, I was twenty years old and I was what you called a hippie in those days. I was travelling round England, we used to go from town to town, kicking round the country. Spend a little time up there and then maybe down near Bournemouth. Cornwall was always favourite, or the West Country. You could be anywhere through the year. You just lived rough. That's what we used to do. Anyway, I was in Hartfield and I got talking to this bloke I knew who told me he was doing a bit of casual work for a builder who was doing work on Brian Jones's house. Well, fuckin' hell, Brian Jones, who got the chance to meet him? So he said if you come along it'd be something like ten bob an hour, half a quid in your pocket an hour and he says, 'Honest, you do fuck all. You can drink when you like, you can take all his dope. Just don't fuck yourself. You've got all these ponces round, pop stars. Just take the piss out of 'em all day.'

Geoffrey: Were you a Stones fan?

Joe: Oh, yeah, I loved them. Anyway, he got me started and it was exactly what he said. All day long you do a bit of this and a bit of that, but nothing much. Just look busy and you'd get paid half a quid an hour.

Geoffrey: Did you have access to the house or was that off limits?

Joe: You could go in and do what the fuck you liked. As I said, they were a bunch of fucking ponces.

Geoffrey: What do you mean by a ponce?

Joe: What would you call it nowadays? A wanker is what he was really. I don't know if you understand that saying, he was a nerd you'd say.

Geoffrey: Did you speak with him?

Joe: Well, sometimes he'd speak to you, sometimes he wouldn't. Sometimes he'd come out there, 'Alright? You doing alright?' And other times he'd walk straight past you not even knowing you were there. He just thought he was a lot fucking better than we was. He weren't, he was just a fucking ponce. He couldn't lay a brick!

Geoffrey: Do you mean a homosexual?

Joe: Oh no, that's a poofter. He looked like one, but I don't know whether he was or not. He always had a lot of women, but he always looked sick. Like a very, very pasty complexion, you know.

Geoffrey: Did you party with him?

Joe: Well, like at night, you wouldn't knock off work and go home. We'd all just stay there and get pissed. Maybe he just wanted people around. I don't know.

Geoffrey: Was there chicks around?

Joe: Oh, fucking loads, I mean, we used to pull birds and take them there. You know, it was, 'Hey, come on, I'll take you up to Brian Jones's house.' And there was lots of parties. It was one big party even when you was working. I mean, we spent virtually all our time there pissed up. Wobbling about with buckets of cement, which was fucking funny looking back really. Imagine trying to build a house up and doing bits of this and bits of that when you're out your fucking head. Somebody said Mick Jagger was there one day, but I didn't see him. But there was so many faces there. I mean, you just took no notice of them. There's always guitars being played. There was always music going on. You know, the record player going really loud. There was always loads going on there, but we was supposed to be working anyway.

Geoffrey: At that time in Brian Jones's life, they said he was on a sort of decline. Did you notice that in any respect? Did you know that he had been plagued with asthma since he was a little boy?

Joe: No, he never said any of that. I've seen him taking those, like you'd put it up to your . . . an inhaler! Put in your mouth and press the top. I seen him doing that but I never seen anyone with asthma so I don't know. I've never seen him coughing or spluttering or anything like that.

Geoffrey: Were you jealous of Brian's chicks?

Joe: I don't know. I mean, I didn't really take any notice, I just thought he was a bit of a ponce.

Geoffrey: Let's talk about the night we're concerned with.

Joe: That he got killed. Well I'll tell you, it was in the evening . . .

Geoffrey: For the record, I've stopped the tape at the request of our friend because he wanted to confer with me on a couple of specifics. Not really being exactly sure what he wanted to talk about and commit to tape. Which, under the circumstances, is understandable and we are continuing with the proviso that at any time he has the right to reach over, or indicate to me to stop the tape so that he can collect his thoughts and we can have some slight discussions off tape. Is that your understanding?

Joe: I don't . . . yeah. I don't want to incriminate meself.

Geoffrey: Tell me about the night that Brian Jones died.

Joe: Yeah, well, you say the night, but from the day really we were working there and in the afternoon me and my mate, Frank, we had a couple of wobblies [Mandrax sleeping tablets]. Well, we had four actually. The longer you take them you sort of build up a resistance so they stop working and you have to have more. The first one I ever had knocked me fucking head off, but that was only one. After a couple of years I'd do six and seven at a time, but that afternoon we had about four. It was a fucking laugh, you know, spending the afternoon fucking about and in the evening the usual thing was just to be pissed up. We got a bottle of vodka. Frank had gone in and got it out of the kitchen. We fucking knocked that back and then there's the beer. Then this sort of party blew up. People starting arriving, drinks going on.

Geoffrey: Let me ask you a couple of questions about Brian's lady at the time, Anna Wohlin.

Joe: Anna, yeah, I didn't really know her. She was just some fucking Swedish bint. She had nothing to do with us. She was sort of aloof. She didn't bother with us. Anyway, it was just a normal night really. A normal sort of party. Everyone's falling about, pissed up. We was pissed as rats, no doubt about it. We were well pissed. We were steaming, I mean, everything was to hand, bottles of vodka, bottles of whisky. And they'd got that fucking Yankee whiskey as well, bourbon. There were plenty of drugs about as well.

Geoffrey: Now the problem I have with that right off is that my research indicates that Brian Jones was basically off drugs at that point.

Joe: I'm not saying *he* did it, but everybody else there did. I ain't saying he did. I mean, he drank a lot. I know that for sure. He fucking knocked the old booze back. There's no doubt about that. And I know he used to like going down the local, The Haywaggon. He used to get down there and put a lot of fucking ale away. There's no doubt about that. [THERE IS A BRIEF BREAK IN THE TAPE.] He could swim like a fucking fish you know. He could go off that springboard and could do like two or three lengths under water.

Geoffrey: He couldn't have been too incapacitated if he was doing all that.

Joe: Looked all right to me, got to be honest.

Geoffrey: He was in a good frame there? He wasn't debilitated? Because a lot of people say that Brian Jones was so physically unfit, that if you will, he just sort of drowned in the pool because he was too high or . . .

Joe: He didn't look it that night. I mean, I've got to be honest, he had been drinking, but I don't know how much. I'd seen him with a drink in his hand . . .

Geoffrey: But he didn't appear to be drunk?

Joe: No, fucking hell, no he wasn't that night. I mean, I've told you before that sometimes he'd talk to you and say, 'Alright, how you doin'?' and other times he'd fucking lord it over you. Well that night was one of those that he was lordin' it. He'd treat you like shit sometimes. He got talking to me and Frank. Frank and I was leaning against the side. You know how you are with your elbows, don't you? On the side of the pool. We was doing that and splashing our feet out and he come by, 'How you doin'?' 'Oh well, we're alright.' 'You do a lot of swimming?' 'Well, not as much as you lot. We can see that you're good.' And then he starts, 'Oh, I can do two lengths of this pool underwater.' He said, 'I'll show you up on the fucking springboard.' And off he went, you know, two lengths. Oh yeah, he'd swim up touching at the end, turn round and kick, you know, like you see on the Olympics, on telly. Then back down the other end, touch that, then he'd come back and say, 'See, you can't fucking do it. I can!' That sort of thing.

Geoffrey: When did things turn ugly?

Joe: Well, round about that time we was talking to him and nobody was really taking any notice. They were jumping in and fucking jumping out. People were more interested in getting pissed and jumping in and out of the pool. Basically, the way he got killed was it was me and Frank talking to him about swimming under water. Now you've got to bear in mind we was well fucking pissed so you don't really know what you're doing and the boy was a fucking ponce. 'Ah, you can fucking swim under water can you, son? You're fucking good under water? Here then, let's see how long you can stay under.' So we fucking pushed him under and held him under for a while.

Geoffrey: Let's break that down. What do you mean you held him under?

Joe: Just a bit of horseplay, that's all.

Geoffrey: What did you do?

Joe: Well, the first time I grabbed him and put me hands on top of his shoulders. I said, 'You good under water, are you, Brian? You're fucking good underwater? Here, try this,' and I pushed him down from the top, from his shoulders, with me hands . . . I'm bigger than him, he was wiggling and fucking panicking and jumping about. But I mean, I'm a powerful bloke, so I fucking held him down there till I thought, 'Right you cunt, now let's see how fucking good you are underwater,' and I pulled him back up again. I mean, he was puffing and panting. Once he started slagging us off then Frank got involved. 'Who are you fucking calling a cunt? Right you cunt, I'll fucking show you how to swim under fucking water.' So then Frank pushed him down, you know. I think somebody did say something at one time. I just said, 'Hey, fuck off! We're only fucking about. He's pissed up, look at him!' So they fucked off. I don't know if you've been to parties where you get pissed yourself and see something going on and you sort of go over and say, 'Here, what's going on?' and they say, 'Fuck off.' So you fuck off, don't you? Case they do it to you!

Geoffrey: You described two episodes of dunking. How many altogether would you say there were?

Joe: I'd say, six, seven, maybe eight. I don't fucking know. It just went on and on.

Geoffrey: Over how long a period?

Joe: Ten, fifteen minutes. Like he did try to get away, but we wouldn't let him go. We thought, 'Fuck this!' We was only having fun at the time.

Geoffrey: Why would you fuck with somebody like that? He's fucking paying your wages, you're not doing any work. You're scamming him . . .

Joe: Don't you think I feel fucking bad about it? I've had twenty odd fucking years of this! You know you're throwing these things in my face. I've fucking fought this for years. I just thought I'd come and tell you about it. Get it off my chest, you know? But it's no good you fucking accusing me and trying to get me arrested. It ain't gonna bring him back, is it?

Geoffrey: But you know that I'm a journalist . . .

Joe: And that's why I've come to see you, because I mean, I've read your books. I know that you do all the pop and rock stuff. I mean, I wouldn't go to the fucking *Sun* or the *News of the World* or something like that. I'll come and see you though, 'cause I respect you.

Geoffrey: All right, anyway, so it went on for between ten and fifteen minutes. And there were maybe seven, eight, nine ducking episodes and he was struggling the whole time?

Joe: Oh, he was trying to get away, you know. He was trying to get away, then he went through one period where it was, 'Ah come on, lads,' you know, 'let us fucking go. *Oh, come on!*' He started pleading, 'Ah, come on, fucking hell, come on, let me go, will you?' But when you're in that frame of mind nobody took any fucking notice, honest. I'm not kidding. Except for maybe that one bloke, nobody took any notice. I reckon it was accidental death, 'cause we didn't *mean* to kill him. Alright, he died, you know, so I suppose a court of law, a fucking judge would say it was murder. But I mean, we didn't think, 'Right, let's murder this cunt!' It just happened. But honest, I'll tell you when it comes to the actual death, you read all these stories about the great climax building up and the death throes and the struggles. It's *nothing* like that. I mean he died just easier . . . When he died it was so fucking easy we didn't even know he was dead! I mean all the time we was pushing him under I remember the last time we both held him down.

And we was only doing it for the fucking crack, you know. For a joke like.

Geoffrey: You have a funny sense of humour, pal.

Joe: Come on, it was twenty-odd years ago. And why do you think I'm telling you? You think I'd do this now? You think I do this every day of my life?

Geoffrey: We just turned off for a minute here so that you could . . .

Joe: I mean, you know, just watch your line of questioning. Let's try and keep this on a low key.

Geoffrey: Look, I'm not playing games here. I mean this is heavy stuff, isn't it really?

Joe: Yeah, yeah, I mean it might be a bit more important to you, though, than it is to me because it was all those years ago.

Geoffrey: Well, I never fucking killed anybody.

Joe: I never fucking killed anybody! How many fucking times do I have to tell you? *It wasn't fucking murder*! You gonna accept that or not?

Geoffrey: You came to me, okay! I didn't come to you, pal!

Joe: It's not fucking murder! I mean you're supposed to be neutral, right? So you just ask fucking neutral questions and I'll give you the answers.

Geoffrey: When he died at the end, what happened?

Joe: To be honest, *nothing*. Nothing happened. I mean all the times we was holding him down, taking the piss out of him and pulling him up again. I mean, we was pulling him up by the hair at one time. Just getting his head out of the water and saying, 'Think you're good underwater, are you?' Then pushing him back down. Let me tell you something, I've never told anybody this; I'm seeing you here today and that's it, I'm fucking gone! This is your one and only chance. I hope you're using that tape recorder 'cause you're not getting it twice. I just want to get it off me chest. Then I think, maybe I can forget about it. I mean, I might find out in years it's done me no good talking to you at all. It might drop me in the shit. I don't know. But I've got to do it. My missus knows fuck all about it. My kids don't know nothing about it.

Geoffrey: Where do you live, in London?

Joe: I'm not telling you.

Geoffrey: What part of London?

Joe: I'm not telling you.

Geoffrey: What do you do?

Joe: I'm not telling you.

Geoffrey: How many kids do you have?

Joe: I'm not telling you.

Geoffrey: Okay, so Brian Jones is dead, what'd you guys do?

Joe: At the time, you've got to bear in mind, we was pissed out of our heads. We'd had those wobblies, bottles of fucking vodka, we'd been drinking beer, drinking that Yankee whiskey. We was fucking well out of it. I think I was more out of it than Frank was. He seemed to know a bit more about what was going on than I did. We pushed him under for the last time and he just didn't fight. You know what I mean? He just went fucking limp. I don't know, it was strange.

Geoffrey: Did you hit him?

Joe: No. No. No. I never hit him once. I put me hands on his shoulders, pushed him under and pulled him up by the hair. It went on for a quarter of an hour or so. The last time he just fucking went down. He didn't fight, didn't do anything. It was Frank that kept pushing him. I mean I'd got my hands on his arse, I think. I'm not sure. But Frank had got him by the shoulders and we was pushing him and he weren't fighting back. He weren't doing nothing. So we thought, 'Fucking hell,' and we let him go and he didn't do nothing. Frank says, 'He's fucking dead!' I says, 'Let's get the fuck out of here for fuck sake!' Now Frank, he'd got this old Ford Anglia and he says, 'Quick, get out, get fucking dressed. No, don't even bother getting dressed, just grab your clothes. You can do it in the car. I'll get the clothes. Let's get the fuck out of here.' We jumped out of the pool and we left him there. He weren't at the bottom, but he weren't at the top. He was sort of halfway.

Geoffrey: Where'd you go?

Joe: We went to London. Well, what we did was funny really, 'cause we was hippies, we'd got fucking hair to our arses. You know, we went skinhead overnight. We had our fucking heads right down to the skin. I mean, we thought they're gonna be looking for hippies, ain't they? So we went fucking skinhead. Shaved our fucking heads, you know. I'll tell you we was shit scared.

Geoffrey: Had you ever been involved in anything like this before?

Joe: No, I'd done like rip-offs and that. I was twenty, let's say I was a little, a bit older. You'd find like a sixteen- or seventeen-year-old kid, tell him you've got some good red Leb [hashish] for sale, you know. Like eighteen quid an ounce. 'I'll meet you at the back of the pub. Like, you bring the money and I'll bring the dope.' When they get outside, you punch them in the face and fuck off. That's basically what you did. I mean I've done a bit of that.

Geoffrey: You keep saying 'Frank', but you told me before we turned on our tape that it wasn't just two people holding him down. Do you want to go into the other people that were there with you on this?

Joe: No, not really, 'cause the only difference between them and Frank is that they're alive and he's not. Heroin overdose. I went down and saw him buried. It was funny really, 'cause his old mum thought he'd died of a heart attack.

Geoffrey: So you're a skinhead, you're living in London . . .

Joe: And I'll tell you, watching the fucking papers and the news, you know. 'Cause we expected they were going to be scouring the country for these hippies what killed Brian Jones. You know, we thought, 'Big murder, big pop star.' I mean, it weren't like killing the bloke round the corner, was it? It's 'Brian Jones', you know. But nothing happened.

Geoffrey: What did the papers say?

Joe: Nothing. They said asthma attack, drugs and his asthma medicine. He'd got some alcohol in his bloodstream.

Geoffrey: So what did you think?

Joe: We thought fucking great! What would you think? Fucking hell, 'cause we thought there'd be police everywhere asking questions of everybody who was at the party wanting to know who'd been working there. Who was invited and who weren't. I mean we was just casual labourers anyway.

Geoffrey: There was an inquest and a police investigation. The media's one thing, but the police are another. Weren't you worried about that?

Joe: Bloody right, yeah. Course we were, but it just didn't come off. I mean we had a lot of worrying. We was fucking scared. Then there was no hue and cry, if you like.

Geoffrey: Now it's been said, not by me, but it's been intimated over the years that Brian Jones's death might not have been purely accidental . . .

Joe: No, no, *no!* You know, I've told you what happened. That's what happened!

Geoffrey: Alright, yeah. But the point is that I've heard stories, you know, as have a lot of people in pop circles, that Brian Jones's death was the result of people with very big business interests that were being jeopardised. Were you paid to kill Brian Jones?

Joe: No!

Geoffrey: What about Frank?

Joe: No, no! I can tell you now, none of us had nothing out of this at all. Nobody was interested in that sort of thing.

Geoffrey: Well, you're the kind of a bloke that stands outside of a pub and hits someone. Gains somebody's trust to the extent that they give you money for drugs that don't even exist. Then when they come out of the pub with their money you beat them.

Joe: Who told you that? Who told you that?

Geoffrey: You just did.

Joe: Did I?

Geoffrey: Yeah, you fucking did.

Joe: Well, I might done a little bit of it . . .

Geoffrey: The point is; you're that sort of bloke, you'll hit someone in the face for ten or twenty quid. Were you given money? Yes or no? Was there any financial consideration for you? How did you live after this happened? How did you keep yourself? You seem to be a man with a lot of expenses. How did you keep it all together? Were you given money, was there a financial interest? I need to know that. I need to know if this is what you say it was. I'm convinced that I know *how* Brian Jones died. I'm not convinced I know *why* fucking Brian Jones died. That's what I want to know. Why did you do it? Were you paid? It's a very important question. Were you paid money? Was Frank paid money? What do you know about this? Come on, look, I can see you want to talk to me. Don't ponce about. Don't you be a fucking ponce. Are you a ponce? I want to make sure that I know *everything* that went down. Not just some kind of fucking watered-down bullshit.

Joe: Well, I'll tell you what I know. I'll tell you what I know. Right, I mean, nobody ever said anything to me. Nobody ever said *anything* to me. As far as I was concerned, what went on that night, it was all sort of off the cuff. But when we shot down the smoke afterwards Frank gave me £350. Now I don't know where he got it from. We couldn't stop to pick our fucking wages up, could we? We were being paid like by the day, but it was always a day late. See, me and Frank then sort of lost contact. He sort of went uptown then if you like. He started wearing smart suits. Ah well, he soon grew his hair again, I'll tell you. Once he found out the law weren't after him he grew his hair to a reasonable length, he didn't grow it long. He'd got some wedge. No doubt about it, he'd got some fucking wedge. I mean he had that fucking beat-up old Ford Anglia, then he got a Rover 2. Quite a decent motor in those days, you know. He like went from strength to strength, I suppose.

Geoffrey: He gives you the money?

Joe: What he said was basically, 'Keep your head down and say nothing.' That's in my interest as well, not to say nothing. So I'm not going to say nothing anyway, would I?

Geoffrey: What else would you like to add?

Joe: There's nothing to add really. I've told you the story. I've told you everything that went on.

Geoffrey: How did you deal with this? Did it make an impression on you emotionally?

Joe: At the time, no. As the years went by I think I was involved in a death. I won't say murder, the *death* of another person. I mean, it don't have to be a rock star, it could have been anybody. I mean, human life is all the same value. It doesn't matter who you are.

Geoffrey: What would you say to Brian's parents now, if you could?

Joe: How 'bout 'sorry'? Think that's good enough? No, I don't think so really.

Geoffrey: Finally, what would you say to the world about what you did? About what you took away from The Rolling Stones and from all the music fans?

Joe: What I'd like to say to the world is that we didn't know at the time what we was doing. We didn't realise that we was killing. Well, *I didn't*. I don't know whether Frank had different ideas being that he had all the money afterwards. We didn't realise it at the time. We was just fucking about. I mean, he [Brian] was a ponce, you know.

Geoffrey: I think that's where we came in. I want to thank you for your time and your honesty.

Joe: Well, thanks for listening to me. I'm glad I've finally done it. I hope it works. I mean, it might not. I know these Catholics go to confession and maybe it'll be a bit like that. I'll feel a lot better after I've told you. I hope I do, you know?

While 'Joe's' memories of the night of 3 July ring true to many close to the debacle, there are those who, in all fairness deny that Brian's death was anything other than a very unfortunate accident. Most of all, Mr Keylock maintains that his lifelong friend and business associate, Frank Thorogood, was at Cotchford only to do his job and take care of Brian. Nothing more.

Geoffrey: You don't think Thorogood did anything wrong, do you?

Tom: No way!

Geoffrey: If he had, what would you have done?

Tom: I would have gone mad.

Geoffrey: Would you have kicked the shit out of him?

Tom: Ahh, Frank, I've known him for fifty years, there's no way. He looked after Brian. See, his job was very difficult, not just a builder. He had to keep all them away, he never opened his mouth. If ever he thought Brian was getting out of hand, he'd phone me, doesn't matter, day or night, he'd phone. Two or three times he wanted this sorted, he said, 'Brian, you don't really want to do that. It's gonna cost this and cost that.' Brian was very money conscious . . .

Geoffrey: Throwing it away or tight-fisted?

Tom: Well, he didn't have a lot, you know. With Brian when he'd have something done we'd send the bill to the office. Frank said, 'Well, I think you'll spoil it.' 'Well, I want it done.' So Frank phoned me and I says, 'Well, if he wants it, he wants it.' Then again Brian changed his mind too many times. You know, he could never . . . he went through a very paranoid thing.

Geoffrey: He definitely told people someone was after him, you know.

Tom: Yeah, but it was all in his mind. I would have given my life for him. A few people have had a go at him and I've stepped in . . .

Geoffrey: How about this? *You* didn't do anything, Thorogood didn't do anything, how about those fucking casual builders? Maybe they got a little pissed up and did something?

Tom: There was no builders there! I can't understand people saying that. *There were no builders there.* They'd gone home.

Geoffrey: Was there a party?

Tom: No party. Mrs Hallet said there was a party going on. If playing sounds is a party with four people! It's a party if you want to call it that. But there was no such thing as a party there.

The fact is, there was a party, whether Tom Keylock knew it or not. After work that evening, as 'Joe' and others tell us, the workmen hung out and started things off by swigging a few beers in the garden. Following that, Elan rolled up, followed by some local friends of Brian. One unconfirmed source even has Suki Potier showing up with the idea of picking up some of her belongings, but in view of the evidence that seems highly unlikely. All night long Brian had his eye on Frank who, as usual, swaggered about like the lord of the manor.

145

'Let him have his fun,' Brian said confidently. 'In a couple of hours he's gonna be out of here for good.'

By around 11.00 p.m., Nicholas Fitzgerald was now convinced that the mystery girl he'd been waiting for all evening wasn't going to show. He was also increasingly concerned about the strange phone call he'd made to Brian's. 'Maybe we'd better get back and see what's up,' he suggested to Cadbury. 'All this is very weird.'

Fifteeen minutes later their car pulled into Cotchford Lane only to be blinded by the headlights of a car parked virtually in the middle of the road in front of Brian's. Combined with everything else, this looked very strange. As they got closer they could see the motor was running, no one was inside, and that the driver's door was wide open. As they inched their way up the bumpy lane both men sat in silence. The windows were rolled down and except for the sound of the car up ahead, everything was totally quiet. No music, no party, no guests – nothing.

'This is fucking spooky,' Cadbury finally said, breaking the eery spell.

'Too right,' Fitzgerald countered. 'Pull over and turn off your lights. I want to see what's up.'

Soundlessly opening his door, Nicholas slipped into the inky night and made his way to the back of the abandoned car. He noticed it was a foreign job, and was just about to note the registration number when Richard called out.

'Let's go in through the back. I'm sure there's something going on.'

Fitzgerald picks up the tale in his book: 'We went back to my car where there was a gap in the hedge leading into Bluebell Wood. We clumsily groped through the trees and emerged behind the beamed stone wall of the summerhouse in shadow, where we heard muffled voices. We skirted the summerhouse, came around to its side and saw the full glare of the lights now over the pool and in the windows of the house . . .

'At the far right-hand corner of the swimming pool three men were standing . . . The power of the spotlights blotted out their features . . . The middle one dropped to his knees, reached into the water and pushed down on the top of a head that looked white.

'At the opposite corner of the pool – far left – stood two other people, a man and a woman, gazing down into the pool where the kneeling man was pushing down on the head, keeping it under. The man to the right of the kneeling man said something. It sounded like a command and I caught the words, ". . . do something." At that, the third man on that side jumped into the water the way an animal might

146

jump, arms outstretched, knees bent. He landed on the back of the struggling swimmer. The man who snapped out the command seemed to be preparing himself also to jump in . . .

'Suddenly, out of the bushes next to me, stepped a burly man wearing glasses. He grabbed my shoulder . . . "Get the hell out of here, Fitzgerald, or you'll be the next." It was a cockney accent. I was terrified. He meant it.'

Tearing back to their car, the two roared off on to Maresfield Road and into the night. Within a few miles the car sputtered and then glided peacefully to a halt. They had run out of petrol. After a couple of awkward moments figuring out what to do, Cadbury decided he would hike back up the road to try and find some fuel. The two men said goodbye.

When questioned about the extraordinary events of that fateful evening, Mary Hallet, her husband Les and their daughter Pauline all feel strongly that foul play was definitely involved. After all these years they are still noticeably frightened and must be gently primed to speak frankly about what went on.

Even after Mrs Hallet was informed that Frank Thorogood had died recently she looked me straight in the eye, leaned forward slightly and whispered, 'Yes, but what about the others?'

I didn't know what to say.

Of what they've revealed, however, it is clear that whatever the truth of that night, the Hallet family were witness to at least some part of it. Mrs Hallet remembers:

Mary: There was a lot of noise down there. We did hear a lot of screaming.
Geoffrey: Do you mean fun screaming?
Mary: No, no, *no*!
Geoffrey: Terrified screaming?
Mary: Yes!
Geoffrey: A man screaming? Or a woman?
Mary: I think it was a woman. My daughter said she heard screaming and I got up and went down to the bottom of the path. I was only in my nightdress so I turned around and came back in quick.
Geoffrey: What did you think had happened?
Mary: I didn't know. We thought maybe it was a raid on the place because these pop stars have raids, don't they? It was during the night. I couldn't tell you what time . . .

147

Pauline, too, backs up her mother's claims with these remarks: 'I remember there was a lot of noise. I looked out the window and saw lots of shouting and hollering going on. And I shouted to mum and dad and later we found out he had died.

'It's so sad. He used to come up to our place quite a lot and when he saw my daughter, he used to play with her. She'd get quite excited and run around. He was very, very sweet.'

Of the many wild stories that have surfaced over the years about how Brian Jones died, there have been few which seem really credible. One absolutely ridiculous scenario has Keith Richards hiding in the bushes surrounding the pool, then leaping out to push Brian into the water. Another asserts that London druglords ordered a hit on Jones when he failed to settle some very large dope debts.

In the book *Rock Diary 1983* this idea is likewise touted: 'Two gangsters were sent to put the frighteners on him. They stuck his head in a bucket of water, prompting an asthma attack. Scared, they dumped him, alive, into the pool.'

Although a large blue plastic bucket was later found by the pool, this theory doesn't really (pardon the pun) hold water, even though some, like Mary Hallet, have suggested the bucket scenario might be reasonable in light of Brian's autopsy report which says he drowned 'from immersion in fresh water'.

'I don't really see how the water in that pool could be considered fresh, with all the chemicals and that they dumped in,' she says.

This distinction, however, was dismissed by a forensic pathologist of my acquaintance, who says there is no significant difference between pool water and so-called fresh water emanating from a garden hose or some other source.

Touted too, over the years, is the equally ludicrous story that Allen Klein put out a Mafia contract on Brian to keep him from forming a group with John Lennon and also from paying him his promised £100,000 a year. It is, of course, totally false, as is the idea that Brian committed suicide over his acrimonious split with both Anita and The Stones.

More stupidity, as Ronni Money confirms: 'Brian was terrified of dying. There's no way he would have drowned himself or not fought desperately to stay afloat if he had experienced trouble . . .'

Two accounts which do seem to match up almost perfectly with what we now know first appeared in lauded author A. E. Hotchner's gripping book on The Rolling Stones, *Blown Away*. The first, an outright admission from a direct eyewitness known only as 'Marty' seems to confirm 'Joe's' story almost word for word, bringing into line the theory that the actual deed was accomplished by two or more casual labourers in the direct employ of Frank Thorogood, though certainly not his steady workers Johnny, Mo and Dave.

'There was two guys in particular had it in for Brian,' 'Marty' reveals in *Blown Away*. 'I mean, always making remarks, "the rich fag", all that kinda stuff. They used to pinch stuff off Brian all the time . . . Anyway, this night Brian was swimming a lot. He could swim good, bounce off the diving board, lots better than any of us lads and the girls was watching him, also because he was a celebrity they sort of gave him attention. These two guys got pissed about that – they was drinking pretty good by then – it was kind of like, when it started, like teasing. Sort of grabbing Brian by the leg and pulling him down, meanwhile saying bitchy things, just horsing around, but kind of rough. Sort of interfering with his swimming.

'. . . Brian tried to get out the pool and they wouldn't let him, kept pushing him back and pulling him under and then it started to get rough and these lads really got worked up at Brian the more he resisted . . . I guess they were just wanting to throw a scare into him, I don't know . . . I could tell it was turning ugly as hell.

'One lad wanted to get Brian out, but the other wouldn't let him and they was kind of tugging on him. It got real crazy and then the next thing I heard was somebody say, "He's drowned . . ." Got to our cars in one hell of a hurry and cleared out.'

Finally, Brian's longtime friend Dick Hatrell has the last word with this recollection of a long-ago conversation with one of The Walker Brothers group, while working as a barman at the Chase Hotel in Ross-on-Wye. It was in September of 1969 and at first the two men didn't recognise each other. When at last they did, however, the talk was all about their old mate, Brian.

'He said that on the evening of the night that Brian drowned, he called Brian to tell him that he and his friend were nearby and could they get together,' says Hatrell. 'Brian said that there was a party going on around the pool and invited them to join, which they did. The fellow said he did not know any of the people at the party and that it was a rough party. He said that he and his friend both felt that some of the men at the party seemed to be hostile toward Brian, I think he used the word "jealousy" to describe the feeling in the air. He said these guys were baiting Brian, poking fun at him, taunting him and at some point he saw that one man was holding Brian down in the pool. Another was clearly discernible standing on Brian's head, the fellow said, to keep him from getting out of the water. The light wasn't all that good, he said, but there was no doubt about what he saw.

'I asked him if he thought they were trying to drown him or just to scare him and simply went too far. He said there was no way for him to tell and that he and his friend left the party right away to avoid involvement . . .'

Checking up on this story in February 1993, I contacted drummer Gary Leeds, late of The Walker Brothers, who, although he admitted knowing Brian, was quite certain he wasn't present at any such party and commented that he would have certainly remembered if he'd witnessed Brian Jones's murder. The only other appreciable connection he had with Jones was drinking with the Stone a couple of times at the Ad Lib and trying (unsuccessfully) to purchase his famous Silver Cloud Rolls Royce.

'Brian wanted too much money,' says Leeds. As The Walker Brothers were a trio, that left only John Maus and lead singer Scott Walker.

Of the two, it is true that Maus used to live in Woking, which is some fifty miles from Hartfield, but unfortunately attempts to reach him at his last-known address in San Diego proved fruitless.

As for Scott Walker, he never gives interviews, so there you are. The mystery endures.

That Frank Thorogood was behind all this is, to me, now without question. Weighing up the testimony of the many people privy to Brian's last days, the one constant is their disdain for the shady builder. Just because he was unpopular though doesn't make him a murderer. The same thing applies if he was a thief, or even the lecher some say. Still, he did have the means, motive and certainly the opportunity to dispose of Jones. Even the police knew that.

It is a fact that still troubles at least one of the officers to this day. Although he now refuses to comment, at the time one of the investigators was intent on laying at least a charge of manslaughter against Thorogood, an outcome ultimately refused by those above him. But why? One can only surmise.

What our friend 'Joe' wouldn't say on tape, but did tell me privately, was that Thorogood personally instructed him and 'Frank' to 'take care of this matter' prior to Brian coming out to swim. Although the words may be slightly ambiguous, the exact nature of Thorogood's demand wasn't lost on the two yobbos, drunk as they were. And they're not lost on me. Twenty-five years on, Brian Jones's spirit cries for justice. Too many people have enjoyed their liberty for too long while a 27-year-old man lies rotting in his grave. As with the crime of murder, there is no statute of limitations on death.

'Those construction guys . . . were there with their girls . . .' Ronni Money later remarked about that final evening. 'They'd all been living off him, fake bills, not doing their work, drinking his booze, all that stuff . . . Brian was foppish, he was rich, he lived luxuriously with beautiful young women, a chauffeur drove him about in a Rolls Royce, and these workers resented him for that, sneered at him.'

Brian Jones didn't deserve to die when he did. As a child he was emotionally abandoned in a polite world of appearances and social status. As a Rolling Stone, he was paraded as a one-dimensional cardboard cut-out, when all he wanted was to be a musician. As a friend and a lover, he was lost in his own oppressive state of mind, compelled to repeat the mistakes of his past like an out-of-sync clockwork toy.

In the end, though, there was a glimmer of hope. A hope drowned in the tepid waters of his swimming pool by people intent on enriching themselves off his skinny back. In short, Brian Jones never found even a hint of justice or mercy. Not in his sweet short life, nor in his murky, murderous death.

6 AFTERMATH
The Cover-Up

BRIAN JONES WAS DEAD. His body lay floating, arms outstretched, near the bottom of the pool, a little to the right of the diving board. His mop of golden hair gently bobbing in the quiet ripples of the water. The two powerful spotlights zeroed in on his lifeless frame illuminating the pool in an artificial daylight that refocused the deadly scene in painful clarity.

There was Brian, as in life, groundless, adrift, floating between two worlds. Waiting for someone to come to the rescue and put things right.

But it was too late.

For a moment or two everyone stood quietly staring into the silver waters. Anna, her head buried in a towel, cried bitterly. Elan was first frightened, then outraged. It was his voice that cut through the night like a razor, causing several people to jump as he screamed out in his shrill American twang:

'You motherfuckers!' he cried. 'Get him out! Get him out! What the fuck are you doing? You bastards!'

Without thinking, he lunged at Thorogood, who fended him off with a single, powerful blow to the back. Elan went flying, landing on all fours on the stone patio surrounding the pool. His knees and one elbow badly scraped.

Instantly, two men were on him, grabbing him by the arms and forcibly escorting him to his car. 'Clear off!' one of them growled.

'Fuck you! You fuckin' moron,' the determined young designer spat back. 'I'm going straight to the police.'

Almost before he had finished speaking, he felt an incredible impact and then the warm thick flow of blood running down his face. Knocked backwards on to the bonnet of his small car, Elan looked up to see one of the men tossing a beer bottle through the open window of his Mini. It was then he realised he'd been bottled.

It must have been at this point that the screaming began. Screaming so loud and terrifying that the Hallet family could hear it from their house several hundred yards up Cotchford Lane. Unfortunately the exact source of the screaming has never been determined.

But whoever it was must have been, by the account of the Hallet family, deeply shocked by what they saw.

Meanwhile, Elan was fumbling desperately in his pockets for his keys.

Sensing his moment had come, he frantically flung open the door, literally dived into his car and slammed the door shut again, pushing down the lock.

Outside Elan's attacker snarled: 'You think I couldn't get you if I wanted to? Now piss off.'

With that, he turned away and disappeared into the darkness. Like Nicholas Fitzgerald a few minutes before, Elan got the hell out of there.

'When I finally got away, all I could think about was Anna and Brian,' he told me in March 1994. 'Was he really dead? Would they kill her too, to keep her quiet? I drove a couple of miles down the road and pulled over. I could hardly see for all the blood and didn't have anything in the car to use as a bandage. Eventually I pulled off my T-shirt and used that. I thought for a minute I was going to pass out, but I somehow kept it together and luckily, the gash stopped bleeding. Later, when I cleaned up I couldn't believe how small it really was. All that blood for such a little wound. I was lucky I guess, a lot luckier than Brian anyway.'

After resting in the car with the windows rolled down for a few minutes, Elan figured he'd better get to a phone and ring the police. Just then, a panda car whizzed by, its lights and siren tearing a gaping hole in the stillness of the countryside. It was then he began to think better of his plan.

'At that point, I was in Britain illegally, so I was very vulnerable. I was worried I would be drawn in, maybe arrested myself, and certainly deported. I was dealing smack at the time as well, and was secretly pretty strung out. Brian didn't know. He wouldn't have let me in his house if he had. I was holding too, that night. I had a good quarter-ounce of amazingly pure China White that wasn't even mine. What was I supposed to do with it? I sure couldn't keep it on me, and if I stashed it somewhere it could get wet, stolen, or even staked out by the law. Obviously, the police had already been called, so I figured Anna must be all right.

'And Brian, well, Brian was already dead so there was nothing I could do to help him now. I told myself I would go home and make an anonymous call to the police, just to tell them what happened. Then I started thinking, I was really the only one who made a fuss when they were working over poor Brian. Everybody else just went dead quiet and got the hell out of there. If any heat came down on Thorogood I'd be the first one he'd come looking for.

'When I finally made it back to my flat, I had a quick wash and then shot-up in the bedroom. The next thing I knew, it was four o'clock the next afternoon and the papers were all buzzing about Brian's death. By then, I figured it was history, so why should I stick my neck out? The cops hated Brian anyway. I'm sure they were as much involved in covering it up as anybody. The only one that stood to lose was me, and I was just too fucked up at the time to really give a damn. *Now*, of course I feel like fuckin' shit about it. Which is why I'm telling my story. But at the time, I was probably more fucked up than Brian.'

After Elan was hustled away, Brian's body was fished out and neatly laid by the pool, a towel under his head.

Speculation had it that Joan Fitzsimmons may have been called in to shuttle certain people off the premises before the police and the ambulance were called. Several months later, when a local man from Chichester was detained by police in connection with another matter, he gave information to DCI Marshall in Lewes Prison, relating to this provocative idea.

On 26 August, the *Daily Express* ran a story indicating that Ms Fitzsimmons might have unwittingly been used by the killers to clear the premises of at least some of the people responsible.

In a piece headed, 'Brian Jones Death: New Probe', it stated: 'New information on the circumstances surrounding the death of Rolling Stone Brian Jones is being studied by the Director of Public Prosecutions. A report compiled by detectives in Chichester, Sussex, may lead to a new inquiry into the pop star's death at his home near Hartfield. The key to the new investigation is a woman patient who is critically ill in a Chichester hospital. She is Mrs Joan Fitzsimmons, a local taxi-driver, who was a regular chauffeur to The Rolling Stones. Detectives want to find out from her whom she drove on the night 27-year-old Jones died – 3 July. And if she was present at Jones's home at any time during the fatal evening.'

Amazingly, this faint glimmer of hope for the continued investigation into Brian's death was scotched when Inspector Laurence Finlay, head of the Sussex CID, commented the very next day in the same paper that the police had 'no interest' in the case, but had made 'inquiries' into 'rumours surrounding Jones's death and found them *without foundation*'.

A cryptic remark tucked away at the bottom of the article read: 'Jones's name had come up several times during their inquiries into a serious case. This was a case of attempted murder which took place after the death of Jones.'

Could they have been referring to Joan Fitzsimmons? She was after all, as the paper said, 'critically ill' in hospital. Perhaps she herself might have been attacked by someone intent on keeping her quiet.

Unfortunately, Fitzsimmons has not been heard from for the last twenty-five years. Her story, however, would certainly be fascinating. Another tantalising brick in the wall.

Even the ever-sceptical Keith Richards was convinced that at the very least several people were moved out of there in a hurry that evening. If true, a reality that makes everyone who claimed to have been there potentially guilty of perjury, if nothing more.

'I still take all the stories from that night with a pinch of salt,' says Richards. 'I've no doubt it's the same with anybody when those things happen. There's a crowd of people, then suddenly there's nobody there. Instead of trying to help the guy, they think of their own skins and run. I don't really know what went on that night. I know there was a lot of people there and suddenly there wasn't and that's about it.

'We had these chauffeurs working for us and we tried to find out. Some of them had a weird hold over Brian. There were a lot of chicks there and there was a whole thing going on, they were having a party. I don't know what happened to Brian that night.'

'There was no one there that'd want to murder him. Somebody didn't take care of him and they should have because he had someone there who was supposed to take care of him, everyone knew what Brian was like, especially at a party. Maybe he did just go in for a swim and have an asthma attack. I'd never seen Brian have an attack. I know that he was asthmatic, I know that he was hung up with his spray, but I've never seen him have an attack.

'He was really easing back from the whole drug thing. He wasn't hitting 'em like he had been; he wasn't hitting *anything* like he had. Maybe the combination of things. It's one of those things I just can't find out. You know, who do you ask?

'. . . "Brian, how could you do that to me, man?" It was like that.

'We were completely shocked about his death. I got straight into it and wanted to know who was there and couldn't find out. The only cat I could ask was the one who I think got rid of everybody and did the whole disappearing trick so when the cops arrived, it was just an accident. Maybe it was. Maybe the cat just wanted to get everyone out of the way so it wasn't all our names involved, etc. Maybe he did the right thing, but I don't know. I don't even know who was there that night and finding out is impossible.

'Maybe he tried to pull one of his deep-diving stunts and was too loaded and hit his chest and that was it. But I've seen Brian swim in terrible conditions, in the sea with breakers up to here. I've been underwater with Brian in Fiji. He was all right then. He was a goddamn good swimmer, and it's very hard to believe he could have died in a swimming pool.

'But goddammit, to find out is impossible. And especially with him not being officially one of The Stones then, none of our people were in direct contact so it was trying to find out who was around Brian at that moment, who he had there. It's the same feeling with who killed Kennedy. You can't get to the bottom of it.

'He was surrounded by the wrong kind of people. Jimi Hendrix was the same way. He just couldn't suss the arseholes from the good people. He wouldn't kick out somebody that was a shit. He'd let them sit there, and maybe they'd be thinking how to sell-off his possessions. He'd give 'em booze and feed 'em, and they'd be thinking, "Oh, that's worth two hundred and fifty quid and I can roll that up and take it away." I don't know.'

Strangely, as the spirit moved him, Richards's take on the tragedy seemed to oscillate according to his mood. In the 1992 biography, *Keith Richards*, he had this to say: 'I wasn't surprised about Brian. I didn't wish him dead and *there were a few guys who did*, but in all honesty it was no surprise. And it was hard to shed a tear at his demise, quite honestly. It was like, "Wow, he's gone, thank God!" Cold-blooded as that sounds, he was a passenger for us. We had to cover his ass. We all revere his memory and nobody deserves to go that young. But if anybody asked for it, he did. You don't leave The Stones singing, you just get carried out. Brian was already effectively dead when he died, he was already out of the band.'

Here then emerges one of the greatest mysteries of this strange case; whether Tom Keylock was present at Cotchford Farm on the night of the murder. Once again, his public pronouncements over the last two-plus decades say he was not. As does his statement to the police. I too would have been willing to leave it at that, except for the man himself telling me otherwise on two separate occasions, and in front of witnesses.

The first time I became aware of the controversy surrounding Keylock's whereabouts was, as I've said, in my London hotel. Mr Keylock showed up on a Sunday afternoon around 3 p.m., along with Pat Andrews, Terry Rawlings, Reg Pippit, Toronto Stones collector Jerry Stone and another long-haired chap (also from Toronto) whose name I was not given. As my daughter Sesa and I sat there chatting with Tom and Terry (the other four had positioned themselves just across from us on the other side of the lounge and ordered coffee), Keylock, in answer to my question about how Brian might have died said this:

'Well, I was out there by the pool with him and went inside for a cigarette. When I came back three minutes later he had drowned.'

At that point I hadn't really studied the case in any great detail and so was not yet apprised that Tom wasn't supposed to have been there. As a result, I simply pressed on casually, asking a few more questions.

'Yeah, but three minutes doesn't really seem like enough time to drown does it? I mean, can someone actually die that quickly?'

'Okay, so maybe it was five,' he said, shrugging his weighty shoulders.

'Five minutes seems a bit light, too, don't you think?' I countered innocently.

'Look, it might have even been ten, you know? It was a long time ago.'

With that, Terry Rawlings, who was sitting next to me on the couch extended his left hand to Keylock saying only, 'Oy,' quite softly under his breath. It was clearly a sign for Mr Keylock to change the subject, which he promptly did.

After they left I asked my daughter to repeat back to me, word for word, exactly what transpired, and she did. So, for what it's worth, I pass on the information.

The next occasion when Tom Keylock seemed to suffer a similar lapse of memory when discussing the events of 3 July, took place during our taped interview of December 1993. When asked if he thought Frank Thorogood had anything at all to do with a plot to kill Brian, he stated emphatically:

'None at all. None at all. I'll tell you here and now, Frank left him to get a cigarette. He was swimming. He said, "I'm going to get a cigarette." Brian said, "Okay." He was at the end of the pool. First of all he told Frank, "I've had a couple of sleepers, I've had a few brandies, I'm gonna swim." Frank said, "I wouldn't advise it." "No, no," he said, "I'm all right. It's only five minutes." Frank left to get a cigarette and Janet Lawson, she was a registered nurse says, "Where's Brian?" He says, "The pool." "Well, keep your eye on him." He says, "I'm getting a cigarette, I'll go back." *And when I come back*, when *he* comes back he looked around, looked in the pool, he was up this end. The end towards the house so he'd probably gone from one end to the other. Personally, I think it was booze, pills and he probably had an asthma attack because the water was real hot. He'd had the heating on for three days, it was very, very hot.' Interestingly, Mr Keylock uses the phrase 'When *I* come back' and then instantly corrects himself.

After everyone was removed from the scene, Thorogood at last got on the phone to the cops. By 12.10 a.m. both the ambulance and the law had arrived on the scene, but where was Keylock? If, as he has alternately insisted, he wasn't about, then one wonders where indeed he was. Mr Keylock himself kindly answered the question during our interview.

Tom: [Keith] said, 'Hey, I've forgot my guitar.' So I went all the way back to Redlands to pick some guitars up and then that's when I found . . . the first person to know about it was my wife.
Geoffrey: Did you go home?
Tom: No, no, no.
Geoffrey: You rang her?
Tom: Frank Thorogood phoned my wife to find out where I was, if she knew. 'As far as I know they're recording at Olympic Studios.' And then she phoned Olympic and asked for Stew and told Stew then.
Geoffrey: When did you find out?
Tom: Halfway up from there I got pulled by the police. They knew the car and they give me a pull . . .
Geoffrey: For speeding?
Tom: No, no. To tell me to go over there, something's gone wrong.
Geoffrey: Who called the police to tell them that?
Tom: The police already knew.
Geoffrey: Oh, I see, they'd been there and they went . . .
Tom: To see where I was.
Geoffrey: Thorogood must have said, 'Hey, we've got to try and get in touch with Keylock and they just pulled you over, right?

Tom: That's right.
Geoffrey: What did you think when they told you?
Tom: I couldn't believe it. And I said, 'You're winding me up.' And they said, 'No, we wouldn't do that, Mr Keylock.' So I said, 'Ta-rah.' Matter of fact, I pulled away so fast I nearly run over his foot. Went straight there.
Geoffrey: And when you got to Cotchford Farm what was the scene you found?
Tom: The cops were out and about, Frank, and then there was Anna Wohlin, the Swedish girl . . .
Geoffrey: You drove your own car back or you came with the taxi driver?
Tom: No, I had Keith's Bentley. I used to drive that all the time.
Geoffrey: Oh, so you drove yourself back to Cotchford?
Tom: Mmmm.

Once again there is controversy, as most published sources insist that Tom Keylock and Les Perrin arrived together at Cotchford at 3.30 a.m. Mr Keylock, however, makes no mention of this. Still, as investigators later recalled the two men walking together by the pool, we can at least assume that they both eventually made it to the scene. Exactly how and when, however, we don't yet know.

The first officer to turn up at Cotchford Farm that evening was Police Constable Albert Evans. In a statement made that same day he described what he found: 'At 12.10 a.m. on Thursday, 3 July, as a result of information received, I went to Cotchford Mill Farm, Hartfield.

'I was shown to a garden swimming pool about thirty-five yards to the rear of the farmhouse. On the pool edge I saw the body of a man on its back with the head slightly raised by a towel. The body was clothed in [black] swimming trunks.

'At the side of the pool I saw a Riker Hodihaler.

'Ambulance attendants were applying resuscitation.

'I went to the house and took possession of half a bottle of brandy, four-fifths consumed; a bottle of vodka, two-thirds consumed, and half a bottle of whisky, half consumed.

'I also took possession of a number of bottles which contained or had contained various types of pills.

'Dr Evans of Hartfield pronounced life extinct in my presence and I accompanied the deceased to the Queen Victoria Hospital, East Grinstead, where I formally identified the body to Dr Sachs, Pathologist, who conducted a postmortem in my presence.'

For PC Evans to confiscate the bottles of booze and pills as evidence was certainly called for, as both drugs and alcohol were later reported as prime factors in Jones's death.

One account from that night has PC Evans confronting Les Perrin, accusing him of deliberately dropping an inhaler by the edge of the pool so that the police would find it and assume that Brian had indeed, suffered an asthma attack.

'A clever trick, Mr Perrin,' he was reported as saying slyly as he bent over to pick it up. Les Perrin's response was unfortunately not recorded.

After the authorities hauled off Brian's body to the morgue they apparently cleared out, not coming back until late the next afternoon. Once again, a serious breach of basic investigative procedure. At this point, no one could be sure if Brian's death was indeed murder, so erring on the side of caution the assumption should have been made that foul play was involved. As such the 'crime scene' should have been roped off, the house locked, a guard posted and everyone escorted off the property. At least until daylight, when a proper search could take place.

Instead, the police simply left, leaving anyone free to do anything they wanted.

The early morning hours after the cops left are still very much unreported. We know that Anna went to bed at about 5.30 a.m. with the help of a sedative and that someone ordered that Brian's mass of expensive clothes be brought outside and burned. Terry Rawlings thinks this must have occurred around 8.30 a.m., but my sources indicate that 7.30 a.m. is the more likely hour, especially in view of the hordes of London media which would surely be heading down to cover the big story.

One imagines having the press witness this little scene wouldn't have really gone down very well.

At any rate, whoever ordered it and whenever it happened, Jones's clothes were definitely burned, along with many of his private papers, his Bible and other personal effects. Surely this act alone was actionable by the authorities. It could be interpreted as deliberately destroying evidence.

In *Golden Stone*, gardener Mick Martin remembers: 'A group of men were burning an enormous amount of stuff. I know, because I had a very nice little Bible and they'd flung that on too. Well, I wasn't having that and went immediately and got it out. But, yes, they were burning Brian's things, his clothes, shirts and what have you. I don't know on whose say so, but they cleared no end of stuff out of his house and burned the lot.'

Although Laura Jackson claims Brian's personal effects were burned following Jones's funeral on 10 July, both Mary Hallet and Terry Rawlings insist that it was, indeed, on the morning of the third that the incident occurred.

Mrs Hallet remembers: 'I think the workmen were there and they were burning it when Mick [Martin] arrived. They said that his parents wanted it burnt . . . I know the workmen took a lorry of iron gates. Inside the house a room was done on one side with iron work. The gate I've got at the top of my steps was the back door. They gave me that. I'd told Mr Jones they'd given it to me and he said, "That's all right, you can have it." Mr Jones later gave me a lovely screen I've got in the other room.'

Terry Rawlings meanwhile, puts a slightly different spin on the events of that morning, claiming that Lewis Jones was perhaps behind the bonfire. In all honesty however, it seems highly unlikely. Mr Jones may have had his troubles with Brian, but he was certainly nobody's fool and as such it doesn't really seem plausible that he would seek to derail any investigation into the death of his only son. Above all, Lewis Jones was a scrupulously honest person and very much a man of his word.

Tom Keylock fervently disavows any knowledge of the fire.

Geoffrey: What about this Michael Martin, the gardener?
Tom: Yeah, what about him?
Geoffrey: It's been said that Lewis Jones told you to tell him to burn the clothes.
Tom: No.

Also taken away that morning was at least one truck-load of Brian's antiques, expensive sound equipment, art work and other household furnishings. Some say Lewis Jones instructed Thorogood to make the arrangements and do the work. Storing away Jones's worldly goods for the protection of the estate. Others, however, insist it was blatant thievery with Thorogood spiriting away everything of real value before Mr Jones could get his bearings and thus, take possession of his son's property.

To this day, the looting of Cotchford is still the topic of speculation amongst locals who had definite suspicions about who and what was behind it. 'I went down late that first afternoon,' says one such person who asked not to be identified, 'and there was quite a bit missing. I'd been down there a lot to see Brian and I knew the layout of the place quite well. When I looked through the window of his music studio, I asked one of the workmen I spotted out in the garden, "Where are all his guitars?"

' "Too bad about Mr Jones, isn't it?" he answered.

' "Yes it is," I replied. That was all I could get out of him. His lips, as they say, were sealed.'

That is not to say that everything was taken away immediately. Mr Johns, Cotchford's current owner, addressed the issue when I interviewed him at the farm late in 1993. 'I wasn't particularly a Rolling Stones fan and it was not widely publicised that it was Brian's house. They wanted to sell it quietly . . . The skulduggery going on that I could smell, but couldn't see, was colossal. . . .

'And they were so busy ripping the place apart. This place was semi-furnished when I first looked at it and they said, "Yeah, it goes with all the kit." By the time I bought it, there wasn't a thing in it but the carpets. The dining-room had some genuine good period furniture in it. . . . He was being ripped off in a huge sort of way.'

Getting back to Anna Wohlin, although she was reportedly fast asleep it seems she was *compos mentis* enough to make at least one phonecall, as Jim Carter-Fea recalls in *Blown Away*:

'Anna telephoned me early in the morning after Brian died. She said that someone had insisted that Anna and Linda Lawrence leave England immediately. Linda was Anna's best friend and Anna had probably phoned her that night. But before she hung up, Anna told me that Brian had not been doing drugs that evening, that he had had a couple of drinks, but he wasn't at all drunk and that he had been in a very good, up mood because he was happy with his music at the time.

'Anna said that she had gone to sleep and at some point came downstairs. She found two people standing by the pool looking down at Brian in the water. Anna said she dived in and tried to fish him out.

The others just stood there watching. Perhaps someone wanted to get her out of the country so that this story couldn't come out.

'I was so upset about all this that I went to see a man I know in parliament, but he said I was just banging my head against a brick wall.'

Around 9.30 or 10.00 a.m. the press started arriving. Only a couple of photographers at first and then dozens, maybe even a hundred of Fleet Street's finest, all stepping over each other to get the story. Outside, Tom Keylock did his best to keep them all at bay. But it was tough. Obviously, they all wanted a shot of the pool and wouldn't take no for an answer.

Within minutes, what was left of the possible crime scene was a joke.

Meanwhile, inside the house Anna was scared. She couldn't bear to speak to Thorogood. But there she was. Holed up with him, frightened, tired and very much alone. She wanted to leave. Leave for good. On that point anyway, she and Mr Thorogood were in complete agreement.

Within a few minutes Joan Fitzsimmons arrived and escorted Anna to her minicab, which was waiting at the other side of the garden on a small back road. She wanted to get her things, but Frank said, no, there wasn't time. Tom would see to that later on. She had no choice but to comply.

'They took her away through the orchard,' recalls Mrs Hallet. 'She was taken away lickety-split, like that. And she went to stay with Bill Wyman for two or three days.'

Mary Hallet was by now quite certain that something was terribly wrong, though she didn't know just what. She went to work at her regular time and was met at the top of the drive by Keylock. Mrs Hallet was then quickly ushered into the house where he told her about Brian.

'I carried on as if it were a usual morning,' she says. 'I got dressed and went down. I was told to keep my mouth shut and say nothing. If I was asked any questions, to just say nothing. But no one asked me any, so it didn't make any difference.'

As word went out that Rolling Stone Brian Jones had drowned in his swimming pool from a deadly combination of drink, drugs and an untimely asthma attack his killers breathed a deep sigh of relief.

The older generation had a field day in the media holding up Jones as example to their cries for a return to 'traditional' values. Meanwhile, the majority of the police were only too pleased to put the whole episode down to Brian's well known self-destructive nature. Everyone just shook their heads and carried on. After all, one less Rolling Stone in this world wasn't exactly bad news for a very large portion of the population. It was a perfect scenario for nearly everyone but Brian.

When I asked Tom Keylock what he thought was the root cause of Jones's decline he had a quick answer.

'Too many pills. We all know [he got them on] prescription, but he could get them anytime. I was against it . . . [Tony] Sanchez didn't get too near me . . . I don't like him for what he done. He was there for the money and drug pushing. I used to keep him away as much as I could, but there was no way I could do anything about it . . . The way [Brian] treated his body and what he was taking, there's no man that's gonna survive that. Keith, he got over his problems, but he was a harder man. A much fitter man. His brain was a lot stronger. Brian was a very weak and mild man. He only used to get a bit violent when he was on drugs.'

If that's so, I asked Tom, and he was Brian's minder, then why didn't he intervene and try and set him straight?

Geoffrey: Couldn't you have just grabbed him and said, 'Listen, you've got to stop . . .'
Tom: I've told him, I've told him!
Geoffrey: 'You've got to stop or you'll die!'
Tom: You're telling me something I've done a thousand times!
Geoffrey: What would he say?
Tom: 'I'll be all right, I'll be all right.' In one ear and out the other. Oh no, I could see it. I could see [it], probably long before they did. Keith used to say, 'Don't worry about me, you . . . go look after him like. Keep your eye on him.'

While the press was in full gear tearing up the garden at Cotchford, Dr Albert Sachs was silently cutting a thin red line into Jones's chest with a scalpel in the morgue at Queen Victoria Hospital, East Grinstead. Opening up the young musician like a melon, the good doctor performed what we now know to be only the most perfunctory of autopsies, ultimately coming to some very unlikely, but nevertheless, highly quotable conclusions on the cause of death.

Although the local coroner's office were initially resistant to supplying the official documents relating to Brian's death, I later asked an associate to contact the cabinet office, historical records section, only to receive the following reply from a very charming young lady with the ironic name of Pat Andrews.

It read in part: 'I have now heard from the Home Office that Coroners' records are covered by an Order from the Lord Chancellor (No 68 dated 16 April 1984). This allows the Coroner to close the records for seventy-five years to protect personally sensitive material from premature public release. Access to records within this period is entirely a matter for the Coroner . . .

'Mr Giuliano also mentions a Home Office report. I am afraid I have had little success here either. Without more detailed information about such a report, who originated it and when, to whom it was sent, title, reference numbers (if any), it simply is not possible to trace it. If Mr Giuliano could provide any of this information the Home Office would gladly carry out a search. However, as you will know, under the Public Records Acts 1958 and 1967, public records are not made generally available for thirty years after their creation. Individual requests for access before thirty years are, of course, given careful consideration, but I am afraid that access to a report of this kind could not be guaranteed even if it could be located.'

After a lot of transcontinental to-ing and fro-ing (including a polite call by my publisher to the standing coroner), a small envelope eventually landed on my doormat some weeks later, containing the mature fruit of the investigation into Mr Jones's death. Underwhelmed, I was at first despondent as what was there was pretty thin. Still, interwoven amongst the various police reports, witness statements and medical findings was some genuinely insightful commentary.

In one document dated 7 July 1969, Dr Sachs revealed that even Brian's psychiatrist was aware that Jones was cutting back on the use of prescription drugs. Those same drugs others would have you believe he was gulping down like Elvis in the mirrored bathroom of Graceland.

Headed 'SUDDEN DEATH – BRIAN JONES', the half-page report went on to say: 'Dr Greenburgh stated that the deceased's drug requirements were becoming less and he had shown considerable improvement of late. Prescriptions were made in small quantities at frequent intervals rather than large prescriptions, which, experience had shown, resulted in the deceased taking larger doses.'

Still, the unsavoury pall of drug addiction clung to Jones like a second skin. Within twenty-four hours of his death it was already a foregone conclusion in the minds of millions that like Beatles' manager, Brian Epstein, comedian Lenny Bruce, and so many others in the business, Jones had left this life on a roller coaster high that simply swept him away. But it was a lie.

As copies of Jones's 9 July death certificate were released to the press, the terrible news printed there in black and white validated the slander and gossip that boldly overtook anything the man ever accomplished in life. Under 'cause of death' it states:

I a   Drowning
  b   Immersion in fresh water
II   Severe liver dysfunction due to fatty degeneration and the
      ingestion of alcohol and drugs. *Swimming whilst under the
      influence of alcohol and drugs. Misadventure*

Twenty-five years later it is now believed that only the first two points are indeed accurate. Yes, Brian Jones did most certainly drown. And yes, it was in fresh water. Beyond that, we should not rush to judgement.

On 7 March 1994, Dr Cyril H. Wecht, perhaps the world's most eminent forensic pathologist and the author of the internationally best selling book, *Cause of Death*, kindly agreed to examine the documents in question with an eye towards rendering an opinion on the nature of Brian's death based on the scientific data contained therein.

One of the first points he made was that at the time of Jones's death the only drugs found in his body were in his urine. And why is that important? Because by the time a drug – any drug – breaks down and enters the urine it is impossible to have any effect whatsoever on the individual in question. In other words, Jones was *not* high. Not at all.

As for the alcohol so widely trumpeted as of enormous importance in the Stone's demise, Brian only registered a scant 0.14 blood alcohol level. An amount Dr Wecht assures me would inflict little or no impairment for a seasoned drinker like Jones.

'. . . it really would not have produced any significant compromise,' he told me emphatically. 'A chronic drinker can handle a 0.14. You and I and other observers might not even be aware that such a person had done any drinking. A non-drinker with a 0.14 might get a little drowsy or behave in a strange fashion, but not a chronic alcohol abuser such as Brian Jones.'

On the night he died Brian was simply not drunk. He'd certainly had a drink but his tolerance was proportionally high and the effect would have been very minimal. As for the popular notion that a combination of drugs and booze were his undoing, Jones plainly wasn't on drugs.

In support of Dr Wecht's findings, here is a lab report dated 7 July 1969, made over the phone by a Mr Cook, a biochemist at the Royal Sussex Hospital in Brighton, presumably to Dr Sachs. It read in part:

1 *Blood barbiturate*	Nil
2 *Blood alcohol*	140 mgs (Approx 7 whiskies, or 3½ pints of beer)
3 *Urine*	Amphetamine like substance 1720 micro-gms. These figures suggest ingestion of a fairly large quantity of a drug
4 *Thin layer chromatography*	Failed to reveal the presence of the following in an unchanged state (a) Amphetamine (b) Methedrine (c) Morphine (d) Methadone (e) Isoprenaline

Read carefully, it states very clearly that other than the relatively insignificant amount of alcohol noted there were *no drugs whatsoever* affecting Jones's system in any way at the time of death.

Now as to the fatty degeneration of the liver which some suggest might have been responsible, Dr Wecht feels that too is a misdiagnosis in this case. 'Although sometimes we say fatty livers can result in sudden death, that's usually in chronic alcoholics who are in a poor state of nutrition, whose health is bad. It's not a diagnosis of death that I would consider at all in this case.'

The other alleged contributing factor to Brian's death is, of course, the infamous asthma attack. Or rather, the attack that never was. Curiously, although it was widely reported in the media, neither Dr Sachs nor his colleagues ever said that asthma was in any way part of the cause of Jones's death. Case in point, a section of the doctor's 5 July 1969 letter to Dr C. Sommerville, coroner for East Grinstead.

'. . . As the interval between his last being seen alive and found in the bottom of the pool face-downwards was only five minutes. I feel it unlikely that he had had an attack of asthma at the time of death.'

Later, at the official inquest held on 7 July 1969, Dr Sachs gave testimony on this very issue:

Coroner: What are the postmortem signs of an attack of asthma?
Dr Sachs: Haemorrhages into the lungs. Lungs bulky, light, and voluminous. Lung collapses when incised. Rib markings. No evidence of water in lung tissue. Bronchial bile – casts of viscid mucus present. In this case, the lungs were heavy and exuding water.

The significance of Jones's lungs being saturated with water is twofold. It certainly proves that he did, in fact, drown, but it also points away from Brian's asthma having anything at all to do with it. Once again, Dr Wecht: 'I don't find evidence in what is set forth to suggest that Mr Jones had an acute asthmatic attack. Furthermore, if we look at it from the standpoint of Jones being a good swimmer, and we've already discussed the fact that he was not under the influence of drugs and so on, there's no reason why, even if he had had an asthmatic attack in a pool, that he would not have been able to simply swim over to the edge and climb out. . . . For an accomplished swimmer that's only three or four strokes, and an asthmatic attack doesn't wipe you out like a massive stroke or a large heart attack. You can swim three, four strokes even if you can't breathe. You'll accomplish that in a couple of seconds and then you're over at the side holding on.'

Of course, once you've successfully ruled out drugs, booze, asthma and liver failure as the cause of death what else is there? Obviously, only Brian swimming along happily in his pool when he suddenly, and quite inexplicably, drowns in the company of several other people. Or murder.

According to all the witness statements, both mouth-to-mouth resuscitation and external, cardiac massage were carried out, but why didn't Brian respond? Tom Keylock initially told me Jones was in the water for only three minutes. The Police say around five. Within that limited time-frame Brian should, in some measure anyway, have responded to resuscitation.

'If he was only in there for three minutes then there's no way he would have drowned because you can live without oxygen for four, five, even six minutes,' Dr Wecht explained. 'He might have had some neurological deficit as a residual effect, but he should not have been unresponsive to resuscitative measures at three minutes or so.'

'I can't rule out the possibility that one or more people may have brought about his drowning by playing games with him, continuing to dunk him, pulling him under and making him swallow water. After a while, even though you may be a good swimmer, as Brian Jones pur-portedly was, if you are not permitted to breathe and you begin to swallow water, then you may drown . . .' In Dr Sachs's postmortem notes several key remarks stick in one's mind, the first of which is that other than Brian being slightly overweight, his general health wasn't really all that bad:

Generative organs, breasts,   Normal for age.
prostate, etc.
Are all other organs healthy? Apparently.

When I spoke to musician Gary Leeds of The Walker Brothers, he told me that after Brian died, rumour had it amongst the in-crowd in Lon-don that when 'they opened him up' Jones had the body of 'a sixty-year-old man'. The tender beginnings of a magnificent, savage myth.

Of course, for those with an interest in maintaining the status quo, there is still much fodder. Also, in the postmortem is the statement that no overt evidence of violence was apparent on the body of Brian Jones.

'If you have a set up whereby someone can be pulled under the water in some fashion and you can do so without inflicting injuries to the individual,' says Dr Wecht, 'it's a diabolically clever way to kill some-body . . .

'But as far as looking at a body and doing an autopsy where the per-son has drowned and that person has been, let's say, pulled under by a frogman or held under by two or three people so they can't struggle. No, you can't look at that body and say this person was homicidally drowned. No way.'

For those with an eye to proving that Brian somehow just magically slipped away when no one was looking, there is amazingly little evi-dence to support this view. A deep look at all the materials, both medical and anecdotal, clearly suggests that Brian was indeed killed as opposed to simply dying. I strongly urge the reader to carefully study both the full content of my conversation with Dr Wecht in the appendices of this book as well as the original documents pertinent to this case.

One person very close to the current groundswell of interest in Brian Jones's amazing life and times is author Terry Rawlings. When we talked in December1993, he touched on the increasingly strange particulars of Brian's death:

Geoffrey: Had he gone swimming alone, with no one else there, would he be dead?
Terry: No, of course not.
Geoffrey: So other people were involved in him leaving the world?
Terry: Yeah, definitely . . . Something happened, something definitely happened.
Geoffrey: Laura Jackson put it this way, 'Brian wasn't meant to die that night.' Is that fair comment?
Terry: Yeah, I think so . . . I don't think he died of natural causes . . . something definitely happened that resulted in his death . . . He just didn't go in the pool and die in like a minute flat or something . . .
Geoffrey: Frank Thorogood and the builders certainly could have been involved. They were the only other people there, right?
Terry: As far as we know . . . A lot of local people over the period he lived there were invited back so who knows if they were there or not . . .
Geoffrey: Do you think someone was harassing him and they just kind of held him under a little too long?
Terry: Maybe [they] even pushed [him] in. You can easily lose your breath that way . . . there's an old army trick that by pulling people backwards underwater it fills up their lungs. It's like piercing a bottle of beer . . . you can take in a lot of water really quickly . . .
Geoffrey: Is that what you think happened?
Terry: It's a possibility . . . I think the whole thing is down to the class structure of England. [Brian] would have been perceived by these builders as being a middle class, twenty-seven-year-old millionaire squandering all his dough. He's got these working-class builders [with] kids at home and they know their time's up . . . They've got the good life for a while [but] it's gonna be taken from them very quickly. They're going to resent him even more . . . I think more than anything it was a result of a building of that resentment over the months . . . [Brian] getting out of bed at twelve o'clock and them being there at eight working. If you look into the class thing in this country, and back

then it would have been even worse, that holds the key to Brian Jones's death . . .

Geoffrey: Do you think Thorogood alone was involved?

Terry: I think Frank was definitely involved in the cover-up . . . The biggest fuck up in that whole story is the routine of phone calls that was made.

Supporting the idea that Brian was indeed murdered is a well-known industry insider who was there at the very beginning of the so-called Swinging London scene, and seemed to be close friends with just about everybody. The Beatles, The Stones, The Who, Jimi Hendrix, you name it, this guy claims he was right there smoking, joking, partying and making deals alongside the newly rich and famous elite of the pop world. Three decades later he is still dealing with these people on almost a daily basis, although in a slightly different capacity. Fortunately, he agreed to talk to me for this book. Unfortunately, he feels he still has too much to lose by allowing me to use his real, instantly recognisable name.

The man I'll call Sean explains why: 'No one would say anything, man. You see with the police in England, you've got to understand how it works there. The police force was formed to protect the gentlemen from the scallywags. It's important you know that. When something happens to people who have money, you know, they might die of cirrhosis of the liver, but they call it pneumonia on the death certificate. People took whoever's word was given.

'I mean, Brian was found drowned in the pool. He had a reputation for being pretty out of his brain. It was all a big mistake. You see, at that time there were the yobs, and then there were the managers and the fucking real hard-core guys who were always causing trouble in one form or another and had loads of money. We were all making so much money and there was great resentment from the working-class types. It was like, "You fucking long-haired bastards!" And I think Brian fell foul of that when no one was looking at that party.

'There were several of them there. But everybody fucking left the minute the word went out. Everybody split. Someone said, "Brian's face down in the pool!" And everyone just freaked. It was just a bunch of fucking yobs who resented this young guy, who's good looking, had all this pussy, all this success, fame and notoriety and all the drugs and the big beautiful house. They resented it, these working class assholes.

And they took advantage of him when he could be taken advantage of. And they fucking blew it, man, you know?'

Although Sean wasn't personally present on the night of Brian's death, he was close friends with Suki Potier who told him all about it in person the very next day, briefed as she was by Nicholas Fitzgerald and several others at the party. Strangely, at the time anyway, Potier wasn't really allowing her emotions to break through regarding Brian. 'I used to see Suki on and off all the time,' recalls Sean. 'I think actually, she was a little bit flawed in some way, or unemotional about it. She was really upset about what happened, but I mean, it wasn't like, "Oh, I'm shattered, man." That one. It wasn't any big fucking movie.'

As Dr Sachs was finishing the postmortem on Brian, the police were busy compiling statements from the principals and trying to figure out exactly what happened.

By the time they got round to returning to Cotchford that afternoon they were very unhappy at what they found. In addition to the crime scene being almost totally decimated by the deadline-hungry media, Thorogood had engineered a clean sweep of the premises, prompting one angry official to personally lock up the house and deliver the keys to Mary Hallet with the stern warning: 'Don't let anyone in that house. If anyone turns up give us a call and we'll come down and sort them out. In the meantime, this property is strictly off limits by order of the Sussex Police. We'd appreciate it if you'd inform us if you see anyone poking around down there.' Mrs Hallet promised them she would.

While the officer was walking back in the direction of Cotchford, one of his colleagues was just finishing taking Tom Keylock's statement over the great oak table in the dining room. Signed in the presence of DCI Marshall at 4 p.m. on 3 July, it emphasised his late employer's alleged drug use, making way for the storm of adverse publicity already gathering momentum around the world.

'I am the tour manager for The Rolling Stones and until four weeks ago Brian Jones was a member of that group, but I continued to look after his interests under the order of Rolling Stones Ltd. He was making tentative arrangements to form a new group.

'I have known Brian for four and a half years. He has always been of a restless, nervous disposition.

'For some time Brian has been under treatment from Dr Greenburgh of 73 Eaton Place, Belgravia, who to my knowledge regularly prescribed tranquillisers and sleeping pills. He also had a supply of "black bombers", but these were restricted on doctor's orders. He always described his sleeping tablets as "sleepers".

'Brian was a good drinker and enjoyed beer as well as spirits such as vodka and brandy. There were occasions when he became under the influence but I have seen him really drunk yet able to swim proficiently.

'Brian was subject to asthma attacks and was issued with an inhaler.'

All very interesting stuff, of course, and on the surface quite true. But on the night Brian Jones died he was clean. A fact at least one officer was very well aware of.

'I'm well retired now and I don't want to get involved,' one of the investigating team told me over the phone late in 1993. 'There were several of us who wanted to bring a charge of manslaughter against Mr Thorogood and one other of his associates. If it had been up to me, we would have. Murder would have been difficult to prove. But manslaughter was certainly an option. An option that someone at the top didn't care to exercise. It still makes me mad when I think about it, but then as now, it's out of my hands.'

By the late afternoon of 3 July, Lewis Jones had been awake for more than twenty-four hours. As he made his way through the bowels of the Queen Victoria Hospital to the morgue to formally identify his son's body he felt slightly nauseous.

Entering the musty, chrome-lined room, he was immediately hit by the overpowering odour of formaldehyde. He choked back hard, but not so that anyone would notice. After a couple of forgotten words to the officers who escorted him, he took the three or four tentative steps necessary to position himself next to the flat metal table that held his heir.

'There are, I'm afraid, some brief formalities, Mr Jones,' one of them said politely. 'I must ask you, sir, is this the body of your son, Lewis Brian Hopkin-Jones?' Pulling back the bright yellow plastic sheet that covered Brian's bloated body, the officer searched the old man's face for some sign of recognition.

'Yes. Yes, it is,' Jones finally answered. He then briskly turned and walked silently out of the room and into the long corridor, his sterling composure never really in jeopardy.

All day long, and for the next week or so, the Fleet Street gossip-mill steadily turned out a blurred mass of hasty mis-information to a waiting world. Accurate or not, it certainly made great copy, which after all, was the only thing that mattered:

ANNA, GIRL IN A BLACK BIKINI GIVES HIM THE KISS-OF-LIFE AFTER DRAMA OF RESCUE DIVE

Brian Jones Dies in Pool After Midnight Party

Jones, who suffered from asthma, almost certainly died either as a result of an attack of the complaint while swimming or from a heart-attack caused by over-liberal use of an asthma inhalant. An inhaler was found beside the fifty-foot-long pool.

Evening News, 3 July

*

2 a.m. BRIAN JONES FOUND DEAD IN SWIM POOL
The Daily Telegraph, 3 July

*

ASTHMA CLUE TO DEATH OF BRIAN JONES
The Daily Telegraph, 4 July

*

BRIAN JONES HAD TAKEN SPIRITS AND DRUGS

Brian Jones, the former member of The Rolling Stones, died through drowning, associated with severe liver malfunction and ingestion of alcohol and drugs, Dr Albert Sachs, consultant pathologist, said at the inquest at East Grinstead yesterday.

Evening News, 8 July

*

BRIAN JONES DRUGS DROWNING HORROR

Pop star Brian Jones had been drinking and taking tablets – his 'sleepers' – when nurse Janet Lawson pleaded with him not to go swimming.

'He would not listen. So he drowned, "under the influence of alcohol and drugs,' in the words of Coroner Dr Angus Sommerville yesterday.

Daily Express, 8 July

*

BRIAN JONES DROWNED AFTER DRINK AND DRUGS

Brian Jones, 27, former member of The Rolling Stones, drowned in the swimming pool of his country home, Cotchford Farm, near

175

Hartfield, Sussex, 'under the influence of alcohol and drugs', a coroner said yesterday.

The Daily Telegraph, 8 July

As the media frenzy continued, the surviving Stones were forced out into the open by the morbid publicity surrounding Brian's death. Charlie and Bill, in particular, were badly shaken. While Ian Stewart and Keith Richards entered into a tight-lipped game of hide and seek with the media, Jagger attended a posh party with Marianne that very evening.

Still, as bad as things looked, in their own way all of The Stones were genuinely upset about Brian. Sean recalls the private, early morning drama when the other Stones first found out Brian was dead:

'Ian Stewart answered the phone and got the word from Keylock's old lady. It was very strange. The phone's just by the main control room. The session ended immediately. They had been talking about getting a new guitarist. In fact, I'd already introduced them to Mick Taylor. Because it was hopeless with Brian. If Jimmy Miller told the truth, he'd admit that I turned him on to Mick Taylor and Keith knows it as well.

'Jimmy told me when the call came in and Ian walked into that control room, somebody was actually doing a Brian [imitation], you know. Ian said, "Brian's dead," and there was a stunned silence in the room. The first thing anybody said, was Jagger and he said, "We'll pay for that." Jimmy Miller was sitting right there and told me.

'The only thing they didn't like about the whole situation was the hint that they had gotten rid of him. There were these sort of ugly rumours that went around.

'Miller then called me from Olympic. I was at Jimmy's old lady's house, Jerry, she's dead now. I was there with my girlfriend and we were just watching TV taking a bit of hash. The phone rang and Jerry said, "It's Jimmy. He wants to talk to you."

'I said, "What's happening?"

'Jimmy said, "Brian died."

'I said, "Oh fuck, no, no, man."

'He said, "Yeah."

' "Well, that fucks that up." Because we were supposed to go down to his house the next day and talk about Brian's new album. Jimmy was going to produce it and I was going to put the package together and play executive producer, like I did with a lot of the things I didn't bother to put my name on, and make the deal. I think Alan White was going to play drums, but I'm not certain. I remember Brian saying it was going to have a "touch of Richie Havens" about it.

'Brian and I talked a lot at that time and he seemed better, man. He seemed relieved of the fucking bullshit. He was relieved of all the pressure. I thought he'd turned the corner. He was just raving about this new album. He was so up on it, his energy was positive and it seemed like someone had taken a ton off his back.

'We were going to do some demos and I was going to go out and get a deal. Which I was already out doing.'

The next day, Friday, 4 July, Mick Jagger faced reporters who demanded firm answers regarding The Stones' plans. Would their scheduled free concert in Hyde Park on Saturday go on as planned now that Brian had died?

'Yes,' said Jagger confidently. 'Brian would have wanted it. We will now do the concert for him. I hope people will understand that it's because of our love for him we are still doing it.' That evening the band (along with new member Mick Taylor) turned up on *Top of the Pops* to promote their new single, 'Honky Tonk Women'. Perhaps that was done out of love for Brian as well?

That afternoon Bill Wyman returned to his hotel to find Tom Keylock and Anna Wohlin sitting there with his Swedish wife, Astrid. Tom told Bill he'd 'rescued' her from the savage media and wondered if the Wymans might consider playing host to the distraught young woman for a few days. They agreed, and Anna hung out quite happily with Astrid, relieved to finally be free of Thorogood and his cronies.

The next day The Stones played to an enthusiastic crowd of over 250,000 in the park, Jones's killers 'Joe' and 'Frank' amongst them, watching on high from the branches of a tree. Ian Stewart was personally appalled. Not only was it the single worst show he'd ever played with the group, but he was none too pleased with Keith's state of mind as the drugged-up guitarist stumbled around 'looking like a derelict'.

Mick too, pissed him off when, after reciting what Stewart termed 'a long boring poem' in memory of Brian, he proceeded to heat things up by whirling into 'Honky Tonk Women' and then cavorting suggestively near the edge of the stage. 'He stripped off his dolly tunic,' Stew recalled, 'and was leaping around in his vest and pants when he suddenly went to his knees, stuck the mike on his crotch and put his mouth over it, leaving nothing to the imagination as to what he was mimicking.

177

'A rather tacky way to commemorate Brian's death.'

Though few people knew it, Brian had been invited to attend the show that weekend by both Keith and Les Perrin. While privately deeply hurt that he should be asked to 'sit in' with his own band he put the best face on, telling them both he was too busy. 'I phoned Brian and asked him if he wanted to come to an open-air concert by The Stones on Saturday afternoon,' Perrin later told the press. 'He said he did not think it right that he should come and horn in on them. He said he was too busy anyway working on his arrangements. He knew what he wanted to do and he was doing it.'

Anna Wohlin was up early Monday morning. Carefully she put on her make-up and slipped into her skimpy, crocheted mini skirt. She must have been in shock. She was now the centre of attention for every newspaper in London. In the space of only a few weeks the pretty Swedish student had become the most talked about woman in Britain – days after holding the lifeless body of Brian Jones in her arms. All the papers were after her story. Some had offered a lot of money. Jan Ollofsson told my editor that she seemed knocked sideways by it all.

The sad truth, of course, is that unexplained deaths like Brian's can be very messy. People tend to ask a lot of questions. Point fingers. Make assumptions. But all that would be over soon and Anna would be free to pick up her life again.

Early on, Tom Keylock turned up to escort Wohlin back down to Cotchford to pick up her things and meet with Frank Thorogood who would accompany her to the coroner's inquest held that afternoon in East Grinstead.

As the two arrived at the proceeding they were mobbed by photographers and besieged by reporters all wondering how she 'felt'. Somebody asked where she got her dress. Underneath her floppy hat the corners of her mouth drooped slightly.

Once inside, the mood was predictably grim as first the police and then Dr Sachs testified as to the imagined particulars of Brian's final exit.

As for the Cotchford crew – Janet Lawson, Frank Thorogood and Anna Wohlin – all said their piece. Anna was admonished by a policewoman to button up her top before sitting down to testify. By all accounts, she faithfully complied.

Like the make-shift police investigation, the official inquest yielded little in terms of any great truth, instead scrupulously going over the same old tired ground. Brian was drunk. He was stoned. He had an amphetamine-like substance in his body. Everyone tried very hard to save him. No, it wasn't the asthma. He'd been seen with his inhaler. His liver was shit. He would have probably died in a few months anyway.

Terry Rawlings comments on the perpetual riddle of the inquest: 'The only thing I found dodgy about the inquest is that Frank Thorogood's story has remained word for word perfect, right to the end. Word for word. Either he's got no imagination or he's very well rehearsed. He says the same thing that's [been] written in every book.'

After Wohlin successfully ran the gauntlet on the way out, sheltered by Thorogood, it was time to seriously consider her next move.

Almost immediately an exclusive interview was set up with senior Fleet Street celebrity writer, David Wigg, who spoke to her, he wrote, 'from a London hideout'. Adhering pretty much to the popular version of events Wohlin, quite unwittingly, became one of the bad guys' greatest assets in spreading the approved gospel of St Brian the Pathetic.

She said in part: 'He was a terribly good swimmer and used to swim every night . . . He didn't want me to leave him. He always wanted me to be where he was.

'He was very fond of me. We had an argument just once because I said I was going to leave him. I remember it made him cry. He talked about marriage and if we could have children.

'I can't believe it. I still think he is coming back. We were so happy. It was accidental. Brian asked me to marry him, but I said it was too early. I thought it was too early for him to suggest it. But he really wanted it and to have children.'

After Jones's death, Wohlin also spoke to journalist Haydon Cameron of the *Daily Mail* and another from *The People*. An article which niggled Brian's dear old dad.

'I could never understand that statement the papers supposedly got from Anna about a party,' Lewis later commented. 'If one were planning a party, would he take sleeping pills first? I was horrified by *The People*'s knowing that a doctor had prescribed the drugs Brian had taken and their saying nothing at all about it. Nobody asked any questions. I wrote the police a letter telling them drugs were prescribed so they could investigate and have that cleared up, at any rate that the drugs were prescribed for Brian by a doctor. I sent the letter on a Friday and by Monday the doctor was out of the country. I have no idea what it means.'

Twenty-five years on, with Anna presumed long dead, Tom Keylock sat sipping orange juice and lemonade in the Gloucester Hotel and commented on the so-called questionable motives of the then 22-year-old model. 'She was after money because that second week she wants to start selling her story and all that crap. Let's be fair, she was only with him a bloody week so what does she know about Brian Jones?'

Anna Wohlin left England on Wednesday, 9 July 1969. According to Bill Wyman, she was down in East Grinstead (why or where, we don't know) and booked a limo on Brian's account to carry her on to Heathrow. From there she would fly home to Stockholm where, according to legend, her young life would end within a year.

'She died over in Sweden,' says Keylock. 'They tell me she stuck her head in a gas oven or something. She committed suicide, or so I'm led to believe, twelve months afterwards. I didn't really know until somebody told me about it.'

Many people believed her dead; for twenty-five years every book or article written about Jones's death claimed she was. But in April 1994, *Daily Mail* reporter David Williams tracked Anna down to a suburb of Stockholm. 'I would certainly give evidence to a fresh police inquiry. I said at the time there was something not quite right about the way Brian died, but no one wanted to listen. I was deeply shocked – numb,' she recalled. 'I should have had a doctor or nurse and been helped, but there was nothing. I had tried to help him and seen him dead – I was young.' She was obviously distraught.

The final chapter in Anna Wohlin's days at Cotchford are as curious as anything yet uncovered about Brian. Mrs Hallet fervently insists that some months later, Anna once again returned to Cotchford Farm and broke in, setting off the alarm. The police came swooping down and were about to drag her off to jail when the soon to be new owner, Alistair Johns, intervened and convinced the cops to turn her loose.

The funny thing is, Mrs Hallet says, she came down only to pick up her few remaining things. But Tom Keylock had already taken care of that on the morning of the inquest. And why would anyone travel all the way from Sweden for a few clothes? If it was actually Anna who broke in that day, it is hard to imagine what she was looking for, but she must have been in a distressed state.

Seeing as all this took place some twenty-five years ago, I might have been inclined to put the whole thing down to an old lady's mistaken memory, but for the fact that Mr Johns told almost the exact same story. And although we'll probably never know the entire truth of it, it seems unlikely both Hallet and Johns are mistaken, especially about an incident in which the police were involved and would therefore become a matter of record.

'She came back down here one day,' Mrs Hallet told me, 'and crawled through the cat hole. She was only a little girl, very small. The other one [Suki] was a bigger person all together. Anna came back and wanted the clothes she'd left behind. She thought she could get through the cat hole without opening the door, you see. So she crawled in, but when she opened the inside back door the burglar alarms went off and, of course, I had to stay here. It was all done through the police. I didn't see anything of her. If only she'd come to me first I could have let her get her clothes.'

And now, Mr Johns's version of the story. Perhaps slightly more accurate as he was personally present and Mary Hallet was not. Still, it's a puzzle.

'Anna in those days was a skinny little thing. She didn't physically break in, she just climbed in through the cat flap. It wasn't the standardised flap, it was a bigger one, but it was still pretty small. She got inside and the alarm went off. I'd signed the contract to purchase and you normally complete such transactions within twenty-eight days. I'd signed in March I think, but we couldn't complete until September because they couldn't prove title. They hadn't cleared everything with the estate duty office. She broke in during that period. We used to come down here a bit, just to see the place was still there. When we arrived the place was crawling with police and this pretty, sort of anorexic creature was sitting outside. The police asked if I wanted to prefer charges of breaking and entering. It seemed a bit of a waste of time so I didn't. She said she wanted to be near where he last was. At least she didn't try and drink the swimming pool.'

Following the inquest, the immediate concern was Brian's burial. Tom Keylock recalls one very strange episode concerning the purchase of Jones's coffin. Apparently, someone got the bright idea that America provided 'better' caskets and so it was decided within The Stones organisation to order a big bronze coffin and have it flown over. Obviously, it wasn't going to be cheap. A point raised by Lewis Jones with Tom.

'He said, "Well, couldn't you get a different coffin?" I looked at him and walked away in disgust. I don't have a lot of love for him, but he never done nothing to me. From what Brian was telling me, their relationship was very hairy, like. I'd hate for anyone in my family to go on terms like that.'

On Thursday, 10 July, Brian was laid to rest in his home town of Cheltenham on a dark, blustery day. Jones's funeral attracted great attention, with the streets literally lined with thousands of people who turned out to pay their respects to the city's famous, errant, fallen son. At last, Brian had found the attention and affection he craved so in life. The next day the *Daily Mirror* ran a full-page spread on the service, as did most of the dailies, complete with a touching photo of Charlie and Bill very close to tears as Brian's coffin was finally lowered into the ground.

'Brian Jones, the former Rolling Stone, wrote his own epitaph,' the article began. 'It said: "Please don't judge me too harshly." A simple, moving plea, read by the rector in the church where Jones once sang as a choirboy.

'Young girls wept in the 900-year-old parish church of Cheltenham as Canon Hugh Evan Hopkins spoke. He said: "I hold in my hand a telegram which Brian's parents treasure more than they can say. He sent it to them some little while ago, after he had come into conflict with the law. I read this with his parents' permission: 'Please don't judge me too harshly.'

' "Here I believe Brian speaks not only for himself, but also for all of his generation, and I pass his words on to any who will hear this service today. Please don't judge him – and them – too harshly."

'The rector spoke of Jones as a rebel and said: 'Brian had little patience with authority, convention and tradition. In this, he was typical of many of his generation who have come to see in The Rolling Stones an expression of their whole attitude to life."

'He added: "Much that this ancient church has stood for for 900 years seems totally irrelevant to them. And yet it is not humbug to come here today to offer our prayers on this tragic occasion."

'The scripture reading was the story of the prodigal son . . . After the service, Jones was buried in his hometown cemetery with much of the adulation he had come to know during his years with The Rolling Stones . . .

'When the last mourners left, Canon Hopkins spoke of the service he had conducted. "I may well be criticised in Cheltenham for presiding over a service for a young man who had given up the Christian way of life. But I did not hesitate, for above all I stand for the love of God.

' "I don't want people to think this whole thing was all a lot of humbug." In death, as in his life, it seemed the singer who quit The Rolling Stones was still not far from controversy.'

Bill Wyman later remembered that throughout the service the press were behaving like animals. Pushing in front of the family for graphic closeups of their grief. Kneeling down, pointing their cameras directly into the grave and screaming out questions to him and Charlie during the service.

Frank Thorogood was there as well. As were Tom Keylock and builders Johnny, Mo and Dave, among others. After it was over and everyone had cleared out, Frank cautioned his men never under any circumstances to discuss Brian's death with anyone. They promised they wouldn't.

A couple of days later someone quietly placed a For Sale sign in the hedgerow at Cotchford. Brian's beloved dogs were sent to kennels and the rest of his things carted away by persons unknown. Cotchford Farm was still as lovely and lush as it had ever been. But, the pastoral beauty of the place bore a dark stain of death and broken dreams. A tiny corner of Christopher Robin's make-believe world was now impossibly altered, a wisp of unfulfilled promise now forever painted black.

7 DYING YOUNG
Remembering Brian

I N THE END, Marianne Faithfull bore the guilt for all those who should have cared about Brian. The lone gasp of conscience on Jones's fast-sinking ship of fair-weather friends. Even though, for Marianne the sweet and gentle-born blueblood, the unnatural burden almost took her life.

Faithfull once said of herself, 'I lived in a Renoir painting; long blonde hair, sunny days, straw hat with ribbons.' Brian could have easily joined her in that painting; two fair, tow-headed waifs strolling down a summer lane, hand in hand.

But that was another lifetime, before she found herself caught up in the mad freefall that was The Rolling Stones. Just like Brian. There was a lot of Marianne that was just like Brian; from their similar cultured backgrounds and childhood respiratory illnesses that left them both in delicate health. Both became entrenched in a world of drugs neither was prepared for or ultimately able to handle. Above all, neither was comfortable with nor cut out for the Stones lifestyle. What Marianne offered Brian was a friendship that was warm and non-threatening. Jones didn't have many platonic relationships with women, and despite their one alleged brief sexual encounter, Faithfull always insisted, 'I was his friend, not his girlfriend.'

'I didn't know much about music then', she explained in Hotchner's *Blown Away*, 'and Brian, who was very knowledgeable, got me interested in it. He could talk about anything. He was a very eclectic person.'

Although they were close and she 'saw him often', she has said, 'Brian was too proud and too cool to discuss his inner turmoil. He just wasn't that kind of person, he kept it all in.'

There was guilt, too, over her own role in the tangled web of band relationships which automatically placed her against Jones in a situation where it was nearly impossible to juggle allegiances. 'Since I was part of the group that was slowly pushing Brian away,' she noted, 'I suppose it would have been regarded as a form of treachery to have taken Brian into my confidence'. Three days after Jones's death, Faithfull flew with Jagger to Sydney, Australia, where they were set to film *Ned Kelly*. 'I was pretty much gone by the time the plane landed,' she discloses. 'I was frightened of flying so I went to the doctor and said I've got a long flight and I need some downers. I must have taken fifteen Tuinals.

In reality, something far more insidious was happening. For the previous six weeks leading up to the film assignment, Faithfull had been playing the role of Ophelia in *Hamlet* at London's Royal Court Theatre. Just as the ill-fated character in the play eventually commits suicide, so the young actress became desperately immersed in a similar mindset. Marianne found herself obsessed with images of Brian, who had not yet even been buried.

'The more I thought of him drowned and wasted the more I began to identify with him and think of myself as also drowned and wasted,' she explained.

'By the time we got to the hotel, I was in a trance. When we got to our room Mick went straight to sleep. I decided to take the rest of the pills. But first, I walked around a bit and had a few visions.'

Looking out of the window, Faithfull saw Jones looking up from the pavement below. At that precise moment, she fell into a six-day coma in which she experienced the following dream: 'The place looked like the illustrations in books by Edmund du Lac and those Dürer engravings of hell,' she says. 'I was very interested in opiate literature at the time and this vision was definitely on an opiate scale. The grandeur and enormity of the place and the general feeling was like one of those engravings. But the surroundings didn't interest me as much as walking along with Brian who had woken up dead and didn't know where he was. "Thank God you're here, Marianne!" he kept saying, and we glided along, our feet not touching the ground, only these long looping glides like skating on ice.

'We talked about everything you could imagine; how he had woken up not knowing where he was and put out his hand for his Valium and there was nothing, and how frightened he was. He was lonely, confused and brought me to the other side to walk with him on this particular bit of journey, which I did with pleasure. Afterwards, he said he was very sorry to have put me in this fix. I didn't mind, I understood how he felt. He didn't know he was dead. I'm sure when people die quickly they must go through terrible confusion. They don't know they're dead. That's why there are ghosts. Death is the next great adventure. That's what Brian and I talked about.

'Then when we got to the end, the edge over which you went or not, Brian slipped off and I didn't. I heard voices calling me back. If Mick hadn't woken me and got me to the hospital so quickly I would have slipped over with Brian.'

The experience left Faithfull with some painful insights: 'People who commit suicide are usually doing it to make people feel bad. I was obviously punishing Mick because Brian had just died and I was angry about the way he and Keith had treated him. Brian was a hopeless mess and they were just so cool. Brian really fucked himself up by letting himself get much, much too involved in drugs, even before Keith got like that. I always felt Keith's way of reacting to Brian's death was to become Brian. But Keith is so strong physically he didn't look like he was disintegrating. Brian really did disintegrate.'

Over time The Stones, too, were finally able to share their recollections of Brian. Bill Wyman remembers his friend this way: 'The sad thing was he had left the group and suddenly he was phoning up people getting a band together. He was coming up to the sessions and telling us all about what he was doing and all of that. I mean, he was still a good friend and then suddenly, wham!'

A more candid and insightful Jagger offered these remarks: 'I always had this feeling that if anyone was going to die it would be Brian. I always knew he wouldn't live very long. He lived his life very fast. He was kind of like a butterfly. A very good musician; he used to jump around from one thing to another. He was the first person in this country to play slide guitar, out of this world. At one point we were very close as a group. Brian Jones lived up to being a Rolling Stone more than anybody; he freaked out more than anybody. But he did it in a nice way, he was very funny.'

Keith Richards typically had a more hard-edged view: 'Although it was a shock when it actually happened, nobody was really that surprised. Everybody knows people that you just have that feeling about. They're not going to be seventy-year-olds, ever. Not everybody makes it.'

In addition, he managed to debunk a long standing myth that Jones was an incomparable, if not brilliant musician. 'Because he's dead I can say, "Oh, Brian was a great musician," but it wasn't true. Brian wasn't a great musician. He did, however, have a feel for certain things.

'Brian was never a purist,' continued Richards. 'He used to like to pretend he was when it was convenient. In actual fact, Brian used to play alto sax with a Cheltenham rock 'n' roll band called The Ramrods, who used to do all Duane Eddy stuff. That was his claim to fame.'

Charlie Watts states, in his reliably heartfelt manner, 'I can't really say anything about Brian. It's such a personal thing and it's impossible to sum up a friend cold-bloodedly. It's a great personal loss that leaves me at a loss for words. No matter what I were to say it would not be enough.'

Yet, back in 1966, he made this understated but revealing assessment of his bandmate: 'He's basically a very quiet bloke. He's really a soft person. His biggest fault is the same as mine; people don't know him. He's generous to people he wants to be generous to. He's very wary of people he doesn't know. This business makes people that way . . .'

Ian Stewart, always one to speak his mind frankly declared: 'Brian really wanted to be a fucking rock 'n' roll martyr. Brian set himself on the road to disaster and went down and down; in a way, it was sad, but he was not a particularly nice person. I never really felt particularly sorry. He told me a lot of lies.'

Just weeks before his death, however, when Jones was dumped from the band, Stewart encountered a changed man. 'I think it was almost a weight off his mind, I think he was pleased to think, "I don't have to worry about that anymore." He seemed to straighten up a lot. He started to phone me which was something he wouldn't have done at all normally. We had some lucid conversations, he was obviously quite straight. He started putting plans together about forming a band. He asked me if I'd come down to play piano, but I thought, "One band with you is enough!"'

The ever-smooth Les Perrin also commented on the Brian Jones he knew: 'I liked Brian tremendously. I make no apologies for that at all. I found him a great conversationalist. A rather remarkable monster. A lovely man. But he would have run out of runway by the time he was thirty anyway, because he was that sort of man. You couldn't live with him without understanding this.'

Conversely, the memories of Tom Keylock revolve around Jones's final days at Cotchford. 'When he found it he thought, "That's it!" Brian said to me many times, "I'm never going to sell this place. I'm here for the rest of my life." Little did he know, it was to be that short.

But he loved it there. In fact, he wanted to be buried at Cotchford. He told me and Frank Thorogood and some of the locals, "I don't want to be buried at Cheltenham." I did tell Mr Jones that.

'Brian didn't speak about death a lot. It was just conversation. I might say to you, "When I die I want to be buried there, want to be buried here, that kind of thing."'

To this day, Keylock keeps a photo of Brian hanging over his commode, granting Jones's request to place it there when he died. 'He said to me, "Don't every let this get lost if I die and you're still alive, you old bastard." I remember he said it may be worth some bread. I said, "That wouldn't interest me, Brian, not now." I still don't make an issue of him thinking he was gonna die. It probably passed through his head, but he never made it an issue to me.'

Shortly after Brian's death, Tom decided he'd had enough of The Rolling Stones and their troubles. And so, after five years of service to the cause, he gave in his notice. 'I was fed up,' says Tom. 'With all the pressures. I said to Stew, "I'm gonna sling it in. I've had enough." I decided when my daughter Alison was born I was gonna spend more time with her than I did with the others. Six years of their life I didn't see much of them and I decided, "Right, I'll call it a day." Keith said, "Don't be silly." I said, "I've had enough. I'm gonna do it. By the way, I'm going to New York." He said, "What for? No, you aren't. I need you down here." I was an associate producer on a video called *Supershow*, with Eric Clapton, Buddy Guy, Steve Stills and Roland Kirk . . . I just jumped on a plane and when I came back I said, "That's it! I'm finished.'

In Tom Keylock's climb from simple chauffeur to superstar minder and then tour manager for the world's greatest rock 'n' roll band, and then finally international film producer, he managed to shoot the final Isle of Wight festival in 1970. 'I shot one of the last concerts Jimi Hendrix ever done on film. For a man called Ronan O'Rahilly. Ronan's got all the stuff on that.'

All in all, quite an incredible journey for the former Second World War serviceman and car-hire company owner.

Another Jones chauffeur whose tenure was abruptly clipped by the strong arm of Keylock, Brian Palastanga, offers recollections of a very different sort: 'Brian had three girlfriends while I was with him. They were Anita Pallenberg, Suki Potier and a Spanish girl called Carmen. He seemed to be fond of them all. Anita was his first; one day he asked me to take the Rolls over to Munich to bring her back to London.

That's the sort of thing he would do if he wanted to see someone. He didn't worry about the expense. With Carmen, he would share a flat for a couple of weeks and then split up. Then they would get together again. And so it went. He was very kind and generous to his girlfriends when he hadn't been smoking. He would think nothing of spending a couple of hundred pounds on clothes for them.

'He kept a German uniform in his wardrobe. He often talked about Germany and how he hated the Nazis for what they had done. One of the chairs in the flat was covered in a large swastika. In a way, I think it was Brian's way of protesting. He often had rows with his friends over politics when he was high and this was sometimes the reason for the fights with his girlfriends. He would say something about politics, they would disagree, and he would become violent.

'I prefer to remember Brian as the simple country boy who loved to go back and have a drink with the locals as just Brian, not Brian Jones of The Rolling Stones.'

Pat Andrews, Jones's first love, recalls: 'Brian was always very insecure and unsure of himself. He wanted terribly to be loved by everybody, but he had a knack of turning people against him. He was afraid of life, I'm sure that's why he smoked hashish, to give himself confidence. Brian only ever wanted to make music and he had a lot of pressure from people who didn't want him to do that. He went through a period of starving for his music. He didn't have anyone to send him money when he started out. He had pressures from childhood. That was why I think he did the things he did. But he certainly started The Rolling Stones and chose the name regardless of what is now believed. It was Brian who put the adverts in the *New Musical Express*. It was Brian who did all the hard slog, checking out all the venues.'

Linda Lawrence, who many thought was always the best woman for Brian, candidly professed, 'I was always in love with him. He was the most gentle and courteous man I have ever known. When I was told of his death I was extremely upset. I had always hoped he would eventually have joined me in America.

'I knew about his other girlfriends, but he seemed closer to me than any of them. Even when he went out with other girls I never gave up hope that one day he would eventually come back to me. He needed love and security and I'm glad I had the chance to give him just that for the three years we were together.'

Suki, too, was another one who felt she had the definitive claim on Jones's love: 'We would have been married by now. We had a big thing going for us. There were other girls in his life but no one else counted. I will never forget him. He was a wonderful, incredible person.

'When I look back now his death seems so pointless and I still can't get over it. I've been so lonely since. He gave me a shoulder to cry on and he picked up the pieces and made me feel a woman again.

'At last he was happy and laughing. He left The Stones because he wanted to get into his own music and he had really got himself together. He had also got over the drug trials and all the hang-ups he went through.

'What happened before we met was something I could accept. I will always remember Brian. There has been no one since. But soon I've got to shake myself out of it. I can't live in the shadows forever.'

One can only sympathise with the tragedy that was Suki Potier. Following the terrible crash that had killed boyfriend Tara Browne in the car in which she was a passenger, Suki eerily predicted that three more men with whom she would become involved would die. In fact, she moved in with Jimi Hendrix, followed by Jones, who both tragically perished. After Brian's death Potier subsequently married a notorious Chinese gambler; when he informed her he wanted a divorce, Suki got behind the wheel beside her disenchanted husband and drove off a cliff, killing them both, thus fulfilling her deadly prophecy.

Back in the early days when he was still the spokesman for the band Jones built up several close relationships with members of the print media. One of those was respected journalist Ray Coleman. Coleman tells the story of having lunch with Jones in 1964 in a swanky London restaurant. The waiter, knowing full well who Brian was, treated the guitarist with a haughty contempt, poking fun at his shoulder-length hair. 'When we reached the coffee stage,' says Coleman, 'the waiter said to Brian, "Would you like coffee, Madam?"

'Now Brian Jones was a sensitive man who often showed anger. It was an electric moment and I expected him at least to punch the waiter in the face. If violence could ever be justified this might have been a fair moment.

'But instead Brian, showing a big heart and far too much self-restraint, burst into laughter. "That's very funny, man," he said to the waiter. "What's your next film?"

'Every time I met Brian since he recalled the moment and often greeted me with the words, "Coffee, madam?" It became a standing joke and he sometimes followed it up by saying: "Those *dirty* Stones! They all look like girls!"'

Jones confided to Coleman he thought the cynical abuse hurled at The Stones for their long hair, dandified clothes and revolutionary din was thoroughly amusing. Except when the band was dubbed 'The Great Unwashed'. 'He told me he had a bath at least once a day and washed his hair five times a week,' remembers Coleman.

'But living through such a stream of knocks finally took its toll on Brian. He developed a mighty chip on his shoulder. He didn't actually resent Mick's leadership, but he was musically unfulfilled. He didn't love The Stones' music, though he realised Mick and Keith Richards wrote songs much more commercial than his, which tended to be more bluesy.

'Brian developed a tortured personality until in the end, he was at odds not only with society, but with people in the pop world whom he had once liked.

'At twenty-six, he was a sad character who believed that, despite earning a fortune, he had achieved nothing. He saw straight through the glitter of instant fame and though he enjoyed it, he was still searching for the real Brian Jones.

'Tragically he never found it.'

Another member of the press with whom Jones forged a particularly keen relationship was *New York Post* journalist, Al Aronowitz. 'Shall I tell you about the time two cops stopped us for doing eighty around Marble Arch? It may as well have been Fifth Avenue and Washington Square, but we were drunk out of our skulls on Scotch. Behind the wheel all Brian did was laugh that asthmatic laugh of his and the cops grinned and let us go. Shall I tell you about the 7.00 a.m. he wanted me to take him to the top of the Empire State Building with his orange blond hair still oozing blood from where a girlfriend had cracked his skull with a Coke bottle? "Well," he used to say, "What do you expect from a pop star?"

'It was Brian who founded The Stones and discovered all those obscure blues records by Bo Diddley, Chuck Berry and Willie Dixon that he somehow imported from America and translated into The Stones' own language. "I was the undisputed leader of the group!" he used to say.

'One of the first things Brian ever told me about was a vision he once had coming out of a nightclub in London's 3.00 a.m. dawn. It was as if the heavens had called upon him to look up and see the face of a goddess angel telling him to work for human good. It was a vision that guided him for as long as I knew him and yet, he always kept cursing himself as one who used his power for evil.

'He died a man whose vision had somehow carried him into decadence. He died as one of the leaders of a generation that was determined to build the biggest monument to itself in the history of mankind, even if the monument turned out to be a whirlwind. He died taking the rap for all the drug users in Britain.'

Don Short of the *Daily Mirror* also had many in-depth conversations with Jones. 'Brian once told me that when the scene with The Rolling Stones was over he would find what he really wanted to do. He had made up his mind to turn his attentions to his own style of music, the rhythm and blues he loved so well.

'Throughout his career Brian was cast in the eternal role of the rebel, the wild man in a wild business. But in his own language, it wasn't his scene. Brian was an intense introvert, far removed from the rebel we knew. He wasn't proud of the drug trials he faced and ultimately came through. He was even less proud of the fact that three teenage girls all claimed to have borne his children. Neither did he glorify the hysteria and uninhibited life of a Rolling Stone.

'Jones once told me, "No one would choose to live the kind of life I live. Do you really thing I enjoy it? But I mustn't complain or be bitter about it. It's brought the bread and the opportunities."'

Mandy Aftel recalls the war of conflicts that continuously raged within Brian: 'I think it all goes back to his Cheltenham roots; right and wrong . . . He had all these opportunities going on all the time, an intense ambivalence. He had this interest in how others saw him, people viewing him as a drug addict, an undesirable, a criminal. For Brian there was this other part of him. He didn't want to be a renegade Rolling Stone, he wanted to play ethnic music . . . He felt the public outrage of The Rolling Stones flaunting all the limits and he was afraid he would be the one to suffer for it and he did not want to be Jesus Christ nailed upon that cross as a martyr . . . I think he was very afraid of authority. It's rather like the bravado of the high school student who sets off firecrackers in class and they get him down to the principal's office and he's crying, "Don't call my parents!"

'I don't think Brian had the ability to reflect himself; I don't think he had a self for himself. But he loved being reflected by others, which is a great part of what fame is. Other people can assure you, you exist.'

Unquestionably, the most offbeat eulogy of Brian Jones was offered by Terry Rawlings: 'He was off his head at times, sweet at times, vicious at times. He was everything; he was real messed up. I mean, he

193

was so pathetic at times, wasn't he? It was brilliant. I loved the way he was so pathetic.'

Of all Jones's cohorts, the much maligned Dick Hattrell remained forever true to his friend: 'He had the negro superstition and wore a black cat's bone round his neck. In spirit, he would play music like a negro and in spirit he became one.

'I feel since Brian left The Stones he would have lived only a matter of weeks unless he had quickly found his full potential. He was on the down road. There was always a sense of doom about him and he was under a psychiatrist's care for years. He did not hold with certain drugs, but he smoked cannabis. It helped him live his life.'

Alexis Korner, who perhaps understood Jones best and truly accepted him for what he was, had this to say: 'Brian was into exciting things; clothes, colours, music, being a rock star excited him. If they ever dulled down he'd immediately ginger them up again so that no one could live with him so they were exciting. Brian was a kickster, feeling everything very intensely. He always wanted to live at a really intense level, which made him very prickly. He would get angry and then suddenly be perfectly all right again. I hope, as his psychiatrist has said, that people give him a better deal in death than they did in life.'

George Harrison too, found something of a soul mate in Brian: 'When we met, I liked him quite a lot. He was a good fellow, you know. I got to know him very well and I felt very close to him. You know how it is with some people, you feel for them, feel near to them. He was born on 28 February 1943 and I was born on 25 February 1943; he was with Mick and Keith and I was with John and Paul so there was a sort of understanding between the two of us. Our positions were similar and I often met him in times of trouble. There was nothing the matter with him that a little extra love wouldn't have cured. I don't think he had enough love and understanding. He was very nice, sincere and sensitive, and we must remember that's who he was.'

Another very close mate was the ever-philosophical Pete Townshend: 'I used to know him quite well. The Stones have always been a group I really dug. Dug all the dodgy aspects of them as well, and Brian Jones has always been what I've regarded as one of the dodgy aspects. The way he fitted in and the way he didn't fit was one of the strong dynamics of the group. When he stopped playing with them I thought that dynamic was going to be missing, but it still seems to be there. Perhaps the fact that he's dead has made that dynamic kind of permanent.

'A little bit of love might have sorted him out. I don't think his death was necessarily a bad thing for Brian. I think he'll do better next time. I believe in reincarnation.'

As time went by even Lewis Jones slowly came to terms with his son's death. Sounding ready to draw the curtain on the entire matter in 1970, Jones stated, 'We've spent the past year trying to settle down. Brian will always be with us and the fans have been very kind. But the past is past and we don't want to see it revived. All I can say is that I think Brian played his part in shaping the world as it is today.'

Later, however, it appeared Mr Jones was anxious to acknowledge the good that lived within his famous son: 'He was extremely sensitive, very deeply hurt. He was naive to the point that he trusted everybody. He was surrounded by people whom he thought were his own friends for his own sake. When he found out that a lot of them could be disregarded as hangers-on, he was most deeply upset. I suppose we all feel like that to a degree in that when we've trusted somebody and then we've found that trust is misplaced, it does leave a feeling of lasting hurt.

'One must always look for some sign of a silver lining to whatever cloud one is presented with, and one of these silver linings is the enormous affection in which Brian was held, not only in this country but throughout the world. This was immediately obvious to us from the over one thousand letters we received subsequent to his death where not one of them spoke of him in anything other than the most kindly and affectionate terms, and it has also been manifested by the fact that Brian's grave has had flowers regularly taken there every week almost without exception since he died.'

That latent affection notwithstanding, the fallout from Jones's questionable upbringing continues to rain down. The forced alienation from his sister Barbara is revelatory in the following anecdote. Barb had a pen-pal in America she'd been corresponding with over the years. Upon Brian's passing, the then 24-year-old mailed her several newspaper clippings about his death as if it were some anonymous celebrity and not her own brother. 'Doesn't sound very personal, does it?' sighed her American friend.

And what of the children Jones left behind? Five are documented, perhaps even others exist. Part of the dichotomy of Brian Jones was his great love of children, as evidenced by his affection for Pauline Hallet's little girl, yet he discarded his own kids seemingly out of hand.

Pat Andrews, having witnessed the Jones family firsthand, offers at least some excuse for Brian's estrangement: 'I guess I knew Brian as well as anyone. He didn't let many people get close.'

Today Pat and Brian's son Julian Mark works for a multinational corporation. The clear resentment of having to bear being almost an exact replica of his father is evident in his remarks: 'I have nothing of his, nothing at all. My mother and my face, which is so like his, are the only two links I have with him. I don't even have his name as my father on my birth certificate.

'I've not had an easy life. My mother feels I've been let down by him. She had no fun as a teenager because of me. She saw her boyfriend become rich, but he left her in abject poverty. She did so much for me, but it would have been nice to have a father.

'It gets to me that I never had the chance to talk to him, it hurts. I never knew we spoke the same way. It was unnerving to hear him. I've had to struggle to get everything I have on my own merits. The little bit of respect I've got is because I'm Julian Mark Andrews and not Mark Jones, son of Brian Jones. When the truth does come out I'm always considered to be rich. At work they think I've got a fortune stashed away. But I'm the poor relation.

'I made a deliberate decision not to be a lookalike. For instance, at a party I can see a girl I like, but get nowhere with her. But when it's mentioned to her who I am I can't get away from her.

'I'm very anti-drugs. That's not just because of my father, but he's a good example of what can happen.'

By contrast there is Julian Brian Lawrence, son of Linda and Brian, a budding musician who works in the studio along with his stepfather, Donovan Leitch, and performs with a reggae band, having inherited something of his father's musical talent. 'I'm very proud of my father,' he confided to Laura Jackson. 'I love him deeply. I've written a couple of songs for Brian. One's called "Heavy Inside", which is all about my dad and my feelings on the way he's been treated.'

Although Julian has regrets about never having had the chance to know his famous father, the memory of a childhood encounter with him helps gets him through the bad times. 'I was frightened and crying and Dad picked me up high in his arms. I can always remember his face as he hugged me close. Sometimes, if I need to, I shut my eyes and I can bring that moment back.'

Even today, a quarter-century later, the Brian Jones mystique lives on. Indeed, his powerful image somehow takes on even greater status with each passing year. Today Brian Jones looms large as the psychedelic James Dean of the sixties, with his own cult following worldwide, including zealots like Boreham Wood hairdresser Margaret Lowe, who every year on the anniversary of Brian's death makes a pilgrimage to Cheltenham to place roses on his grave.

'Most of my friends think I'm mad,' she says, 'but he was such a smashing bloke.'

Then there is Jacqui Saunders, who claims she has regular contact with Jones via the spirit world. Eighteen months after his death the Bristol-born Saunders was lying in bed when she saw his face on the wall. 'I sat up and everywhere I looked I could see his face. I knew it wasn't my imagination. Brian came to me because we were so alike and he wanted to find his grave in Cheltenham, so I took him there, and to the church where he was a choirboy. It was an incredible experience for me.'

She also claims the power to cure a host of afflictions including nervous complaints, drug problems and even migraines was acquired from the dead musician. 'Brian has taught me not to be afraid of death,' she affirms. 'He will always guide me through life.'

But perhaps Jones's most devoted keeper of the flame is Phil Kent of Lydeard St Lawrence, founder of the Brian Jones Appreciation Society. A talented jazz musician whose admitted obsession with Jones began in 1963, Kent is responsible for setting up yearly memorial services and is hoping to someday organise an international rock festival in his memory. 'Brian was beautiful, sensitive, intelligent and exceptionally talented. A huge amount of abuse was pitted against him, but he was made an example of because he broke all the rules. Without him, there would not have been the greatest rock 'n' roll band in the world. It is that memory that needs to be kept alive.'

Brian Jones is remembered today as a highly inventive artist whose musical accomplishments were many. But in the end it was Jagger and Richards whose engine fired his band, and who have kept it running for the past thirty years.

Still, the tragedy of Brian Jones was one of unfulfilled promise. Just as he ultimately found the courage for his own reclamation, he collided with a cruel and untimely destiny. Like every victim of violent crime, there would be no reprieve for Brian and there should likewise be little mercy for those who robbed both him and the world of his promising presence.

Yet, had Jones found the love and attention he craved as a child, had he not been forced to suffer the hurtful alienation from his sister, had he never got into drugs, had he not lived his life on the edge, would we still remember him today?

The bigger part of Brian Jones, I'm convinced, was good and simmering just below the surface. He was more a naughty boy than a heinous criminal. He abused drugs, but was no junkie; he waved the renegade banner of rock but his heart wasn't really in it; by the end even his infamous womanising was in question, as Dennis Burke once observed: 'He didn't even look at pretty girls; I couldn't believe it.'

Deep down Brian was actually the kind of boy Lewis and Louisa Jones always wanted; talented, introspective, creative, dedicated, innately disciplined and hard-working. The little boy who loved toy trains, buses and animals grew up to be a person of great dignity and heart.

Eventually, Lewis Jones was finally able to meet Brian halfway: 'I used to think he was a young fool and told him so and he used to think that I was an old fool. But in the end he proved his point, that he was capable of building the kind of career in music that he had dreamed of. He proved that I was wrong and he was right.'

In the end, Brian Jones was very much his father's son.

APPENDICES

The Forensic View
by Dr Cyril H. Wecht

Geoffrey: Could you tell me your general impressions after having read through the coroner's report and other materials?

Dr Cyril Wecht: After I reviewed the materials regarding the death of Lewis Brian Jones, with particular emphasis on the autopsy report and the coroner's discussions, it does appear to be a death due to drowning. The findings of a positive nature, specifically, frothy fluid around the nostrils and some slightly blood-stained fluid in the mouth, the heavy, wet lungs, all of these would be consistent with a death due to drowning.

The absence of any other significant pathological findings, that is to say, in drowning deaths it's sometimes just as important to negate other possible causes. They talk about the liver being somewhat fatty, or extensive fatty degeneration. This certainly suggests alcoholism. There are other causes of fatty liver, but not very many, especially in someone of Brian Jones's age. He was a little obese and obese people can have some fatty changes of the liver, but not extensive changes.

Although sometimes we say fatty livers can result in sudden death, that's usually in chronic alcoholics who are in a poor state of nutrition, whose health is bad. It's not a diagnosis . . . that I would consider *at all* in this case.

Mr Jones evidently did a lot of drinking. He had a 0.14 alcohol level at the time of his death which is significant by itself . . .

Geoffrey: It's not roaring drunk though, is it?

Dr Wecht: No, it's not a lot. And for somebody who does a fair amount of drinking it really would not have produced *any* significant compromise. A chronic drinker can handle a 0.14. You and I and other observers might not even be aware that such a person had done any drinking. A non-drinker with a 0.14 might get a little drowsy or behave in a strange fashion, but not a chronic alcohol abuser such as Brian Jones.

I can't rule out the possibility that one or more people may have brought about his drowning by playing games with him, continuing to dunk him, pulling him under and making him swallow water. After a while, even though you may be a good swimmer, as Brian Jones purportedly was, if you were not permitted to breathe and you begin to swallow water, then you may drown.

There's no way I could rule that out. But I cannot find any evidence of physical injuries on Brian Jones's body that would be consistent with defensive type trauma . . . Nothing that was noted in the autopsy, by way of any bruises on the face or the head or anywhere else on the body . . .

Geoffrey: Sorry to interrupt, but would such actions necessarily cause bruising? Could not two very strong people hold someone firmly under the water without bruising?

Dr Wecht: Sure, absolutely. And they could certainly dunk him and push him under without bruising him also. So no, I don't think the autopsy rules out that kind of situation at all.

It's not a really detailed autopsy. I was surprised at the limited amount of commentary, especially since they knew they were dealing with a celebrity. However, I think it's most likely that the absence of any great discussion means that they did not see anything . . .

Geoffrey: The newspapers and, by and large, the public, embrace the notion that Brian Jones was some kind of junkie that just got too loaded and fell into his swimming pool. But the blood barbiturate levels, blood alcohol levels, urine samples and various pharmacological reports here don't indicate that he was intoxicated on either alcohol or drugs, is that correct?

Dr Wecht: No, no, no. They did report an amphetamine-like substance in the urine, but what's in the urine doesn't count because that's already out of your system. That has no effect on your brain at all. As far as the autopsy findings are concerned and the toxicological analysis *there is no reason to attribute his death to a drug overdose, or to even suggest that drugs played a role in his death.*

Geoffrey: All the headlines said they did, of course.

Dr Wecht: The records that were sent to me mention all these different drugs he had gotten from his doctor. Some of it reminds me of Elvis Presley. I'm sure in many cases these stars . . .

Geoffrey: Get just what they want.

Dr Wecht: Exactly. So, regarding his blood, the alcohol, the barbiturates were negative and in the thin layer chromatography there were no amphetamines, morphine or methadone found and so on. As I've already said, that which is in the urine *has nothing to do with death*.

Geoffrey: So, in your estimation with an experienced drinker like Brian Jones you don't think the blood alcohol level would have impaired him to the point that he would have been in *any* peril from that factor alone?

Dr Wecht: No. That is correct, exactly.

Geoffrey: Do you also feel that the level of drugs active in his body would be sufficient to rule out the fact he had some kind of drug overdose in the pool.

Dr Wecht: That is correct. In fact, the report says that the findings were negative, except for the urine and that doesn't affect *anything*.

Geoffrey: I have a letter here, which I sent you, from a Dr Sommerville. It reads, 'In an asthmatic attack, the bronchi are in spasm: this would tend to seal the lining of the tissue and prevent the entry of water while the spasm lasted.' A lot of people have always felt Mr Jones might have died from asthma. Do you think Brian Jones died from some kind of asthma attack?

Dr Wecht: I don't agree with the statement Dr Sommerville made, that an asthmatic attack is going to seal the bronchi and prevent water from getting in. It's true, that in an asthmatic attack you get *some* bronchospasm, but it's not spasm that is complete and seals it off like some kind of trap door. After all, water is a fluid that doesn't need much space to get through.

We also note the lungs being rather large, wet and heavy. So I don't agree with that statement at all. That if Mr Jones had had an asthmatic attack he would not have had water getting into his system. Are they saying that since he had water therefore he did not have an asthmatic attack?

Geoffrey: Right.

Dr Wecht: Well, asthma is a difficult diagnosis to make as far as an autopsy is concerned. More specifically, an acute asthmatic attack leading to death is very difficult to determine. Spasm of the bronchi does not remain in place following death like spasm of arteries. When you die all spasmodic contractures loosen, whether it's a vessel or a tube structure like the bronchus, the airways or the larynx. Some people go into laryngeal spasm. For example, people who have an acute reaction to penicillin or some other kind of substance to which they have a severe sensitivity. I would like to examine the slides before making a more definitive comment on that, but the findings *do not* show a lot of inflammation, or a lot of mucus to suggest an asthmatic attack. I don't know if the autopsy was superficial, but the autopsy report is quite sparse as you can see. If I sent you a copy of my autopsy reports the most perfunctory of cases are eight, nine, ten pages long, and I'm not holding myself up as some paradigm. I'm just saying that if you do a decent autopsy report and describe things properly then that's the way it comes out. This is very, very short and I don't have the slides. *I don't find evidence, however, in what is set forth to suggest that Mr Jones had an acute asthmatic attack*. Furthermore, if we look at it from the standpoint of Jones being a good swimmer, and we've already discussed the fact that he was *not* under the influence of drugs and so on, there's no reason why, even if he had had an asthmatic attack in a pool, that he would not have been able to simply swim over to the edge and climb out. After all, he was not swimming the English Channel. He was not out in the middle of the ocean. He was at no time, I imagine, more than ten feet away from the side. I don't know the dimensions of the pool, but I doubt . . .

Geoffrey: Ten feet is accurate.

Dr Wecht: Okay, so if he were in the centre of his pool he was probably no more than ten, twelve, or fifteen feet maximum from any edge. For an accomplished swimmer, that's only three or four strokes and an asthmatic attack doesn't wipe you out like a massive stroke or a large heart attack. You can swim three, four strokes even if you can't breathe. You'll accomplish that in a couple of seconds and then you're over at the side holding on.

Geoffrey: In the same letter, it comments that 'individuals with liver dysfunction due to fatty degeneration can die suddenly.' Can you please comment on that, because people have suggested that that is perhaps what happened.

Dr Wecht: Well, in certain cases with malnourished individuals on a drinking binge the fatty liver can sometimes lead to sudden death with fat emboli and so on. *That is not the situation here.* In this particular case, I would say that it is total conjecture *with no scientific basis at all,* to even think that his fatty liver caused his death.

Geoffrey: How long does it generally take people to drown?

Dr Wecht: Well, to drown in the sense of dying would be five or six minutes at the minimum. You would need to have the brain deprived of all oxygen for that period of time.

Geoffrey: Witnesses have stated that Mr Jones was only really under-water for about three minutes, they then fished him out and a state registered nurse and another young lady gave him CPR and external heart massage.

Dr Wecht: Well, if he was only in there for three minutes then there's no way he would have drowned because you can live without oxygen for four, five, even six minutes. He might have had some neurological deficit as a residual effect, but he should not have been unresponsive to resuscitative measures at three minutes or so.

Geoffrey: What would be the outside perimeter wherein resuscitation would be futile?

Dr Wecht: I would say that if somebody has been without any oxygen whatsoever, which in the context of a drowning would mean such a person has been submerged totally in water, for perhaps five minutes. Usually someone that doesn't have a bad heart is going to live for five, six minutes, sometimes even longer. As I say, there might be some damage to a portion of the brain after four or five minutes, however.

Geoffrey: So you're saying approximately five or six minutes in total.

Dr Wecht: Without any oxygen whatsoever. I'm not talking about struggling, swallowing water or bobbing up and down. I mean, after you've been submerged and you are not getting *any* oxygen at all.

Geoffrey: To murder someone by drowning them seems a pretty good way to go, doesn't it?

Dr Wecht: Sure, it's a clever way. If you have a set-up whereby some-one can be pulled under the water in some fashion and you can do so without inflicting injuries to the individual. It's a diabolically clever way to kill somebody.

Geoffrey: And it would be difficult for someone even of your expertise, in many cases, to discern that?

Dr Wecht: You *can't* discern it from the drowning itself. You can only discern it from the collateral findings; injuries on the individual, either inflicted or in some kind of a struggle, circumstances based upon police investigation, interrogation of other individuals and so forth. But as far as looking at a body and doing an autopsy where the person has drowned and that person has been, let's say, pulled under by a frogman or held under by two or three people so they can't struggle. No, you can't look at that body and say this person was homicidally drowned. No way.

Geoffrey: Does anything seem suspicious to you about this case?

Dr Wecht: It would not be suspicious from the autopsy report. But obviously, when I read all the other information about what people have said, then that would make me suspicious. If I were aware of that at the time then I would ask homicide detectives to look into this if it happened here in America under the jurisdiction in which I work as a forensic pathologist.

Geoffrey: If you were handed this case today, with all the information I have given you, the newspaper clippings, the statements of the various witnesses and the police reports, would you recommend that homicide review it?

Dr Wecht: Oh yes. If people were prepared to give this kind of testimony under oath. In America, since there's no statute of limitations on murder I would recommend such a case being re-opened and people then being asked to testify under oath where they're subject to perjury. With this case it isn't as if there was a murder case considered and then thrown out. We're not talking, therefore, about double jeopardy or even a homicide investigation. We're talking about a case which was *assumed* to be an accidental drowning and while there was a coroner's inquest, that's rather perfunctory in England in unnatural death cases. But as far as I can see from the materials, it's not a case that was even investigated as a possible homicide. So now that this new information has come forward, if people are prepared to make these statements, some of which might even be a little self incriminating, or certainly potentially embarrassing, then sure. Questions might be asked such as, 'Where were you?' 'Why didn't you say something about this before?' 'What does this say about your moral character, your sense of ethics?' If this case happened in America I think both the homicide detectives and the district attorney's office would pursue it.

7 March 1994

Dr Cyril H. Wecht, widely recognised as one of the world's leading forensic experts, has performed over 12,000 postmortem examinations and reviewed 25,000 more. His long experience and expertise in the areas of both medicine and law have made him a sought-after expert witness in many controversial cases.

Diary of Events

11 September 1966 – 24 September 1969

1966

Sunday, 11 September: The Rolling Stones on *The Ed Sullivan Show* in New York. The segment was originally taped two days earlier.

Tuesday, 20 September: Two freelance journalists approach Brian Jones in trendy Blazes nightclub, London and speak to him about his drug use and general feelings on LSD. When the story turned up five months later in banner headlines in the *News of the World*, Mick Jagger was mistakenly named as the Stone who gave the interview, and not Jones. Jagger immediately sued for libel. As a result, in The Stones' office Brian was thereafter given the nickname, 'Liability Jones'.

Thursday, 22 September: The Stones appear on *Top of the Pops* via a film flown over from the States.

Friday, 23 September: The Rolling Stones play two shows at the Royal Albert Hall in London. Their opening act on this tour is American R&B legend, Tina Turner.

Saturday, 24 September: The Rolling Stones play two shows at the Odeon Cinema in Leeds.

Sunday, 25 September: The Rolling Stones play two shows at the Empire Theatre in Liverpool.

Wednesday, 28 September: The Rolling Stones play two shows at the Apollo Theatre in Manchester.

Thursday, 29 September: The Rolling Stones play two shows at the ABC Cinema in Durham.

The Stones are presented with several gold discs in Kensington: taped originally on 23 September, the segment appears on *Top of the Pops*.

Friday, 30 September: The Rolling Stones play two shows at the Odeon Cinema in Glasgow.

Saturday, 1 October: The Rolling Stones play two shows at the City Hall in Newcastle.

Sunday, 2 October: The Rolling Stones play two shows at the Gaumont Cinema in Ipswich.

Thursday, 6 October: The Rolling Stones play two shows at the Odeon Cinema in Birmingham.

Friday, 7 October: The Rolling Stones play two shows at Colston Hall in Bristol.

The Stones appear on *Ready Steady Go!* in a segment taped originally on 4 October.

Saturday, 8 October: The Rolling Stones play two shows at the Capital Theatre in Cardiff.

Sunday, 9 October: The Rolling Stones play two shows at the Gaumont Cinema in Southampton.

Early November: Brian Jones poses for the cover of a German magazine dressed in a Nazi SS uniform with his girlfriend, Anita Pallenberg. Beneath his jackboots is a child's doll; around his neck a Chivalry Cross. Predictably, there is an immediate media furore to which Jones responds with the cryptic remark, 'I wear a Nazi uniform to show that I am anti-Nazi.'

Friday, 2 December: Brian attends a birthday party for Guinness heir Tara Browne at the family's rambling County Wicklow estate in Ireland.

Sunday, 4 December: Jones first meets Suki Potier.

Sunday, 18 December: Jones's close friend Tara Browne dies when his blue Lotus Elan collides with a parked lorry in Redcliffe Gardens, Kensington. Suki Potier was with him but sustains only minor injuries. A few days later Brian flies to Ireland for the funeral.

Tuesday, 20 December: The London papers carry a report that Brian and Anita will soon marry. Although the couple deny it, the rumours persist.

1967

Sunday, 15 January: The Rolling Stones appear on *The Ed Sullivan Show* in New York.

Sunday, 22 January: The Rolling Stones appear on the ITV show, *Sunday Night at the London Palladium.*

Thursday, 26 January: The Rolling Stones appear on *Top of the Pops* in a segment taped the previous day.

Sunday, 5 February: The Rolling Stones appear on the *Eamonn Andrews Show.*

Wednesday, 8 February: Brian, Keith and Anita fly to Munich to visit the set of *Mord und Totschlag.* Jones is composing the film's score.
Saturday, 25 February: Jones and Pallenberg, along with Richards and mutual friend Deborah Dixon, leave Paris in Keith's Bentley on a cross-country trip to Morocco. Ex-military man Tom Keylock is their driver.
Tuesday, 28 February: Jones spends his 25th birthday in a Toulon hospital suffering from pneumonia. The rest of the entourage, however, pushes on. Richards and Pallenberg soon begin having an affair.
Saturday, 4 March: Reports appear in the press that Jones has recorded the soundtrack for the German film, *Mord und Totschlag* ('*A Degree of Murder*'), at IBD Studios, London, where Brian employs the talents of drummer Kenny Jones and Mike Leander, among others. The film, starring Anita Pallenberg, receives only lukewarm reviews, but Jones's work on the project is almost universally lauded. In an article on Brian's music published in *Record Collector* magazine, writer Mark Paytress comments on the now ultra-rare recording: 'Listening to an audio tape of the movie reveals a score not untypical of the time. A variety of instruments can be heard (Brian played sitar, organ, dulcimer, harmonica and autoharp; engineer Glyn Johns recruited Jimmy Page to play guitar and pianist Nicky Hopkins), and the film's main theme reappears in several styles. It opens in a fairly light pop vein led by strong wailing harmonica, then segues into a distinctly psychedelic mode, with considerable variations on the theme. As the film progresses, the music is less apparent, though eastern, country, blues/soul and R&B styles are all covered. There is one vocal on the soundtrack, sung by Peter Gosling, a Bill Wyman discovery and leader of the group Moon Train.'
Sunday, 5 March: After four nights with Keith in Marbella, Anita joins Brian in Toulon.
Friday, 10 March: Jones jets back to London from Nice for further medical treatment at a hospital in West London. The Stones' office formally announces that *Mord und Totschlag* has been selected as Germany's entry in the Cannes Film Festival.
Wednesday, 15 March: After several days' rest Jones flies to Morocco where he rejoins The Stones' party which has now grown to include Mick Jagger and Marianne Faithfull.
Thursday, 16 March: Returning from the surrounding hills after recording the Master Musicians of Joujouka with his friend Brion Gysin, Jones discovers Mick, Marianne, Keith and Anita have all returned to London without so much as a word. Predictably, Brian falls to pieces.

Saturday, 18 March: Jones flies home from Morocco with the intention of confronting Anita. Brian's accusations, however, only serve to widen the rift with his former girlfriend. Although still extremely distraught, he is finally convinced the affair is over. A story appears in the *Record Mirror* touting Brian's film score for *Mord und Totschlag.* Says director Volker Schlondorff, 'Brian's music has worked out marvellously for the film. It fits in wonderfully with the story. He came to Munich three times to see the finished film for timing purposes.' Brian too, expressed great pleasure in the project noting, 'In writing and producing the track, I used a series of different groups . . . from one musician to ten. I ran the gamut from the usual brass line-up to country and western, using violin and banjo. Mostly they were session men, but some of the group boys helped out.'

Saturday, 25 March: The Rolling Stones travel to Malmo, Sweden, to kick off their current European tour. Not surprisingly, there is still considerable tension between Jones and Richards who barely speak.

The Rolling Stones play two shows at the Indoor Hall in Malmo.

Monday, 27 March: The Rolling Stones play two shows at the Indoor Hall in Orebro, Sweden.

Wednesday, 29 March: The Rolling Stones play two shows at the Stadthalle, Bremen, West Germany.

Thursday, 30 March: The Rolling Stones play two shows at the Sporthalle, Cologne, West Germany.

Friday, 31 March: The Rolling Stones appear at the Westfallenhalle, in Dortmund, West Germany.

Saturday, 1 April: The Rolling Stones play two shows at the Ernst Merck Halle in Hamburg, West Germany.

Sunday, 2 April: The Rolling Stones play two shows at the Stadthalle in Vienna, Austria.

Wednesday, 5 April: The Rolling Stones play two shows at the Palazzo dello Sport in Bologna, Italy.

Thursday, 6 April: The Rolling Stones play two shows at the Palazzo dello Sport in Rome, Italy.

Saturday, 8 April: The Rolling Stones play two shows at the Palazzo dello Sport in Milan, Italy.

Sunday, 9 April: The Rolling Stones play two shows at the Palazzo dello Sport in Genoa, Italy.

Tuesday, 11 April: The Rolling Stones play two shows at the Olympia Theatre in Paris, France.

Thursday, 13 April: The Rolling Stones play two shows at the Sala Kongresowej (Palace of Culture) in Warsaw, Poland.

Friday, 14 April: The Rolling Stones appear at the Hallen Stadium in Zurich, Switzerland.

Saturday, 15 April: The Rolling Stones appear at the Hautreust Hall, The Hague, Holland.

Monday, 17 April: The Rolling Stones appear at the Panathinaikos Football Stadium in Athens, Greece.

Wednesday, 10 May: Jones is busted in his South Kensington flat for unlawful possession of drugs along with his close friend, Prince Stanislaus Klossowski (known to friends as Stash). They are carted off to Chelsea police station to be charged, after which Brian is released on £250 bail.

Thursday, 11 May: Jones is formally arraigned at the Marlborough Street Magistrates Court.

Friday, 12 May: Jones teams with The Beatles at Olympic Studios in Barnes for the recording of 'Baby, You're a Rich Man' on which he plays soprano saxophone.

Friday, 2 June: Brian appears at West London Magistrates Court where his case is formally set down for trial.

Friday, 16 June, Saturday, 17 June & Sunday, 18 June: Jones joins the cream of the pop world at the Monterey International Pop Festival in Monterey, California. There he spends time in the company of his great friend, Jimi Hendrix, introducing him on stage.

Tuesday, 27 June: Keith Richards, Mick Jagger and friend Robert Fraser go on trial at Chichester Crown Court. Jagger, who was accused of possession of amphetamines, is found guilty and remanded to Brixton Prison until sentencing. Richards fares no better, being found guilty of allowing his premises to be used for the consumption of illegal drugs; he is then incarcerated at Wormwood Scrubs. Fraser, too, is found guilty of possession of heroin and remanded into custody. According to Stones expert, Massimo Bonanno, the bust was dirty from the very beginning. 'It becomes clear during the trial,' writes Bonanno, 'that the *News of the World* has played a major part in setting up the raid. Particularly, in planting a "Mr X" as a spy. Suspicion falls upon one David Schneidermann, a California drug dealer who mysteriously disappears following the bust, never to be seen again. Says Marianne Faithfull, 'We believed information was supplied by that fink, Schneidermann, who, despite having an attaché case chockablock with drugs, was not searched. When a cop asked to see the contents of his case, Schneidermann said it was full

211

of exposed film and couldn't be opened and the cop let it go at that.' In the end Mick is sentenced to three months in jail; Robert Fraser, six months, and Keith, an astounding one year behind bars. Upon appeal Jagger is granted a conditional discharge, Richards's conviction is overturned, but Fraser goes to jail. Brian Jones is quite naturally extremely apprehensive about his own legal problems, and according to friends, is becoming increasingly paranoid.

Wednesday, 5 July: Jones, accompanied by Suki Potier, enters Priory Nursing Home in Roehampton suffering from severe emotional distress.

Our World, on which The Beatles perform the classic, 'All You Need Is Love' is aired in Britain (although it was recorded earlier). Mick, Keith and Brian are in the audience of superstar friends.

Wednesday, 12 July: Suki leaves the Priory Clinic, checking into the Richmond Hill Hotel. She remains an out-patient.

Brian Jones attends a Rolling Stones recording session at Olympic Studios, where they have been working since 7 July.

Thursday, 20 July: Sessions are completed for the album which will later be known as *Their Satanic Majesties Request*.

Monday, 24 July: Jones checks out of the Priory Clinic.

Thursday, 27 July: In an attempt to shake off his current state of mind, Brian jets to Marbella with Suki Potier and their close friend Nicky Browne (widow of Tara). 'It's been a year of pressure,' he commented to the press upon his departure from Heathrow. 'Don't make a big thing out of this. No one is getting married or anything. We are just going on holiday, relaxing, behaving ourselves. I decided on the spur of the moment. I have been under pressure for some time and I need a rest.'

Thursday, 10 August: Jones is sent $300 by The Stones' office to pay his hotel bill at the New Marbella Club. At one point, Jones is so broke he has to borrow money from one of the other guests, a Major Dawson.

Thursday, 24 August: The *Sun* runs a story stating that a three-minute promotional film made by The Rolling Stones which satirises the trial of Oscar Wilde has been rejected as 'unsuitable' for screening by the BBC. The film was to have accompanied the song, 'We Love You'. In the piece, Mick Jagger plays Wilde, while Keith Richards is the judge in a wig of rolled newspaper. Marianne Faithfull, meanwhile, portrays Lord Alfred Douglas, Wilde's lover. Johnnie Stewart, producer of *Top of the Pops*, commented that a BBC official had deemed the film, 'Unsuitable in the context of the programme.'

Friday, 25 August: Brian, Jimi Hendrix and Nicholas Fitzgerald contemplate joining The Beatles and Mick and Marianne in Bangor, North Wales, the next day to meet the Maharishi Mahesh Yogi. In the end the trio decides against it.

Saturday, 26 August: Jones, Fitzgerald and Hendrix go to the Pink Flamingo Club to see the The Animals who perform 'Paint It Black'.

Sunday, 27 August: Jones attends a Jimi Hendrix concert at Brian Epstein's Saville Theatre on Shaftesbury Avenue.

Friday, 1 September: Brian attends a Rolling Stone recording session in London. During this period he is introduced to the Maharishi Mahesh Yogi and his philosophy of Transcendental Meditation. Although he pays lip service to the guru's cosmic concepts for a few days he then promptly forgets the entire episode.

Saturday, 2 September: Jones checks into the Skindles Hotel in Maidenhead.

Sunday, 3 September: Perhaps the most frightening news ever to emerge from the turbulent sixties; Brian Jones announces to the press that he intends to apply for a pilot's licence.

Tuesday, 5 September, Wednesday, 6 September & Thursday, 7 September: The Rolling Stones begin to record at Olympic Studios. Following the sessions, Jones once again returns to Marbella for a few days.

Thursday, 14 September: The Stones arrive in New York via London.

Friday, 29 September: Jones and the rest of the group return from New York. On this day their manager, Andrew Oldham, officially splits with the group. Henceforth, The Stones will produce themselves.

October: Jones is questioned by police in reference to a murder investigation in the office of The Stones' solicitors, Joynson-Hicks. After making an official statement he is released and no further action is taken.

Sunday, 15 October: The approximate date Jones embarks on a lone motoring trip to the West Country visiting Taunton, Penzance, Wells and St Ives.

Friday, 20 October: Jones jets off to the Spanish coast for a brief holiday in anticipation of his forthcoming court appearance on drug charges.

Monday, 30 October: A hearing is held at the Inner London Sessions. Although Jones has been under the care of psychiatrist Dr Leonard Henry for several months, by the time he enters the courtroom he is on the verge of a severe breakdown. During the proceedings, Brian admits to both the possession of cannabis and allowing his premises to be used for the consumption of unlawful drugs. He does, however, plead not

213

guilty to the possession of methedrine and a small amount of cocaine. Jones is subsequently sentenced to nine months in prison and is remanded to Wormwood Scrubs. As Brian is taken handcuffed from the courtroom; a group of friends, including Mick's brother, Chris, begin a loud verbal protest.

Tuesday, 31 October: A demonstration on behalf of Jones is held on the King's Road in Chelsea. Seven so-called Stones fans, as well as Chris Jagger, are subsequently charged with abusive behaviour and damaging police property. Jones's lawyer, Michael Havers, arranges for his client to be released on £750 bail pending an appeal.

Wednesday, 1 November: Stones representatives announce that if Jones were to be hospitalised for any reason the band would continue without him. Manager Allen Klein, however, is subsequently quoted as saying that Brian's position within the band is secure and they are not considering a replacement.

Thursday, 16 November: 'Ruby Tuesday' is recorded at Olympic Studios with Brian playing piano and recorder.

Sunday, 3 December: The BBC airs an interview with Mick, Charlie and Brian on the radio programme, *Top Gear*. The show was originally taped on 30 November.

Saturday, 9 December: Brian, Keith and Anita visit the Watts district of Los Angeles.

Tuesday, 12 December: Jones's sentence is set aside after three different psychiatrists testify that he is not emotionally sound enough to weather a prison term. One even suggests he might possibly attempt suicide if incarcerated. Brian is then placed on three years' probation and given a £1,000 fine. His probation officer, William Hornung, declares that he does not intend to treat the Rolling Stones guitarist as a celebrity.

Thursday, 14 December: Jones is admitted to St George's Hospital, London, after collapsing at home. He is diagnosed to be suffering from a severe nervous breakdown as well as a dental infection which requires the extraction of two teeth.

1968

Saturday, 20 January: Jones plays saxophone on a track for an album by Mike McGear, formerly of the group The Scaffold, who is Paul McCartney's younger brother.

Wednesday, 28 February: Jones celebrates his 26th birthday with friends in Paris.

Saturday, 16 March: Model Linda Keith attempts suicide at Brian's flat after being spurned by Jones. Comments Brian, 'I came home after an all-night recording session in Barnes. Last night before I left the flat I told her I would only be about three hours. I didn't bother to telephone even though I had been out all night. I got home about 9.00 a.m. and she was sleeping peacefully. I went out again to see about a recording studio and when I came back I found the police at the flat. They had smashed the door down and had taken some prescribed bottles of tranquillisers to the hospital to be examined. She may have been upset and thought I wasn't going back, but we hadn't had a row or anything. I was absolutely shattered when the landlord of the flat called the police up to have me removed. I asked him why he was doing this and he said: "Because you are trespassing here. We don't want your kind in this place."'

Sometime during the day Brian and Mick are interviewed for the BBC radio programme, *Scene and Heard.*

April: Builder Frank Thorogood meets nurse Janet Lawson through a girlfriend.

Wednesday, 3 April: The approximate date that Brian attends a Rolling Stones recording session at Olympic Studios in the company of both Anita and Suki. Around 8.00 p.m. he meets devoted fan Helen Spittal for the first time.

Saturday, 11 May: Brian confides to friends that a so-called crooked cop is trying to extort money from him threatening that if he doesn't pay up, Jones will be set up and busted.

Sunday, 12 May: The Rolling Stones appear at the *New Musical Express* Poll-Winner's Concert.

Wednesday, 15 May: Mick and Brian appear on *Top Gear*. Brian is interviewed for *Scene and Heard.*

Thursday, 18 May: The Rolling Stones appear on the ITV show, *Time for Blackburn*. The segment was originally taped on 12 May.

Tuesday, 21 May: Jones is once again arrested for possession of cannabis at his flat in Royal Avenue House on the King's Road. Charged at Marlborough Street Magistrates Court he is later released on £2,000 bail.

Wednesday, 5 June: Cult film director Jean-Luc Godard films The Stones recording 'Sympathy For The Devil' at Olympic Studios. As is evidenced by the completed film, Brian does not look at all well.

Tuesday, 11 June: At Marlborough Street Magistrates Court Jones is to be tried for possession of Indian hemp.

Further shooting of The Stones by director Godard at Olympic. At 4.15 a.m. a fire of unknown origin breaks out causing Jean-Luc's entire film crew as well as The Rolling Stones to take shelter in the street.
July: The Rolling Stones appear on *Top of the Pops* in a segment taped originally on 26 June.
Tuesday, 23 July: Jones once again visits Morocco, this time in the company of Suki Potier.
Saturday, 17 August: Sources close to The Stones suggest that Eric Clapton will leave Cream to take Brian's place in The Stones. Clapton denies it. Jones comments, 'At least I still have one friend out there.'
Saturday, 21 September: It is reported The Stones will star in the Carlo Ponti film, *Maxigasim*. Filming is to take place in Hollywood and North Africa. The plans, however, ultimately come to nothing.
Thursday, 26 September: Jones is fined £50 plus court costs of £105 after being found guilty of cannabis possession. Jagger, Richards and Suki Potier pose with a greatly relieved Brian outside the court.
October: Jones returns to Morocco to record material for what was to be the closest thing to a solo album he ever accomplished. The LP, entitled *Brian Jones Presents the Pipes of Pan at Joujouka*, was released posthumously in October 1971.
November: Frank Thorogood begins work for Brian Jones.
Thursday, 21 November: Jones purchases Cotchford Farm, the former home of *Winnie-the-Pooh* creator A. A. Milne, for a reported £30,000.
Saturday, 30 November: The Rolling Stones appear on London Weekend Television's *Frost On Saturday* programme on a segment taped the day before.
Thursday, 5 December: The Rolling Stones hold a luncheon in the Elizabethan Rooms of the Kensington Gore Hotel to mark the release of their ground-breaking *Beggars Banquet* album.
Monday, 9 December: A rehearsal is held at the London Derry House Hotel for The Rolling Stones' *Rock'n'Roll Circus.*
Tuesday, 10 December: The *Rock'n'Roll Circus* is filmed at RSG Studios in Wembley. Brian parties well, but contributes little to the actual film. Here John Lennon first suggests forming a new group with Jones.

1969

Saturday, 4 January: Jones travels to the island of Ceylon, but is refused accommodation in the tiny village of Kandy by hotel staff who accuse him of being 'a penniless beatnik'. Brian's answer is to wave a huge wad of notes in their faces and demand service. 'I am not a beatnik,' declares Jones defiantly. 'I work for my living. I have money and I do not wish to be treated as a second-class citizen . . . Things have changed since last year. Some people jeered at us on the streets thinking we were beatniks. Every person who has long hair is not a beatnik. Quite a lot of people do it as a fashion.'

Monday, 13 January: Jones's appeal against his 26 September conviction is formally denied.

Tuesday, 11 February: Jo Bergman of The Stones' office cables Allen Klein in New York to inform him that Electra Records wishes to buy Brian's *Joujouka* album. 'What's happening?' she demands; 'Brian's hysterical.'

Tuesday, 18 February: Bergman writes to Brion Gysin in Morocco to inform him of progress on the *Joujouka* project. 'Brian spent considerable time in the studio editing the material and this was finished about the end of September,' she says. 'The art-work and the tapes for the album were then sent to our New York office. Klein, who looks after business affairs for The Stones in America, promised to handle negotiations for this album and to make sure that it was released in the best possible way and with the right sort of promotion. During the time that Brian was in Ceylon, we made repeated inquiries to Klein to find out what was happening, and since Brian has been back, he also has been in touch with Klein. Klein's office keep telling us that they are arranging everything, that it will be done, etc., but we have heard no concrete facts about what label will release the album and when. I know that Brian is most anxious that Hamri and the musicians should be aware of the state of the album, and that Brian has been trying to arrange its release. Brian sends his regards and will be contacting you soon himself.'

Monday, 5 May: Jones rings Nicholas Fitzgerald to warn him not to discuss the plans to form a group with John Lennon and Jimi Hendrix. Alexis Korner has advised Brian that such a group would threaten the continued existence of The Stones, The Beatles and The Jimi Hendrix Experience.

Saturday, 10 May: Brian's parents spend the weekend with him at Cotchford Farm.

Comments Lewis Jones some time later, 'My wife and I were pleased that a few weeks ago we were able to spend some days with Brian at Cotchford. Brian seemed to be so perfectly happy and reconciled and we had high hopes that he would soon achieve his new ambition to form a group, more in keeping with his ideas. When success came to him, Brian was never arrogant or boastful. He never said: "I told you so!"'

Monday, 12 May: Jones joins the local Sussex horticultural society.

Sunday, 8 June: Mick Jagger, Keith Richards and Charlie Watts travel down to Cotchford from London to advise Brian he is no longer a member of The Rolling Stones. On the surface, Jones takes the news well, but is inwardly crushed and confides to friends he feels betrayed.

Monday, 9 June: Stones publicist Les Perrin and his wife receive a telegram from Brian stating: 'I'm very unhappy. So unhappy, I've done things. But I've sorted out things financially and morally. I've done the best I can for the people I love. I love you and Les very much.' Jenny Perrin then phones him to see if he's all right. Jones tells her he plans on writing some music that afternoon and was thinking of soon going off to Morocco for a holiday. He also wondered out loud if he had done the right thing by breaking with The Stones.

Tuesday, 10 June: Generic guitarist Mick Taylor is pegged to replace Jones in The Rolling Stones. The group gathers in London's Hyde Park for a photo session with their new member.

Thursday, 12 June: Anita Pallenberg phones Brian at Cotchford sounding extremely distressed and upset. Afterwards Jones refuses to discuss the exact nature of the call.

The approximate date of Lewis Jones's last telephone conversation with his son, at which time Mr Jones comments that Brian was 'quite normal' and 'full of beans'.

Stones fan Helen Spittal visits Brian at Cotchford. He tells her, 'The Stones don't want me.' He also mentions that when he dies he wants to be buried at Cotchford. Says Spittal, 'At one point Brian and I were up in his bedroom. He was looking out of the window at Frank swanning about, acting as if he owned the place, and he began talking to me about him, saying that he just wasn't doing anything he was supposed to. I said surely he must have a contract he was tied to and couldn't he get his solicitor to do something about breach of contract to get Frank off the premises. But it was no use. I guess it was for the sake of peace and quiet, but Brian just let things carry on as they were.'

Tuesday, 17 June: Swedish student Anna Wohlin moves into Cotchford Farm.

Sometime between Sunday, 22 June and Saturday, 28 June: Disc jockey John Peel entertains Jones at his flat in London. Peel remembers his friend: 'He was generally speaking greatly misrepresented. He was a pretty quiet person, gentle and kindly. When I saw him last week he was just beginning to be much happier. Before he was very nervous. He was excited about the new group he was going to form. He wanted me to look out for musicians as I travelled about the country.'

Monday, 30 June: Brian Jones phones his psychiatrist, Dr A. L. Greenburgh, urgently requesting a prescription of Durophet (black bombers). The doctor later confirms that 'ten or so' were given. Janet Lawson alleges she rang Frank Thorogood at Cotchford sometime in the early evening to arrange a train trip from London to East Grinstead. Thorogood meets her at the railway station. She then spends the evening in the builder's garage flat at Cotchford.

8.30 p.m.: Suki Potier rings Jones's friend Nicholas Fitzgerald at his flat in London warning him she feels Brian is in some kind of danger. She begs him to drive down to Sussex to make sure he's all right. The Guinness heir calms her down, promising to think about it.

9.00 p.m.: Janet Lawson claims to have had dinner at Cotchford Farm in the company of Jones, Frank Thorogood, Anna Wohlin and 'friends'. She also mentions that when they all went outside for drinks by the pool the floodlights were on. Nicholas Fitzgerald, however, insists they weren't installed until the following afternoon. She also notes that Brian swam that night, adding, 'He was a good swimmer and was *acrobatic* in the water.'

11.00 p.m.: Fitzgerald calls Jones only to hear the receiver picked up and then promptly laid down without a word being spoken. He rings back several times, but the line is always engaged.

According to Lawson, Jones is still enjoying himself in the pool. She says goodnight and returns to the flat alone.

Wednesday, 2 July:

10.30 a.m.: Fitzgerald receives a call from one Ralph Hampton, saying that Brian has asked him to see that Nicholas phones Jones at home that morning. He further admonishes him to keep on trying until he gets through.

11.00 a.m.: Nicholas Fitzgerald and student Richard Cadbury leave London for Cotchford to check up on Jones.

Brian and Anna get out of bed and go downstairs to watch a tennis match on television. She claims they watch television 'for most of day,' have 'a salad lunch' and 'another snack' later in the day. She further states that during the 'evening of that day', she and Brian watched yet more television together. Why is there no mention of the early afternoon visit of Nicholas Fitzgerald and Richard Cadbury, or indeed, Brian's lunchtime visit to the Haywaggon with one of the workers?

12.00 p.m.: Mary Hallet chats with Brian in the dining room at Cotchford. She notices that the pollen seems to have set off an asthma attack. Jones, however, fends it off with the aid of his ever-present inhaler. He tells her he's having several people over that evening.

In his witness statement, Tom Keylock states that he spoke to Brian on the telephone at Cotchford and that they discussed the former Stone's holiday plans and the formation of his new group.

1.00 p.m.: Mrs Hallet finishes her housework and leaves Brian alone in the house. She remembers seeing Frank Thorogood roaming around outside.

1.30 p.m.: Fitzgerald and Cadbury arrive at Hartfield and go directly to the Haywaggon for lunch. There they run into Jones and an unidentified construction worker in the bar. In the toilet Brian confides to Fitzgerald he feels he's being held hostage by Thorogood and his cronies.

2.30 p.m.: Jones, Fitzgerald and Cadbury arrive at Cotchford Farm where casual workmen 'Joe' and 'Frank' are installing a pair of spotlights above the pool. Brian, Nicholas and Cadbury stay in the garden for about an hour.

4.00 p.m.: Fitzgerald falls asleep in the garden while Cadbury and Jones chat together in the house.

6.00 p.m.: Jones and his guests retire to his ground-floor music room to listen to some tapes of Brian's music. Fitzgerald recalls hearing Jones jamming with the likes of John Lennon and Jimi Hendrix. Brian complains that several of his new demo tapes have gone missing. He suspects Frank Thorogood.

6.15 p.m.: Thorogood claims to have returned from a trip to London. Mrs Hallet, however, remembers seeing him at Cotchford when she left work at 1.00 p.m. It is possible that the builder could have driven to London and back in that time. Allowing for rush-hour traffic on the return trip, however, he would have had virtually no time to spend in town, so why bother making the trip?

7.00 p.m.: Jones speaks to a girl on the telephone who identifies herself as Luciana Martinez Delarosa, who says she's at Haywards Heath station and needs to be picked up.

7.15 p.m.: Cadbury and Fitzgerald volunteer to collect the young lady from the station.

7.30 p.m.: Friends begin to arrive at Cotchford for the party Jones had mentioned to Mary Hallet that afternoon. Among the guests is designer Elan and an unidentified member of The Walker Brothers. Mixed in amongst the dozen or so guests is Frank Thorogood and at least four of the builders.

Between 9.30 and 10.00 p.m.: Thorogood claims that Brian came to his flat to invite him and Lawson to the house 'for a drink'. Obviously, his time conflicts with that of his companion, Lawson, by approximately a full hour.

9.50 p.m.: Thorogood states that he, Lawson, Wohlin and Jones finished watching *Rowan and Martin's Laugh-In* after which Brian suggests going for a swim in the pool. One wonders how anyone could be watching television with Brian at the farm when, according to both Thorogood and Lawson, he hadn't yet showed up at their flat to invite them over.

10.30 p.m.: Janet Lawson says that Brian visited Thorogood's flat inviting the couple to join him at the main house.

11.15 p.m.: Nicholas Fitzgerald and Richard Cadbury return to Cotchford Lane. There they see a foreign car (with the headlights on) blocking the drive to Brian's house. The driver's door is open and the motor is running.

11.20 p.m.: The two men make their way on to Jones's property via Bluebell Wood. There, through the bushes they glimpse the pool brightly lit with the newly installed spotlights. Moving slightly forward, they observe Brian being held underwater by three men. (Author Geoffrey Giuliano's independent investigation some twenty-five years later confirms Fitzgerald's claim after obtaining a taped conversation from one of the three.)

11.25 p.m.: Fitzgerald claims, 'A burly man wearing glasses with a Cockney accent' appears and threatens the two men, who run back to their car and quickly drive away. Later that evening Cadbury is separated from Fitzgerald, never to be seen again.

11.30 p.m.: Jones is reportedly 'discovered' floating face down near the bottom of his swimming pool.

Between 11.30 p.m. and 12.00 a.m.: The estimated time of death given by Dr Albert Sachs following his examination of Brian Jones's body.

Thursday, 3 July:

12.10 a.m.: Police Constable Albert Evans arrives at Cotchford Farm where he is led through the garden to the edge of the pool where he first sees Brian's body.

3.30 a.m.: The alleged time of arrival at Cotchford of Les Perrin and Tom Keylock.

5.00 a.m.: Anna Wohlin goes to sleep in Brian's bed at Cotchford Farm.

Early morning: An autopsy is performed on the body of Brian Jones at Queen Victoria Hospital, East Grinstead, Sussex.

12.20 p.m.: Nicholas Fitzgerald awakes in his Cheyne Walk flat only to discover the world is being told a very different story about the previous evening's events.

4.00 p.m.: Tom Keylock signs a sworn witness statement in the presence of Detective Chief Inspector Marshall and Detective Sergeant Peter Hunter at Cotchford Farm.

5.00 p.m.: Lewis Jones identifies his son's body in the morgue at Queen Victoria Hospital in the presence of Police Constable Duffett.

9.30 p.m.: Mick Jagger and Marianne Faithfull attend a party in the back garden of Prince Rupert of Loewenstein's Kensington home. Other guests include Princess Margaret, Lord Harlech and Peter Sellers. The groups Yes, Stalactites and Al Wynn perform. The theme of the party is that everyone must dress entirely in white. In memory of Brian, however, Marianne dresses in black from head to toe.

Friday, 4 July: Mick Jagger replies to rumours that The Rolling Stones' free concert in Hyde Park will be cancelled due to Jones's death. 'Brian would have wanted it to go on,' says Jagger. 'We will now do the concert for him. I hope people will understand it's because of our love for him we are still doing it.' That evening the band appears on *Top of the Pops* with new man Mick Taylor on guitar to perform their latest single, 'Honky Tonk Women', backed by 'You Can't Always Get What You Want'. The Stones are widely criticised for so callously moving on without even a moment's mourning for their fallen comrade.

The *Daily Mirror* runs a story that Linda Lawrence and Pat Andrews intend to file claims against Brian's estate for the maintenance of the two boys they had with Jones.

5.00 p.m.: Bill Wyman returns to his hotel to find Tom Keylock and Anna Wohlin in the company of Wyman's wife, Astrid. Wohlin stays with the Wymans for the next four days.

Saturday, 5 July: Dr Albert Sachs officially concludes his postmortem report on the body of Brian Jones.

The Rolling Stones perform as scheduled at their free concert in Hyde Park. Jagger comments on Brian's demise, telling a reporter, 'I am just so unhappy about Brian's death. I am so shocked and wordless and so sad. Something has gone, I really lost something. I hope he is finding peace.'

Brian Jones's killers, occasional builders 'Joe' and 'Frank', happily watched the concert from a tree in Hyde Park.

Monday, 7 July:

9.15 a.m.: Dr Greenburgh is interviewed by police about Brian at his surgery at 73 Eaton Place in Belgravia.

Anna Wohlin returns to Cotchford Farm to pick up her belongings and then goes on to testify at the official inquest into Brian's death held in East Grinstead.

While at the inquest the 22-year-old Wohlin is asked to cover up her see-through crocheted dress by a female police sergeant.

In a newspaper article entitled 'The Girl Who Gave Brian Jones The Kiss Of Life' it is revealed that Anna Wohlin made two visits to the East Grinstead police station, then left to stay at the home of Stones bassist Bill Wyman.

Tuesday, 8 July: The *Daily Express* runs a story with the headline 'Brian Jones (After Drink and Drugs) Ignored Swim Warning From Nurse'. In the same piece Anna Wohlin is quoted at the coroner's inquest as saying that although she'd never seen Jones have an asthma attack he had often used his inhaler, 'particularly when he was in the pool and had difficulty in breathing'. Frank Thorogood, meanwhile, had this to say about that fateful night: 'Brian was not really under the influence of drink, but he staggered slightly. We watched television and finally, he suggested a swim. We had had quite a bit to drink.' (A rather contradictory statement, to say the least.) Dr Albert Sachs, the pathologist assigned to the case, stated that Jones 'had all the signs of natural disease', that he suffered from pleurisy and his heart was larger than it should have been for his age. His liver was also apparently twice its normal weight.

Marianne Faithfull suffers a drug overdose in the suite she shares with Mick Jagger at the Chevron Hotel in Sydney, Australia. She is rushed by ambulance to St Vincent's Hospital, where she is in a coma for several days. Faithfull later intimates she took the pills out of a feeling of empathy for Jones. 'I found myself thinking about Brian who had not yet been buried and the more I thought of him drowned and wasted the more I began to identify with him and think of myself as also drowned and wasted.'

Wednesday, 9 July: Brian's death is officially registered at Uckfield, County of East Sussex. His occupation is listed as 'entertainer' and the cause of death entered as 'drowning, immersion in fresh water. Severe liver dysfunction due to fatty degeneration and the ingestion of alcohol and drugs. Swimming whilst under the influence of alcohol and drugs.' The verdict? 'Misadventure,' according to Bill Wyman's book, *Stone Alone*. Anna Wohlin charges a chauffeur-driven limousine to Brian's account, motoring from East Grinstead to Heathrow airport, from where she flew home to Stockholm. Within twelve months she will disappear from view, presumed dead until 1994.

Thursday, 10 July: Lewis Brian Hopkin-Jones is laid to rest in St Mary's churchyard, Cheltenham. Canon Hugh Hopkins reads Brian's own epitaph taken from the telegram he sent to his parents after he was busted on drug possession charges. It reads simply, 'Please don't judge me too harshly.' From The Rolling Stones' inner circle only Charlie Watts and Bill Wyman attend the service. 'Everybody was around Brian's grave,' remembers Wyman. 'All his family and relatives were tranquillised. As the coffin was being lowered into the ground, the press were terrible, cameras poking into the grave, everyone asking questions. There was no respect. But when he drove away through Cheltenham, there were thousands of mourners, men with their hats off and women crying. I'd never seen anything like it.'

An account published in the *Daily Mirror* says, 'Dozens of girls, many dressed in black and carrying red roses, had converged on the Gloucestershire spa town. Typists and shop girls interrupted their lunch hour to stand in the rain outside the church. About 500 people stood silently as the funeral procession left for the cemetery. Hundreds more lined the route and filled the quiet cemetery, nestling in a fold in the Cotswolds.'

Friday, 11 July: The Rector of Cheltenham, Canon Hugh Evan Hopkins, rationalises his decision to allow Brian to be buried in the church yard of St Mary's. 'I may be criticised for holding a service here for a young man who had given up the Christian way of life. But when I was asked by his parents, with some understandable diffidence, whether I would allow the service to take place in the church, I did not hesitate.'

Saturday, 12 July: The *Record Mirror* memorialises Brian with the fitting headline: 'The Drugs, The Girls, The Hang-Ups Are Superfluous To This Obituary. Let Us Remember Him For What He Was: BRIAN JONES–THE MUSICIAN . . .' The article went on to say: 'Let his friends write his epitaph: "He was just getting everything together . . ." "He was really beginning to open up . . ." "Everything seemed to be go going right for him at last . . ." He was a victim of the pop machine that turns a boy who wants to make music into a mixed-up man searching for who-knows-what? And ironically, it seemed Brian Jones died at a time when he was about to fulfil that elusive ambition. Or was he? "Brian was just too sensitive for the pop world," said a friend last week. Maybe that was the cause of all his problems. Only his psychiatrist knows . . . "He had really opened up since he left the group," said a close friend. "He had been unhappy for some time that the music they were making was not what he wanted. And in the last few weeks he really seemed to be getting things together at last. He was really happy. He would ring up at 2.00 a.m. to discuss what he was doing – then he'd call back back twenty minutes later apologising for ringing so late." We shall never know what the new Brian Jones group would have sounded like. But the pop world can remember Brian as the man who really set The Stones rolling – he was a prime factor in their conception and in many European countries he was The Stones with a far greater fan following than Jagger. He was one of the first people to develop the use of the sitar in pop music in this country and will be remembered too as a fine exponent of the bottleneck guitar.'

Sunday, 13 July: A Rolling Stones secretary, who asked that her name not be revealed, speaks to journalist Peter Oakes about her former employer, Brian Jones. 'Even with millions of girls clamouring to meet him, and ready to do anything for him, he was lonely. He just couldn't communicate with people – he was frightened of people, especially girls. I know about his children, but they were the result of his early days when he thought he had to prove himself by being a tearaway. By the time I joined the group he had outgrown all that and built a protective shell around himself. Brian was no womaniser. Girls meant nothing to him. He would use them when he was high, perhaps, but he never loved. Brian couldn't love anybody except himself or his own music. Kindness, yes – but love, no. That was his problem. He used to use drugs and drink to try to overcome his deep loneliness.'

Tuesday, 26 August: The *Daily Express* runs an intriguing story indicating that Brian's last driver, Joan Fitzsimmons, may have new information regarding Jones's death. In a piece headed, 'Brian Jones Death: New Probe' it states: 'New information on the circumstances surrounding the death of Rolling Stone Brian Jones is being studied by the Director of Public Prosecutions. A report compiled by detectives in Chichester, Sussex, may lead to a new inquiry into the pop star's death at his home near Hartfield. The key to the new investigation is a woman patient who is critically ill in a Chichester hospital. She is Mrs Joan Fitzsimmons, a local taxi-driver, who was a regular chauffeur to

The Rolling Stones. Detectives want to find out from her whom she drove on the night 27-year-old Jones died – 3 July – and if she was present at Jones's home at any time during the fatal evening. Jones was found dead in the swimming pool of his fifteenth century, £35,000 [*sic*] farmhouse a few days after he had quit The Rolling Stones. Five days later an inquest decided that Jones was under the influence of drink and drugs when he went for a late night swim.'

Wednesday, 27 August: The *Daily Express* runs a story with the headline: 'Police: "No Interest" In Brian Jones's Death.' The article went on to say, 'A CID chief yesterday made a "clear the air" statement about Rolling Stone Brian Jones. Detective Chief Inspector Laurence Finlay, head of the Chichester, Sussex, CID, said that they had "no interest" in the death of Jones. But he added that Jones's name had come up several times during their inquiries into a serious case. This was a case of attempted murder which took place after the death of Jones. Mr Finlay explained that they had made inquiries into rumours surrounding Jones's death, but that they had found them "without foundation". Jones, aged 27, was found drowned in the swimming pool of his converted farmhouse near Hartfield, on 3 July, and later an inquest decided that the cause of death was misadventure. A spokesman for the Director of Public Prosecutions said yesterday that they could not discuss the matter.'

Wednesday, 24 September: It is announced that Cotchford Farm is to be sold in an effort to wind up Brian Jones's financial affairs. It is ultimately purchased by Alistair Johns who owns the property to this day.

A Brian Jones Discography 1963–1984

Compiled by Brenda Giuliano

Brian Jones with The Rolling Stones

1963

SINGLES

BRITISH SINGLES

F 11675	COME ON/I WANT TO BE LOVED	Decca Records
F 11742	POISON IVY/FORTUNE TELLER (Withdrawn)	Decca Records
F 11764	I WANNA BE YOUR MAN/STONED First pressing listed 'B' side as STONES.	Decca Records

AMERICAN RELEASES

9641	I WANNA BE YOUR MAN/STONED (Withdrawn)	London Records

FOREIGN RELEASES

AT 15032	COME ON/TELL ME (YOU'RE COMING) Black label.	Decca Records

ALBUMS

BRITISH RELEASES

LK 4554	*Thank Your Lucky Stars (Volume Two)* Monaural One track: COME ON.	Decca Records

1964

SINGLES

BRITISH RELEASES

F 11845   NOT FADE AWAY/LITTLE BY LITTLE   Decca Records

F 11934   IT'S ALL OVER NOW/GOOD TIMES, BAD TIMES   Decca Records

F 12014   LITTLE RED ROOSTER/OFF THE HOOK   Decca Records

AMERICAN RELEASES

9657   NOT FADE AWAY/I WANNA BE YOUR MAN   London Records

9682   TELL ME/I JUST WANNA MAKE LOVE TO YOU   London Records

9687   IT'S ALL OVER NOW/GOOD TIMES, BAD TIMES   London Records

9708   TIME IS ON MY SIDE/ CONGRATULATIONS   London Records

9725   HEART OF STONE/WHAT A SHAME   London Records

FOREIGN RELEASES

AT 15040   LITTLE RED ROOSTER/OFF THE HOOK   Decca Records

AT 15035   EMPTY HEART/AROUND & AROUND   Decca Records
Black Label.

F 22180   HEART OF STONE/WHAT A SHAME   Decca Records
Picture sleeve.

EXTENDED PLAYS

BRITISH RELEASES

DFF 856 C   THE ROLLING STONES   Decca Records

DFE 859 C   FIVE BY FIVE   Decca Records

FOREIGN RELEASES

SDE 7501	THE ROLLING STONES (VOLUME TWO)	Decca Records

ALBUMS

BRITISH RELEASES

LK 4577	*Ready, Steady, Go!*	Decca Records

Two tracks: COME ON/I WANNA BE YOUR MAN.

LK 4588	*Saturday Club*	Decca Records

Monaural
Two tracks: POISON IVY/FORTUNE TELLER.
First track: POISON IVY.
Second track: THIS IS THE STONES.
Also on their first Extended Play.
Second single (Withdrawn).

LK 4605	*The Rolling Stones*	Decca Records

Monaural

LK 4645	*Fourteen*	Decca Records

Monaural
One track: SURPRISE SURPRISE.
Royalties donated to the Lord's Taverner's Playing Fields Association.

AMERICAN RELEASES

LL 3375	*England's Newest Hit Makers: The Rolling Stones*	London Records

Monaural

PS 375	*England's Newest Hit Makers: The Rolling Stones*	London Records

Stereo

LL 3402	*12 × 5*	London Records

Monaural

PS 402	*12 × 5*	London Records

Stereo

1965

SINGLES

BRITISH RELEASES

T 12104   THE LAST TIME/PLAY WITH FIRE   Decca Records

F 12220   (I CAN'T GET NO) SATISFACTION/   Decca Records
           THE SPIDER AND THE FLY

F 12263   GET OFF OF MY CLOUD/THE SINGER   Decca Records
           NOT THE SONG

AMERICAN RELEASES

9741   THE LAST TIME/PLAY WITH FIRE   London Records

9766   (I CAN'T GET NO) SATISFACTION/   London Records
           THE UNDER ASSISTANT WEST COAST
           PROMOTION MAN

9792   GET OFF OF MY CLOUD/I'M FREE   London Records

9808   AS TEARS GO BY/GOTTA GET AWAY   London Records

FOREIGN RELEASES

AT 15043   (I CAN'T GET NO) SATISFACTION/   Decca Records
           THE UNDER ASSISTANT WEST COAST
           PROMOTION MAN
           Picture sleeve.

F 22265   GET OFF OF MY CLOUD/I'M FREE   Decca Records

AT 15039   TIME IS ON MY SIDE/   Decca Records
           CONGRATULATIONS
           Black label.

EXTENDED PLAYS

BRITISH RELEASES
DFE 8620   GOT LIVE IF YOU WANT IT!   Decca Records

FOREIGN RELEASES
SDE 7502   GOT LIVE IF YOU WANT IT!   Decca Records

RFE 8620   GOT LIVE IF YOU WANT IT!   Decca Records

ALBUMS

BRITISH RELEASES

LK 4661   *The Rolling Stones Number Two*   Decca Records
           Monaural

LK 4733   *Out Of Our Heads*   Decca Records
           Monaural

SKL 4733   *Out Of Our Heads*   Decca Records
           Stereo

LK 4725   *Out Of Our Heads*   Decca Records
           Monaural
           Export release.
           Featuring (I CAN'T GET NO) SATISFACTION.

AMERICAN RELEASES

LL 3420   *The Rolling Stones, Now!*   London Records
           Monaural

PS 420   *The Rolling Stones, Now!*   London Records
           Monaural

LL 3430   *England's Greatest Hit Makers*   London Records
           Monaural
           One track: SURPRISE SURPRISE.

PS 430   *England's Greatest Hit Makers*   London Records
           Stereo
           Royalties donated to The Lord's Taverner's Playing
           Fields Association.

LL 3429   *Out Of Our Heads*   London Records
           Monaural

PS 429   *Out Of Our Heads*   London Records
           Stereo

LL 3451   *December's Children (And Everybody's)*   London Records
           Monaural

PS 451   *December's Children (And Everybody's)*   London Records
           Stereo

1966

SINGLES

BRITISH RELEASES

F 1233	19TH NERVOUS BREAKDOWN/AS TEARS GO BY	Decca Records
F 12395	PAINT IT BLACK/LONG LONG WHILE	Decca Records
F 12497	HAVE YOU SEEN YOUR MOTHER, BABY, STANDING IN THE SHADOW?/ WHO'S DRIVING YOUR PLANE	Decca Records

Cover and label changed.

AMERICAN RELEASES

9823	19TH NERVOUS BREAKDOWN/SAD DAY	London Records
901	PAINT IT BLACK/STUPID GIRL	London Records
902	MOTHER'S LITTLE HELPER/LADY JANE	London Records
903	HAVE YOU SEEN YOUR MOTHER, BABY, STANDING IN THE SHADOW?/ WHO'S DRIVING YOUR PLANE	London Records

FOREIGN RELEASES

F 12331	19TH NERVOUS BREAKDOWN/AS TEARS GO BY	Decca Records

EXTENDED PLAYS

FOREIGN RELEASES

SFE 7503	THE ROLLING STONES (OUT OF OUR HEADS)	Decca Records
DFE 8650	THE ROLLING STONES	Decca Records

ALBUMS

BRITISH RELEASES

LK 4786	*Aftermath* Monaural	Decca Records

SKL 4786	*Aftermath*	Decca Records
	Stereo	

SKL 4838	*Have You Seen Your Mother LIVE!*	Decca Records
	Stereo	
	Export release.	

SKL 4495	*Hits LIVE*	Decca Records
	Stereo	
	Original title.	
	Export release.	

TXL 101	*Big Hits (High Tide And Green Grass)*	Decca Records
	Monaural	
	Gatefold.	

TXS 101	*Big Hits (High Tide And Green Grass)*	Decca Records
	Stereo	
	Gatefold.	

AMERICAN RELEASES

LL 3476	*Aftermath*	London Records
	Monaural	

PS 476	*Aftermath*	London Records
	Stereo	

LL 3493	*Aftermath*	London Records
	Monaural	

PS 493	*Aftermath*	London Records
	Stereo	

NP 1	*Big Hits (High Tide And Green Grass)*	London Records
	Monaural	
	Gatefold.	

NPS 1	*Big Hits (High Tide And Green Grass)*	London Records
	Stereo	
	Gatefold.	

1967

SINGLES

BRITISH RELEASES

F 12546	LET'S SPEND THE NIGHT TOGETHER/ RUBY TUESDAY	Decca Records
F 12654	WE LOVE YOU/DANDELION	Decca Records

AMERICAN RELEASES

904	LET'S SPEND THE NIGHT TOGETHER/ RUBY TUESDAY	London Records
905	WE LOVE YOU/DANDELION	London Records
906	SHE'S A RAINBOW/2000 LIGHT YEARS FROM HOME	London Records
907	IN ANOTHER LAND/THE LANTERN	London Records

FOREIGN RELEASES

F 22706	2000 LIGHT YEARS FROM HOME/ SHE'S A RAINBOW	Decca Records
F 12546	LET'S SPEND THE NIGHT TOGETHER/ RUBY TUESDAY	Decca Records
F 12654	WE LOVE YOU/DANDELION Picture sleeve.	Decca Records

ALBUMS

BRITISH RELEASES

LK 4852	*Between The Buttons* Monaural	Decca Records
SKL 4852	*Between The Buttons* Stereo	Decca Records
PS 509	*Flowers* Stereo Export release.	Decca Records

| TXL 103 | *Their Satanic Majesties Request* Monaural | Decca Records |

| TXS 103 | *Their Satanic Majesties Request* Stereo | Decca Records |

AMERICAN RELEASES

L 3499	*Between The Buttons* Monaural	London Records
PS 499	*Between The Buttons* Stereo	London Records
L 3509	*Flowers* Monaural	London Records
PS 509	*Flowers* Stereo	London Records
NP 2	*Their Satanic Majesties Request* Monaural	London Records
NPS 2	*Their Satanic Majesties Request* Stereo	London Records

1968

SINGLES

BRITISH RELEASES
| F 12782 | JUMPIN' JACK FLASH/CHILD OF THE MOON | Decca Records |

AMERICAN RELEASES
| 908 | JUMPIN' JACK FLASH/CHILD OF THE MOON | London Records |
| 909 | STREET FIGHTING MAN/NO EXPECTATIONS (Withdrawn) Picture sleeve. | London Records |

FOREIGN RELEASES
| F 22825 | STREET FIGHTING MAN/NO EXPECTATIONS | Decca Records |

ALBUMS

BRITISH RELEASES

LK 4955   *Beggars Banquet*   Decca Records
Monaural

SKL 4955   *Beggars Banquet*   Decca Records
Stereo

AMERICAN RELEASES

LL 3539   *Beggars Banquet*   London Records
Monaural

PS 539   *Beggars Banquet*   London Records
Stereo

1969

SINGLES

BRITISH RELEASES

F 12952   HONKY TONK WOMEN/YOU CAN'T   Decca Records
ALWAYS GET WHAT YOU WANT
Picture sleeve.
Promotional copies.

AMERICAN RELEASES

910   HONKY TONK WOMEN/YOU CAN'T   London Records
ALWAYS GET WHAT YOU WANT

FOREIGN RELEASES

F 12952   HONKY TONK WOMEN/YOU CAN'T   Decca Records
ALWAYS GET WHAT YOU WANT
Picture sleeve.

ALBUMS

BRITISH RELEASES

LK 5019   *Through The Past, Darkly (Big Hits*   Decca Records
Volume Two)
Monaural

236

SKL 5019	*Through The Past, Darkly (Big Hits Volume Two)* Stereo	Decca Records
LK 5025	*Let It Bleed* Monaural Free poster included in initial release.	Decca Records
SKL 5025	*Let It Bleed* Monaural Free poster included in initial release.	Decca Records

AMERICAN RELEASES

NP 3	*Through The Past, Darkly (Big Hits Volume Two)* Monaural	London Records
NPS 3	*Through The Past, Darkly (Big Hits Volume Two)* Stereo	London Records
RSP 1	*The Rolling Stones Promotional Album*	Rolling Stones Records
NPS 4	*Let It Bleed*	London Records

Note: Recent Rolling Stones compilations featuring contributions from Brian Jones have not been included.

Brian Jones Solo Recordings

1971

ALBUMS

COC 49100	*Brian Jones Presents The Pipes Of Pan At Joujouka* Gatefold. Inner fold-out. Yellow or beige label.	Rolling Stones Records

Paint It Black

No Catalogue Number	*The Four Thousand Year Old Rock'n'Roll Band*	Rolling Stones Records

Deluxe press pack for the 'Joujouka' album.
A 12 × 12 promotional kit containing a photo of
  Jones.
A twenty-page booklet by Dr Timothy Leary.
A three page reproduction of a *Rolling Stone* feature
  on Joujouka.
A three-sided press release.

Brian Jones Session Work with Other Artists

Unknown	YELLOW SUBMARINE (The Beatles)	Parlophone Records

Jones reportedly contributes hand claps.

Unknown	ALL YOU NEED IS LOVE (The Beatles)	Parlophone Records

Jones contributes hand claps.

Unknown	YOU KNOW MY NAME (LOOK UP THE NUMBER) (The Beatles)	Parlophone Records

Jones plays alto saxophone.

Unknown	I'M NOT SAYIN'/THE LAST MILE (Nico)	Immediate Records

Jones plays guitar.

Note: Although several of these recordings appeared on various Beatles albums and compilations over the years, for the sake of brevity, these have not been included.

Motion Picture Soundtrack Recordings

Unknown	*Mord und Totschlag ('A Degree Of Murder')*	Polygram Video

Jones composed and recorded the music for this film starring Anita Pallenberg. Although no soundtrack album was ever released, a home video of the film was recently issued in Germany.

Radio Recordings and Shows

Unknown	*A Bo Diddley Radio Performance*	BBC Radio

Jones reportedly accompanied the blues legend on harmonica.

| October 1964 | *Dust My Pyramids* | BBC General Overseas Programme |

October 1964 — *Dust My Pyramids* — BBC General Overseas Programme

This is the only official song which credits Brian Jones as the composer. It is less than thirty seconds long.

March 1971 — *A Story Of Our Time: The Rolling Stone Brian Jones* — BBC Radio Four

Written and Presented by Michael Wale.
Interviews by Michael Wale and Rita Dando.
Produced by Michael Raper.

July 1984 — *Rock & Roll Never Forgets: Brian Jones* — Westwood One

Presented by Mary Turner.
Five LP set.
US radio promotion.

Unreleased Demonstration Recordings

1963 — BRIAN'S BLUES — IBC

An instrumental featuring bottleneck guitar.

May 1964 — (Title unknown)

It is rumoured that Jones was about to record an original instrumental written by him and Andrew Oldham. Assisting him with the project was supposedly Jet Harris of The Shadows. The single never materialised.

1969 — GO TO THE MOUNTAINS — Apple Custom Recording

A recording of an original composition by Brian Jones, John Lennon, Denny Laine and a drummer rumoured to be Alan White. At least two acetates were cut.

June 1969 — (Title unknown)

Various unknown recordings with Alexis Korner. The existence of these tapes has been confirmed both by Jones and Korner. While most of Brian's private tapes disappeared following his death, it is believed that several recordings were placed behind a panel wall at his Sussex home where they remain to this day. Janie Perrin says she owned an acetate of one of the finished songs, but it has since been lost.

Recordings Alleged to Have Been Made by Brian Jones

Unknown SHADES OF ORANGE/LOVING
SACRED LOVING

These two tracks were long purported to be original
Brian Jones outtakes. In actual fact, they were Bill
Wyman produced compositions by The End. They
have both been widely bootlegged under Jones's
name.

Compositions Created in Memory of Brian Jones

1969 A NORMAL DAY FOR BRIAN (THE   Unreleased
MAN WHO DIED EVERYDAY)
Pete Townshend

1969 'On the Death of Brian Jones'
A poem by Jim Morrison

1971 JANITOR OF LUNACY   Reprise Records
Nico

1986 GODSTAR   Temple Records
Psychic TV
This tune actually made the charts and was a
memorial to Jones.

Examples of Brian Jones's Contributions to Specific Rolling Stones Recordings

PAINT IT BLACK
Jones plays sitar.

WE LOVE YOU
Jones plays Mellotron.

LADY JANE
Jones plays dulcimer.

NO EXPECTATIONS
Jones plays bottleneck guitar.

RUBY TUESDAY
Jones plays recorder.

MIDNIGHT RAMBLER
Jones plays percussion.

DANDELION
Jones plays saxophone.

YOU GOT THE SILVER
Jones plays autoharp.

ON WITH THE SHOW
Jones plays harp.

OUT OF TIME
Jones plays marimbas.

GOMPER
Jones plays flute.

SALT OF THE EARTH
Jones purportedly plays bottleneck guitar.

LITTLE RED ROOSTER
Jones plays bottleneck guitar.

2000 LIGHT YEARS FROM HOME
Jones plays Mellotron.

Brian Speaks

INTERVIEWS WITH A LEGEND

TODAY, THERE IS precious little left of the biting wit, charm and intelligence of Brian Jones. Sadly, this is more a measure of The Stones management's moratorium on Brian getting any press than the inevitable erosion of time. Still, any attempt to comprehend both the turbulent life and tragic death of the man must hinge on an understanding of Brian Jones the person. A person of great compassion, talent and insight. A young man gone too soon.

There follow four brief interviews with Brian Jones, conducted by various news reporters and television presenters in the mid-sixties.

Question: Brian, how tall are you?
Brian: Five feet eight inches . . . but people think I'm even shorter.
Question: When did you get interested in music?
Brian: At school, Cheltenham Grammar School. But I was eighteen before I started working properly . . . that was at the Marquee Jazz Club in London.
Question: Do you own a car?
Brian: Yes, a Humber Hawk at this moment. But before I used to hire a different car each week, just to try each one out. I suppose you could say I'm kinky for cars.
Question: It's said your hair is the longest of all The Stones. Right?
Brian: Well, I don't know. We don't measure it. Anyway, I think there's a bit too much said about our hair and our clothes. I've always felt it is the music that matters.
Question: Any special influence on your career, musically speaking?
Brian: All the great R&B people affected me. Jimmy Reed, Bo Diddley, Chuck Berry. One of the best things about the times we were out of work was that we could stay in and just listen to the American imported records.
Question: What are your views of adults who criticise The Stones?

Brian:	A lot of it is due to the fact that we wear clothes and do things that they wouldn't dare. I just get fed up to the back teeth when they say we should conform. After all, we don't say they should conform to our standards.
Question:	Are you a day person, or a night person?
Brian:	I seem to come to life during the night. Except that I can't buy clothes during the night-time, which is a drag. Contrary to what people think, we spend a lot of money on clothes, even if it's not on hackneyed old mohair suits.
Question:	You play guitar and harmonica. Any preference?
Brian:	This is odd. You can play a guitar costing £250. Or a harmonica, like mine, which is just over ten bob. But I honestly prefer harmonica. You get more out of it. You can get a wide variety of sounds and really 'feel' the blues.
Question:	Would it have worried you if The Stones had never attained wide recognition?
Brian:	Difficult to say. There were times when we felt we'd never get anywhere, but I know for sure that I'd never give up my music. There was a time when all I lived on was an egg beaten up in mashed potato.
Question:	Do you really smoke as many as seventy cigarettes a day?
Brian:	That number seems to go up every time it's quoted. No, but I smoke when I'm thinking. So it's easy to see how I could cut down.
Question:	Any big ambition for The Stones?
Brian:	I'd love us to do well in the United States. Visiting there is a gas of an idea and it'd be marvellous to have a hit record in a country which has produced so many greats.
Question:	Any special memory?
Brian:	With the help of the fans, there've been a lot. But I think actually playing harmonica with the great Bo Diddley was probably the greatest. You don't forget the day a long-standing dream comes true.

London

* * * * *

Question:	How long have you been playing harmonica, Brian?
Brian:	About two years, I would say.
Question:	Have you ever had any lessons on it?

Brian: No. We only use very small 'vampers', they call them. They only cost ten bob. They're not musical instruments really in the proper sense of the word. The secret of playing this little harmonica and getting our sort of sound is bending the notes. It's a completely different method of playing a harmonica. You don't play the notes straight, you have to bend them to get this whining sound. In actual fact, they're not chromatic at all. You don't even have the eight straight notes of the octave, you have to make something yourself and this you do by bending, as well. I couldn't possibly give anybody any tips on playing the harmonica. It's just a matter of getting to know the feel of it. You mess about with the harmonica for a few months and all of a sudden you can get this sound. I don't even know how to do it myself. It's done in the throat. You alter the volume of your throat, you know. It's very difficult to explain really.

Question: How long do you reckon a harmonica lasts you?

Brian: Well now, we don't use harmonicas so much as we used to, but when we used to play in the clubs and we were playing three hours a night, every night, they would only hold up a single evening.

London

*   *   *   *   *

Question: Don't you agree that 'Street Fighting Man' is very similar to 'Jumpin' Jack Flash'?

Brian: I don't agree it's similar in concept at all. It's certainly not similar musically. It was done within a similar time to 'Jumpin' Jack Flash', but I think that the concepts of the two records are so completely different I don't see how you can possibly compare the two and accuse us of bringing one record out after another in an attempt of one copying the other.

Question: What do you think of The Beatles' *'Sgt. Pepper'*?

Brian: I think it goes to show what great writers John Lennon and Paul McCartney are. The fact that somebody like Joe Cocker can pick up a song like 'With A Little Help From My Friends', which let's face it, nobody thought was very good, and do something marvellous with it is great.

Question: Experimental pop music didn't bring much success for your group. Will you return now to the commercial beat, to your old style?

Brian: Well, I understand by that question you're talking about *'Their Satanic Majesties Request'*. I think everybody should experiment. And we don't consider that we have failed. We haven't gone back on our new album to a very, very funky 'crash bang'. It doesn't mean that we failed, it just means we don't want to continue along a tangential line. Every now and then we want to go out and experiment.

Question: Did you finish your new movie [*Mord und Totschlag*] or not?

Brian: Yes, we did. In actual fact we are going to see it very soon. A fresh showing and apparently it has been very successful.

Question: The last question. Who do you consider to be the biggest personality in show business?

Brian: Well, unfortunately he passed away, but Otis Redding will always be my favourite, I think. And to all you cool dudes in Austria, I'll see you again soon.

Austria

*　　*　　*　　*　　*

Question: What do you think your generation has offered to the world?

Brian: Our generation is growing up with us and they believe in the same things we do. Our real followers have moved with us, some of those we like most are hippies in New York, but nearly all of them think like us and are questioning some of the basic immoralities which are tolerated in present day society, the war in Vietnam, persecution of homosexuals, illegality of abortion and drug taking. All of these things are immoral.

We are making our own statement; others are making more intellectual ones. Our friends are questioning the wisdom of an almost blind acceptance of religion compared with total disregard for reports related to things like unidentified flying objects which seem more real to me.

Conversely, I don't underestimate the power or influence of those unlike me, who do believe in God. We believe there can be no evolution without revolution. I realise there are other inequities; the ratio between affluence and reward for work done is all wrong. I know I earn too much, but I'm still young and there's something spiteful inside of me which makes me want to hold on to what I've got. I believe we are moving on to a new age in ideas and events.

London

Bibliography and Sources

For brief extracts quoted from the following works, I would like to thank:

Aftel, Mandy. *Death of a Rolling Stone/The Brian Jones Story*. London: Sidgwick & Jackson, 1982

Bockris, Victor. *Keith Richards*. New York: Poseidon Press, 1992

Cooper, Michael. *Blinds and Shutters*. Guildford: Genesis/Hedley, 1990

Cooper, Michael, Terry Southern and Keith Richards. *The Early Stones*. New York: Hyperion, 1992

Dalton, David. *Rolling Stones*. New York: Amsco Music Publishing Company, 1972

Fitzgerald, Nicholas. *Brian Jones/The Inside Story of the Original Rolling Stone*. New York: G.P. Putnam's Sons, 1983

Giuliano, Geoffrey. *Not Fade Away/The Rolling Stones Collection*. London: Paper Tiger, 1993

Herman, Gary. *Rock 'n' Roll Babylon*. New York: Perigee Books, 1982.

Hotchner, A. E. *Blown Away*. New York: Fireside, 1990

Jackson, Laura. *Golden Stone/The Untold Life and Tragic Death of Brian Jones*. New York: St Martin's Press, 1993

Norman, Philip. *The Stones*. London and New York: Penguin Books, 1984, 1993

Russell, Ethan. *Dear Mr Fantasy*. Boston: Houghton Mifflin Company, 1985

The Rolling Stones Monthly Book. London: Beat Publications Ltd

Sanchez, Tony. *Up and Down with the Rolling Stones*. London: Blake Paperbacks Ltd, 1991

Scandal – Inside Stories of Power, Intrigue and Corruption/Brian Jones/ The Life and Death of a Rolling Stone. London: Orbis Publishing Ltd

Schofield, Cary. *Jagger*. New York: Beaufort Books, 1985
Wyman, Bill with Ray Coleman. *Stone Alone/The Story of a Rock 'n' Roll Band*. New York: Viking Penguin, 1990

VIDEOGRAPHY

Finch, Nigel (director). *25 × 5/The Continuing Adventures of The Rolling Stones*. New York: CBS Music Video Enterprises

OTHER SOURCES

Wale, Michael (writer and presenter), Rita Dando (interviews), Mitchell Raper (producer). *A Story of Our Time: Brian Jones The Rolling Stone*. London: BBC Radio Four, March 1971
Turner, Mary (presenter). *Rock & Roll Never Forgets: Brian Jones*. New York: Westwood One, July 1984

A complete list of all sources utilised in this book has been compiled and placed on file. These include periodicals, newspaper reports, government documents, personal correspondence, radio shows, video tapes, audio tapes and other anecdotal material. To all those who shared with me their precious memories and insights into the life of Brian Jones, my sincere thanks:

Ian Anderson (musician and friend of Jones); Pat Andrews (early girlfriend); Brian Auger (musician and friend of Jones); Mick Avory (musician and friend of Jones); Ginger Baker (musician and friend of Jones); Pete Bennett (Rolling Stones promotional executive); The Brian Jones Appreciation Society; Peter Brown (The Beatles' former manager and a friend of Jones); Jack Bruce (musician and friend of Jones); Dennis Burke (publican and friend of Jones); The East Grinstead Coroner's Office; Chris Eborne (author and Rolling Stones expert); 'Elan' (designer and friend of Jones); Kathy Etchingham (a friend of Jones); Les Hallet (Jones's maintenance man); Mary Hallet (Jones's housekeeper); Pauline Hallet (a friend of Jones); Richie Havens (musician and friend of Jones); the Home Office; A. E. Hotchner (author); Neil Innes (musician and friend of Jones); 'Joe' (former employee of Jones); Alistair Johns (the current owner of Cotchford

Farm); Phil Kent (Brian Jones archivist and early friend of Jones); Tom Keylock (Rolling Stones tour manager); Ben E. King (musician and friend of Jones); Denny Laine (musician and friend of Jones); Jo Jo Laine (friend of Jones); Gary Leeds (musician and friend of Jones); Donovan Leitch (musician and friend of Jones); 'Derrick' (a friend of Jones); Steve Marriott (musician and friend of Jones); Jan Ollofsson (a friend of Anna Wohlin and Jones); Anita Pallenberg (Brian's lover); Reg Pippit (actor and Brian Jones aficionado); Terry Rawlings (author and researcher); Noel Redding (musician and friend of Jones); 'Sean' (a friend of Jones); Vivian Stanshall (musician and friend of Jones); the Sussex Police; Dr Cyril Wecht (forensic pathologist).

The Official Documents

Notes of the Post-Mortem Examination of

Name of deceased __Lewis Brian Jones.__   Age __26__   Sex __Male__

Address of deceased __Cotchford Farm, Hartfield, Sussex.__

Name of G.P. ____

Observers present at examination __C.I.D.__

Date and time of examination __Mortuary, Queen Victoria Hospital,__

Place where examination performed __E. Grinstead, 3rd July 1969.__

Estimated time of death __11.30 – midnight 2nd July, 1969.__

If a histologial or bacteriological examination is to be made the pathologist will initial here:

Chief points in the history of the case.	Deceased apparently went for a swim in a pool at his home with friends. Friends left the pool and the deceased decided to stay in the water. Last seen alive 11.30 p.m. 2nd July, 1969. Found dead shortly afterwards.

EXTERNAL EXAMINATION

Height(length), Weight	5' 9".
Apparent age	26 years of age.
Nourishment	Powerfully built, with a tendency to obesity.
Temperature at rectum	Not taken.
Rigor mortis, hypostasis, decomposition	Rigor mortis present. Hypostasis present.
Evidence of violence, burns	Nil.
Identification (tattoo marks, old scars, special deformities	Nil seen.
Body surface - Pallor, abnormal coloration	Pallor of face. Frothy fluid round nostrils.
Orifices of body, hair, teeth	Own teeth.

INTERNAL EXAMINATION

Cranial Cavity Skull, scalp and face	N.A.D.
Brain - weight, etc.	Wt. 1553gms. Congested and oedematous. Punctate haemorrhages in white matter.
Meninges and blood vessels	Congested.
Spinal column, cord and meninges	N.A.D.
Thoracic Cavity Mouth, tongue, tonsils, oesophagus	Little blood stained fluid in mouth. Could be due to artificial respiration.
Larynx, trachea, bronchi, thyroid and thymus glands	Respiratory tract. Mucosa congested. Bronchi contains a few flakes of glairy mucus, but this is not the viscid adherent mucus associated with death due to an asthmatic attack.
Lungs, pleurae, diaphragm	Wt. L 632gms, R 643gms. Adhesions left base to chest wall. No free fluid to pleural cavities. Both lungs voluminous. Some areas of collapse. Lungs
Pericardium	pit on pressure. Frothy blood stained fluid exudes from lungs on section. Few subpleural petechial
Heart (size, weight, cavities and contents, valve orifices and valves), heart muscle and coronary arteries	haemorrhages. Heart Wt. 411gms. General hypertrophy. Both sides dilated. Myocardium fatty and flabby. No evidence of vascular or valvular disease.

Aorta, pulmonary and other blood vessels	Blood from left side of heart showed 29% Hb plasma due to haemolysis. Aorta. Narrow but n.
Internal injuries (thoracic)	Blood alcohol 140 mgs % Nil
Abdominal Cavity Stomach and contents	About 1oz. of undigested food in fluid. Mucosa congested.
Peritoneum, intestines and contents, appendix, mesenteric glands, etc.	N.A.D.
Liver and gall bladder	Wt. 3000gms. Congested. Architecture lost. Sections show liver dysfunction due to extensive
Spleen	fatty degeneration. Gall bladder. Empty. Spleen Wt. 247gms. Congested.
Kidneys and ureters	Wt. L 190gms R 181gms. Congested.
Bladder and urine	Little urine present. Analysis showed 1720 micro-gms. % of a basic amphetamine-like substance.
Suprarenals, pancreas	Apparently normal.
Generative organs, breasts, prostate, etc.	Normal for age.
Internal injuries (abdominal)	Nil.
Are all other organs healthy?	Apparently.
Cause of death as shown by the examination :	In my opinion the cause of death was :-

I Disease or condition directly leading to death * ... ... Antecedent causes ... ...) Morbid conditions, if any, } giving rise to the above } cause stating the under- } lying condition last ... }	**I** (a) Drowning. due to (or as a consequence of) (b) Immersion in fresh water. due to (or as a consequence of) (c)
II Other significant conditions, contributing to the death, but not related to the disease or condition causing it ø	**II** Severe liver dysfunction due to fatty degeneration and the ingestion of alcohol and drugs.

* This does not mean the mode of dying, such as, e.g. heart failure, asphyxia, asthenia, etc., it means the disease, injury or complication which caused death.

ø Conditions which do not in the pathologist's opinion contribute materially to the death should not be included under this heading

These notes should be short and concise records of the facts observed; if opinions are expressed the grounds upon which they are based should also be stated. Scientific terms should be avoided when possible.

Any further remarks . In death from an asthmatic attack lungs are light and bulky.

Signature and qualifications Albert Sachs, CB. CBE. MD. MSc. FRCP. F. C .Path

Address Queen Victoria Hospital. E. Grinstead. Sussex.

Date 5th July. 1969

11/67

CLE/394/3650/250

Pathological Report No.   669   Date received: 3.7.65   HISTOLOGY

T QUEEN VICTORIA HOSPITAL,   PM.   Specimen Liver—frozen.

EAST GRINSTEAD.   Ward: Site Lungs x 2.

Name: Brian Jones.   Age:26   Surgeon or Physician: Dr. Sommerville.

Lungs.   The alveolar spaces are dilated and show bullous areas due to
breakdown of the alveolar septa. Albuminoid material is present
in the alveolar spaces. Subpleural haemorrhage is present. This
is the histology found in drowning.

69 " " -

Signed: Pathologist.

Date:

INQUISITION

123

An inquisition taken for our Sovereign Lady the Queen

At THE MAGISTRATES COURT in the PARISH of EAST GRINSTEAD SUSSEX.

On the SEVENTH day of JULY, , 19 69

[And by adjournment on the ~~day of~~ 19]

[Before and by] (1) me Angus Christopher SOMMERVILLE.

one of her Majesty's coroners for the said County of Sussex.

~~[and the undermentioned jurors]~~ touching the death of (2) Lewis Brian JONES.

whose body has been viewed by me (3)

~~[concerning a stillbirth]~~

1. Name of deceased: Lewis Brian JONES.

2. Injury or disease causing death: (4) 1 (a) Drowning

(b) Immersion in Fresh Water.

II. Severe liver dysfunction due to fatty degeneration and the ingestion of alcohol and drugs.

3. Time, place and circumstances at or in which injury was sustained: (5) Approximately 11.30 p.m., on the 2nd July, 1969, at Cotchford Farm, Hartfield, Sussex. Deceased had been drinking earlier in the evening, and was seen to be obviously under the influence of Alcohol and apparently Drugs. Insisted on going for a bathe. Seen to stagger on the Diving Board before jumping off into Swimming Pool, but managed to swim with other companion in Pool. Latter left to get Towel, returned to find deceased at bottom of Pool.

4. Conclusion of the ~~jury~~/coroner as to the death:
Drowning whilst/under the influence of Alcohol and Drugs.
                 Swimming
MISADVENTURE.

5. Particulars for the time being required by the Registration Acts to be registered concerning the death :

(1) When and where died	(2) Name and surname of deceased	(3) Sex	(4) Age or probable age	(5) Occupation and address
11.30 p.m. 2nd July, 1969. Cotchford Farm, Hartfield, Sussex.	Lewis Brian JONES.	M	27	Entertainer. of Cotchford Farm. Hartfield. Sussex.

Signature of jurors:

Signature of coroner:

P.T.O.

PATHOLOGICAL LABORATORY   7th July, 1969.

Telephone report from Mr. Cook, Biochemist, Royal Sussex
Hospital. Brighton.

1. <u>Blood barbiturate.</u>   Nil.

2. <u>Blood alcohol.</u>   140mgs. (Approx 7 whiskeys, or
                                    $3\frac{1}{2}$ pints or beer)

3. <u>Urine.</u>   Amphetamine like substance
                                    1720 micro-gms. (in normal
                                    urine this never exceeds
                                    200 micro gms.) These figures
                                    suggest ingestion of a fairly
                                    large quanity of a drug

4. <u>Thin layer chromatography.</u> Failed to reveal the presence
                                    of the following in an
                                    unchanged state.

                                    (a) Amphetamine.
                                    (b) Methedrine.
                                    (c) Morphine.
                                    (d) Methadrone.
                                    (e) Isoprenaline.

But did show the presence of 2 dense spots, one <u>yellow</u>
orange which has not been identified and the other a
<u>purple spot</u>. This could be due to diphenhydramine, which
is present together with methaqualone in mandrax, which
the deceased is known to have taken.

Sudden Death - Brian JONES

The Deceased was under the care of Dr. A.L. GREENBURGH of 73 Eaton Place, Belgravia, W.1., telephone Belgravia 3232.

Dr. GREENBURGH was away in Majorca until the late evening of Sunday, 6th July. Was contacted at his surgery at 9.15 a.m. on Monday, 7th July.

The Doctor confirmed that the Deceased was regularly prescribed:

MANDREX - as sleeping tablets, 2 to 3 per day.

VALIUM - (10 mg) - as tranquillizers, 3 per day, which, 'he needed all of the time'.

MEDIHALER - regular prescriptions - Doctor has never been consulted by the Deceased for asthma.

DUROPHET - ("black bombers") infrequently.

PIRITON - 4 mg., was prescribed day before death as a result of a telephone call from Deceased, complaining of hay-fever.

About ten days ago, the Deceased made an urgent telephone call to Dr. GREENBURGH, requesting Durophet and a prescription for ten or so was given.

Dr. GREENBURGH stated that the Deceased's drug requirements were becoming less and he had shown considerable improvement of late. Prescriptions were made in small quantities at frequent intervals rather than large prescriptions, which, experience had shown, resulted in the Deceased taking larger doses.

Kuranhau
D.C.1.
7/7/69

CERTIFIED COPY   **OF AN ENTRY**
· Pursuant to the Births and   Deaths Registration Act 1953

use a false certificate or a copy of a false certificate intending it to be accepted as genuine to the prejudice of any person, or to possess a certificate knowing it to be false without lawful authority.

DEATH	Entry Number	108

Registration District *Uckfield*	Administrative area
Sub-district *East Grinstead*	*County of East Sussex*

1. Date and place of death   *Second July 1969*
Cotchford Farm, Hartfield

2. Name and surname	3. Sex *Male*
Lewis Brian JONES	4. Maiden surname of woman who has married —

5. Date and place of birth   *28th February 1942*
Cheltenham Glos.

6. Occupation and usual address   *Entertainer*
Cotchford Farm Hartfield

7. (a) Name and surname of informant   **(b) Qualification**
Certificate received from A.C. Sommerville. Coroner for East Sussex. Inquest held 7th July 1969

(c) Usual address

8. Cause of death

1a *Drowning*
b *Immersion in Fresh Water*
II *Severe liver dysfunction due to fatty degeneration and the ingestion of alcohol and drugs. Swimming whilst under the influence of alcohol and drugs.*
MISADVENTURE

9. I certify that the particulars given by me above are true to the best of my knowledge and belief.

—   Signature of informant

10. Date of registration	11. Signature of registrar
Ninth July 1969	*M. P. Lacey Registrar*

Certified to be a true copy of an entry in a register in my custody.

...*J Purcell*............. *Deputy*. Superintendent Registrar   *10th July 1992*   Date

GA 538615

MR AND MRS L B JONES 335 HATHERLEY ROAD
CHELTENHAMGLOS .

PLEASE DONT WORRY DONT JUMP TO HASTY CONCLUSIONS
AND PLEASE DONT JUDGE ME TOO HARSHLY ALL MY
LOVE - BRIAN .